San Cai Historical Memoirs in Television

Rhythmic Writings of Music Background

San Cai Historical Memoirs in Television

Rhythmic Writings of Music Background

Zi-Jian Cai

EXCELLER BOOKS™
A GLOBAL PRESS

San Cai Historical Memoirs in Television:

Rhythmic Writings of Music Background

Cover by Exceller Books using resources from Pixabay.com

ISBN: 978-81-19524-53-2

First published in India in 2024 by Exceller Books, An imprint of GE Group

Address: G1, Dream Apartment, Degree College Road, Belgharia,

Kolkata, 700056, India

EXCELLER BOOKS™
A GLOBAL PRESS

www.excellerbooks.com

Preface

"San Cai Historical Memoirs in Television" records and summarizes the real experiences and social activities of Zi-Jian Cai as the author in making use of the support from the satellite operators of China and the United States to promote political and scientific progressions. The historical facts that under his leadership, the Chinese people strove for the legal right of democracy are described as real as possible. For the first time in history to make use of the force of law principle, the country belonging to the people practised democracy calling for law execution, thereby becoming one of the turning points in history for democracy and law to acquire the winning force. It is described, as real as possible, that the author, the Chinese people and the people worldwide worked together, with democracy calling for law execution as the basis of force, to create and compile the new theory of armed troops for war - the armed police. It is described, as real as possible, that the author and Chinese people won bravely over the exaggerative fallacy that nuclear weapons can destroy all humans, changing the strategic doctrine of humans in consideration of nuclear weapons and becoming the turning point in history for the humans to win over the nuclear weapons. The author Zi-Jian Cai thereby acquired the laurel as one of the San Forces to facilitate these three progressions and achievements. It is described as real as possible that the author and the satellite operators actively led the people in the whole world to amend and innovate physics altogether, successfully unifying the four forces in physics with the electromagnetic force. It is described as real as possible that people in the world investigated and expected civil intelligent robots and ocean chemical intelligent creatures to appear in the future. Meanwhile, the people in the Middle East proposed laws to revive the species and its history. It is described as real as possible that the people in various countries altogether inspected and compared the examination system with the democratic system and the presidential system with the parliamentary system, applauding and demonstrating the advantages of the democratic parliamentary system. It is described as real as possible that the author, the satellite operators and the people in various countries investigated together and practised for the first time the strong measures to control democratic crimes with the party disciplines, party flags and symbols, supplementing the present method of democratic management by changing the prime minister. It is described as real as possible that the author and the people in various countries made use of "Marx-MingXun calling for competitive election" to revise the disciplines and flag of communist parties, to improve the democratic image of communist parties in various countries, to promote all the communist parties in the whole world to control the democratic crimes with their party disciplines, and accordingly to synchronously revive the communist parties in various countries, while in further along with "Provincial and municipal legislation to republics," to promote the construction of democracy and republics in China. It is described as real as possible that the author improved the method of writing in Chinese and English, using the rhythm of music to adjust and restrict the undulation of rhythms in writing and using the literary works from this innovative manner of writing to spread the theory of armed police, the colloquia of physics, the memoirs in television, the natural principles and tactics of Chinese chess, and so on. All of these facts could be checked and verified in the videos of television in public during that time in various countries, composing an important depiction of the people's history, fully demonstrating the people's history recorded in the media of television as not only splendid and glorious but also interesting and wonderful, while enriching the historical knowledge and technology to the society and politics. Even if there are some mistakes somewhere in the contents of the book, it is easy to identify and correct them according to the videos on television. The author welcomes numerous readers to further investigate and supplement the illustrated history.

Musical Backgrounds for Rhythmic Writing

Blue Danube Waltz

Blue Danube Waltz (Beginning Session)

Blue Danube Waltz (Middle Session)

Please read the following text sentence-by-sentence to feel the musical background of the rhythmic framework.

Supporting Words: Whereas, Accordingly, Merely, In order to, Wish, Occur, and so on.

The theme song as "The Blood of Steel and Heart of Faith" in "The Legend of the Condor Heroes."

Music for "The Blood of Steel and Heart of Faith"

Please read the following text sentence-by-sentence to feel the music background of the rhythmic framework.

Supporting Words: Whilst, Hence, By, Hope, Solely, Shortly and so on.

The Same Song

Music for the Same Song

Please read the following text sentence-by-sentence to feel the musical background of the rhythmic framework.

Supporting Words: While, Therefore, Before, Capable of, However, Only, Expect and so on.

Photo Album

Photographs of Zi-Jian Cai:

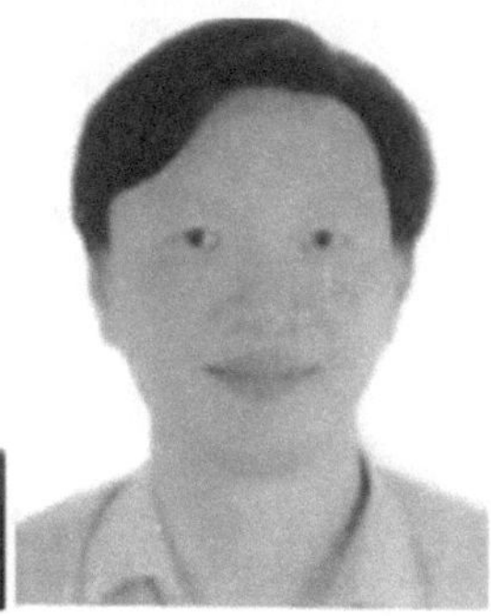

Photographs of His Parents:

Contents

Chapter | 1

Publication of Brain Theories

Musical Background of Rhythmic Writing: Blue Danube Waltz

Please read the following text sentence-by-sentence to feel the musical background of the rhythmic framework.

This book of memoirs records and illustrates a period of personal experience and relevant historical events in the life of author Zi-Jian Cai as one of the San Forces at present. Prior to January 26, 2005, the contents were written according to the self-memories and were not accurate to date and month. Since that day, the author has maintained a diary every day, and the corresponding contents have also been written and edited according to their importance, and they are accurate to date and month. In addition, the contents of television in this book of memoirs have just been written according to the real situations the author faced. However, there should certainly be many contents of television at present not witnessed by the author, and the historians should supplement them according to their social influences.

I am Zi-Jian Cai, a male in gender. I was born in HeFei, the capital of AnHui Province in China, on July 21, 1965. I was the only child in my family, with WaWa as my childhood name. HeFei was a city of medium size, very beautiful, abundant in universities and colleges, with a high ratio of intellectuals in the population and a prosperous light industry. My father,

MingXun Cai, was a technician at AnHui Printing and Dyeing Factory, whereas my mother, RuJue Jiang, was a physician in a governmental hospital in the city. My parents were both intellectuals. They came from Shanghai and arrived at HeFei while reinforcing the inland. My father was a little more than 170cm in height, with high and wide shoulders, a long and elliptical head, an upright nose, rigid eyebrows, white skin, big ears, thin lips, a purple face and single-fold eyelids. He wore nearsighted spectacles, for which he was called "Blind Cai" in his factory. The length of the vertex of his head was greater than its width, like that of Newton and Einstein. His hair was fine, soft and long. There was an insightful shadow between his eyebrows. He was heroic, introvert and beautiful. He was not only agile but also clever. He was fond of novelty and curiosity, good at speech and proficient in mental arithmetic.

He was the elite member of the Shanghai Youth Conquering Team of Bridge in the 1950s. They successfully retained the bridge championship for many years, with overwhelming dominance at the highest level in the nation at that time. According to many relatives and friends, ShiKang Liu, the leader of the team, was the most proficient, and my father was ranked second. In addition, the team member GuanGen Ding played bridge accompanied by the highest Chinese leader XiaoPing Deng later.

My mother was around 160cm in height. She had wide and flat shoulders. Her head was trapezoidal on top and round at the base. The vertex of her head was nearly the same in length and width. She had a small ball in the forehead and a protuberant in the cheekbone. She had white skin, big ears, thin lips, a red face, an upright nose and bright eyes, double-fold in eyelids and light-coloured eyebrows. Her hair was thin, rigid and straight. She looked like a heroine in her youth, somewhat like Elizabeth in the British novel "Pride and Prejudice", whereas she became intractable and competitive after middle age. She was picky on food, good at life and advertent on dress throughout her life. In the time of my childhood, prior to going to school, I took after my mother, who had a big face, cheekbone, and white skin, just like ZiRong Yang, played by XiangLing Tong in the model opera "Taking Tiger Mountain by Strategy" at that time, whereas I had single-fold eyelids.

Within three years after I was born, my family shifted to the home of my maternal uncle's grandfather, with a very high living standard and a maid in service. My maternal uncle's grandfather was the uncle of my mother. He was slightly over 160cm in height with an oblate and round-shaped head, protuberant cheekbone, rigid eyebrows and wide nose. He had a black complexion, big ears, thick lips and a red face. His head was bald with an oblique vertex. His black and thick beard was usually shaven, clean and bright. He was nearsighted, so he used spectacles. He was the head of the AnHui Institute of Prevention and Treatment of Tuberculosis, a member of the Chinese Peasants' and Workers' Democratic Party, and a member of the People's Political Consultative Conference of AnHui Province. He was born in the Chinese year of the mouse. He was not only optimistic and nice but also realistic and charismatic. He adopted my mother when he was young and brought her up like his real daughter.

At that time, the highest Chinese leader, ZeDong Mao, started the Cultural Revolution, plundering the people to consolidate his might and status, incriminating and criticizing the orthodox Communist Party of Soviet Union as revisionism. After 1967, the Cultural Revolution started to influence our family. My father and my maternal uncle's grandfather were both censored as the Cultural Revolution struck the intellectuals at that time. In December 1968, ZeDong Mao and the educated youths in Beijing, deviating from the basic knowledge of the Communist Party, fell into fantasy and aberration and started the movement of going to the mountainous and rural areas, and calling on the young people in cities to learn in reverse from the poor and lower-middle peasants. My mother was, as well, forced to go to the countryside along with the hospital she was affiliated with. Accordingly, I followed my mother to translocate from HeFei, the capital of AnHui Province, to SuSong County in southwestern AnHui, a beautiful county near the LuShan Mountain scenic areas. Since then, as my parents were forced to live separately, my mother had no choice but to raise me on her own, and accordingly, she sometimes sent me to my granny's home in Shanghai to live. At that time, Shanghai was the most developed and internationalized metropolis in China, with a population of ten million, many high buildings and foreign houses standing like trees in the forest and nice and modern people. It was the place every Chinese wished to reside in. In the family of my granny and uncle in Shanghai, I learned to speak Shanghainese. After returning to AnHui, I usually spoke Shanghainese at home with my parents.

After 1972, the politicians in the faction of ZeDong Mao had most of the control of the country, and the turmoil of Cultural Revolution as well calmed down to some extent. For special relations and sending gifts, my mother was relocated back to work in HeFei much earlier than others. When I was about to go to primary school in 1972, I left Shanghai and returned to HeFei to live with my parents. I entered the primary school for the children of the Printing and Dyeing Factory my father was affiliated with. Despite spending very little, if any time, on my study, I nearly always came first in the class. This is because I learnt with complete attention and understood everything clearly. My father was, somehow, afraid of his wife, and my mother was the queen in our family, coddling me much and cultivating my habit of lying in bed without getting up in the morning at weekends. As my parents spent little effort on my studying, I acquired the ability of independent thinking and matured earlier in my mind. When I fell ill, my father would read the stories in the novel "Water Margin" to me. However, he turned to read "The Romance of the Three Kingdoms" to me after I attended the third grade in school. I liked Chong Lin and Yun Zhao and sometimes played Yun Zhao as a vanguard with a bamboo spear on my own. Learning to read "Water Margin" and "The Romance of the Three Kingdoms" symbolized that I started to be serious and mature, whereas I felt that it was impossible for ZeDong Mao, who took after ZiCheng Li, to be successful. In 1976, I was transferred to the bigger middle school of AnHui Textile Bureau to study in the primary class. I nearly always came first in the class and had no problem with my studies. In primary and early middle school, I was often elected as one of the "Three good" students and "Excellent" little red guard in class, with almost 100% votes. All my classmates in HeFei called me Shanghainese since I was able to speak

Shanghainese. Nonetheless, my parents frequently reminded me that the political situation in China could be jeopardized and, therefore, oriented me to study to become an intellectual in the future.

In 1976, ZeDong Mao deposed the very popularly admired leader XiaoPing Deng once more. On April 5, 1976, the April 5th Movement broke out in Beijing against the cultural revolution of ZeDong Mao in the commemoration of EnLai Zhou. ZeDong Mao sent a militia of workers to suppress the movement. In September 1976, ZeDong Mao passed away. He was a great leader, who led the Communist Party of China to establish independent regimes of workers and peasants, create guerrilla tactics, and eventually win over the military troops of JieShi Jiang armed with US weapons and establish the People's Republic of China. Accordingly, the Chinese people thoroughly threw away the restrictions of feudal tradition and stood up in real, and China stepped into the class of strong countries in the world. In regret, he made the mistake of left doctrinairism at his old age and started the Proletarian Cultural Revolution, plundering the people. In these regards, ZeDong Mao was not democratic but a progressive personage, establishing a republic country led by the Communist Party of China that believed in science and welfare. Since 2016, in the process of promoting democracy in China, ZeDong Mao's thoughts and socialism reacquired the admiration of me and the Chinese people.

After ZeDong Mao had passed away, GuoFeng Hua took over the chairman of the Communist Party of China. He started the surprising raid to arrest the "Gang of Four" headed by Qing Jiang, the widow of ZeDong Mao. Soon, he further negated the Proletarian Cultural Revolution, which brought misfortune to the country and disaster to the people, leading China to go to normalization, which was accordingly called by the newspaper "Set Things Right" at that time. In 1977, the very popularly admired Chinese leader XiaoPing Deng regained the position as vice prime minister, whom ZeDong Mao had put down. He promptly associated with the international modernization to consolidate his own status. Under the leadership of XiaoPing Deng, the "Reforming and opening up" movement, which is well-known all over the world, was carried out in China. The theory of market economy was established within socialism, correcting the defect of the non-marketing economic system, which was unable to accurately reflect the various needs in the lives of people, greatly improving the lives of people and elevating the strength of the country. The theory acquired applause from Western countries such as the United States. A significant progression was made in international communism, influencing all countries of communist parties that were facing difficulties at that time. Also, family planning in China was promoted under the leadership of XiaoPing Deng and Guofeng Hua, who similarly possessed some historical values as a reference. In 1977, XiaoPing Deng further recovered the system of entrance exams for universities, which had been prohibited in the Cultural Revolution, making the people eligible to enter the universities by taking exams.

As I was very clever and agile at studying, under the encouragement and education of my father in 1978, I jumped two grades to pass into the HeFei 10th Middle School, the key middle school of the city, at the age of just 13, and further passed into the top class of that school, with my reputation rising sky-high. Since that time, I studied more seriously, but still felt easy. The teachers of the 10th Middle School were very good with their teaching and exercise content for the university entrance examinations. In the first year, I made progress and became one of the top 6 students in the class, whereas in the second year, I was the topper in the class. In the university entrance examination in 1980, I achieved the top score in the school and passed into the University of Science and Technology of China (USTC), the key national university. I was just 15 years old at that time and was the famous "wonderful child" in the east district of the city. My father learned from his friend teacher Yang Lu in USTC that studying biophysics had the most promising future, and he helped me apply for the Department of Biology, and I soon got admitted. My parents were quite happy and vigorously active in spirit.

The University of Science and Technology of China (USTC) was located in HeFei. While I lived and studied at the university, I nearly always went back home at weekends. After I had gone to study at USTC, I started to study and learn seriously. During my 5-year tenure at USTC, I came first in all key courses. Nonetheless, I was influenced by the significance of the contents required to study, while in the 5-year system of USTC, there were incorporated many irrelevant and trivial courses. My interest in studying got reduced, and I spent time on learning to play bridge. In addition, going back home every weekend further reduced my time for studying, and as a result, my average grade was influenced, and I was ranked down to 10 or so. At that time, my father led his bridge team to drastically defeat the university bridge team of USTC, and I certainly felt very glad and proud. My father made use of the method of a high natural bid to block and disturb the information exchange of opponents, indicating the predominance of natural bid over the precision bid the university team of USTC adopted.

After having gone to study at USTC, I started speaking Chinese Mandarin in daily life while studying. However, I still spoke Shanghainese at home with my parents. I was a good student, silent and conservative, but I was disgusted by the autocracy in my mind and disliked the political life required by the university. I was fond of singer LiJun Deng from Taiwan. The students at USTC were industrious in their studies and broad and profound in their basic knowledge. However, they studied without deep comprehension and pursued fragrant recognition. In the later period, while studying the specialized courses, I thought of many problems of Pre-Darwinian chemical evolution on my own, following the models in molecular biology, while my classmates were not so deep in consideration. In speciality, I selected protein clearance and hydrolysis as my direction, which played important roles in regulation within eukaryotic cells, and I wished to share the biological achievements at the molecular level with DNA double helix.

From 1980 to 1985, with the instigation, conspiracy and flattery of my mother, my father made friends with and flattered the municipal cadre of human resources who retired from the army. They visited and gifted each other, and my father was promoted continually in the factory. ZhiLiang Wang, another cadre, retired from the army, cooperated with my father to struggle for might and reform and promoted my father to enter the core of factory management of AnHui Printing and Dyeing Factory, a middle-sized key enterprise at that time. Rewarding in relevance to merits was the cultural tradition of AnHui. Therefore, the workers there were sensitive to the bonus for performance. My father not only adopted and encouraged this tradition but also added the culture of giving exams to determine job assignments, which was unwelcome there. He promoted many intellectuals, realizing the dual champions in both production and quality and was glorious in achievements of reform. Accordingly, he was admitted to join the Communist Party of China. In the election campaign of the whole factory, which was required by the superior level, he defeated the opponent with glorious achievements and excellent speech and was accordingly elected by the factory employees to be the plant manager of the factory. In this regard, he became one of the earliest members of the Communist Party running for election in the primitive period of socialism under the leadership of the Communist Party, whereas, at that time, Gorbachev had not taken over yet. Under the leadership of my father, the factory continuously progressed and developed, acquiring the admiration of DaWei Zhang, the mayor of the city, who was the trusted follower of ZiYang Zhao in the reforming faction of the Communist Party of China. In the early stage of reformation in the city, it was precious for my father to have such encouragement and achievements.

In 1985, at the age of 20, I finished my 5-year studies at the University of Science and Technology of China (USTC), graduated from the university and passed the exam to enter the Shanghai Institute of Biochemistry, orienting to the topic of protein hydrolysis. At that time, the municipal leaders of HeFei received the new regulation from the Central Committee on the restriction of age as plant manager, allocating my father away from the Printing and Dyeing Factory and promoting him as the vice-chairman of the Municipal Association of Science and Technology. Unfortunately, my father was severe in the psychology of relying on administration and technology due to his nearsightedness. He did not consider taking advantage of this new position to play a more important role or step to a higher level of reformation. In contrary, he resorted to his special relation to move to SuZhou, a city very close to Shanghai. My family left AnHui and returned to the rich area southern to the Yangtze River.

In 1985, I was 20 years old and had grown up, with a height of little more than 170cm, high and broad shoulders, and very thin arms. I inherited the genes of thinness from both my paternal and maternal grandmothers. My head had turned long and round in shape, with a vertex longer than its width, like that of Newton and Einstein, and bulgy with a small ball in the forehead. I had a protuberant in my cheekbone, an upright nose, big ears, thin lips, a red face, a white complexion, single-fold eyelids and light-colored eyebrows, thin, soft and long hair and an insightful shadow between eyebrows. I was fond of novelty and curiosity, picky on food, good at life and advertent on appearance, and accordingly attractive to social eyes.

As I had an excellent interview held by the Institute of Biochemistry in 1986, I was recommended by my adviser, Sir

Chi, to study with Professor Castellino at the University of Notre Dame in the United States of America. At the University of Notre Dame, I had excellent grades in courses and worked hard in the lab. As a result, Castellino became fond of me. I had two other classmates, Mei and Li. In 1986, there broke out the parade of students from the University of Science and Technology of China (USTC) in AnHui, where I had graduated. After being repressed by the authorities, its president, LiZhi Fang, was expelled from the Communist Party, and accordingly, many students from its Department of Physics went to the University of Notre Dame. I introduced Luo as the child of my previous teacher to my adviser to come to study. I, my classmate Li and other classmates in physics from USTC sometimes talked about and commented on physics while having meals in the dining hall.

In the spring of 1987, Luo turned outside to ask for a transfer to California because her boyfriend would go there. Accordingly, the long-term relationship between me and my adviser Castellino was somewhat influenced, while my personality and interests gradually turned from concerning personal relationships to paying attention to grades and papers. During that time in university, I watched the fashionable movie "Top Gun," sweeping the whole United States, and was deeply affected by the major characters in the film. Accordingly, I upgraded grossly and became independent in academics. At that time, I was preparing for the Ph.D. qualifying exams. I took the chance to comprehensively scan the biological sciences to see whether there was any problem I could independently solve and whether there was any chance I could take to become a professor earlier in future. I happened to win the fellowship from the department, and I certainly prepared well to rise high, create new and win glory. If I had not made any important achievements as a graduate student in biology, I would have managed to become either a laboratorian or a veterinarian in the future and would have even been inferior to my mother as a physician. I had a wonderful childhood, while my father chose biology as my major subject just to make achievements and earn fame in society.

At that time, I sometimes walked around the lake at the University of Notre Dame and thought of problems one by one, whereas I usually perceived them as solved or insignificant. I once more read the novel "The Romance of the Three Kingdoms," where Yu Guan was rushing desperately in battle to win fame while young, admiring Bei Liu as ambitious as a big eagle while sad in heart, was learning Liang ZhuGe and picky about choosing a good king to assist while bowing to contribute till death. I adopted the mood of unhappiness to resist and prevent slanders from colleagues on my studying and investigating other topics. Just then, my father in SuZhou promoted production whereas the local workers blew their own trumpet and were ungrateful, sometimes quarreling with my parents on trivial things. They wrote letters to me, telling me that they were unfairly treated, and I felt sad and occasionally wept. The Americans around were so stupid and meddlesome that they misunderstood that I was so bullied by Luo as to become unhappy, consoling me all day. Especially, Mei thought that I fell into psychosis. Nonetheless, I, after all, made all the progressions somewhat and discovered there were not only chances in immune regulation and evolutionary development but also some unsolved problems in neurosciences.

Soon, my adviser, Sir Chi, at the Institute of Biochemistry, was planning to be a visiting scholar there. The US advisor, Castellino, was not good at managing the scholars in the lab, arranging for me to follow a British scholar and Li to follow my adviser, Sir Chi from the Institute of Biochemistry, to do an experiment. In this way, my Chinese adviser and I would have been considered thieves, making it difficult to pass away time in the lab. Meanwhile, I passed the Ph.D. qualification exam and started working and behaving seriously. On the other hand, the Americans around me were still meddlesome with me. Li flattered Luo once more, while the Americans were hypersensitive once more to take them apart. Li and Luo denied any special intimate relationship and reversely imitated me as sad in pretence, implicating that I had been sad and cold and that Luo should decide to transfer to the school close to her boyfriend. I was under heavy pressure and apprehended Luo to transfer away with me. Luo yielded and agreed to help me transfer. I told my US adviser that I wanted to be transferred as well. Surprisingly, my adviser Castellino was upset, made a decision inappropriate as a teacher and insisted on getting me out of his lab. Unfortunately, this time, Luo behaved like a Chinese coward, unwilling to help me transfer as equivalent to my girlfriend, and accordingly, I was very embarrassed and immediately gave up. Besides having passed the written exam to qualify for a Ph.D., I was qualified to get a Master's degree, and I had the opportunity to transfer to another university if I faced any difficulty.

My Chinese adviser, Sir Chi, arrived at the University of

Notre Dame. He considered that it was possible to get a solution for temporary disinhibition of my temper and actively helped me to reconcile, persuading me to work with Castellino for several more years. I, after all, was a student sent by the government, while what the Chinese adviser said usually represented the Institute's opinion, with which I had to agree. Sir Chi adopted the opinion of Mei and told Castellino in my absence that I was stimulated to require psychological treatment, and Castellino gave permission. With regard to psychosis, the Fathers at the University of Notre Dame were much more severe, and so was the hysterical reaction of Castellino. I was studying science then, believing that any behavior was subjected to the restriction of law. Even though I learned and mimicked Yu Guan and Liang ZhuGe, it belonged to the most common behavior of learning. With regard to the criteria of the university to evaluate students, those with good grades and hoping to be transferred to a better university were good students, while those hoping to be transferred to a worse university were nonetheless bad students. In 1976, when I went from primary school to middle school, I was transferred to another school, and the teachers in primary school were unsatisfactory. But soon, I jumped two grades to become a famous child.

Prior to returning to China, I called my previous classmate, Biao Zhao, from the Institute of Biochemistry, and learned that he had become a student of Professor Kandel at Columbia University in New York. At that time, Kandel was the main contributor to the cellular mechanism of learning and memory and one of the most famous scientists in the biological field. This was the first time I learned the mechanism of neuronal plasticity. I decided to take the chance to return to China this time to read and study more and see more of the chances in the sciences. I printed many pieces of literature, purchased the textbook of neuroscience that Kandel wrote, and wished to study broadly and deeply, and accordingly, I was not yet bad in mood.

Actually, I progressed much in the period of two years while I was at Notre Dame. I learned the advantages of American culture, realizing that most Americans were reasonable and brave. I made continuous progress in academics and learned to deal seriously with the problems in science while accumulating a solid and broad basis of knowledge. I learned to scan to find out the big unsolved problems. Accordingly, I was higher than others in academics, which laid the foundation for my success in the future. I also increased my knowledge of the society of the United States. One day, my classmate Mei was late when returning home from the lab in the evening, and she called the police to protect her, making me realize for the first time that the police had the duty of protecting and serving the people. On another day at a party, a classmate said that once, a US police officer surprisingly drew out a gun, making a Chinese female colleague severely scared, as he wanted the Chinese woman to stop her car, but she did not. I was impressed to know that US police were allowed to use violence to shoot.

In November 1987, I departed for China, taking a flight from New York to Shanghai. In New York, I met with my classmate Biao Zhao, who was working under Kandel at that time. I talked with him frankly and sincerely about sciences. This time, while I boarded the airplane from the United States back to mainland China, contrary to the tide of going from China to the United States, which is much more advanced than China, I started to feel lingering. In the 1980s, with the powerful promotion of Xiaoping Deng, China reformed and opened up to learn from developed and advanced countries such as the United States and Western Europe. At that time, the average income of Chinese people was less than $700 per year, while China was even a relatively autocratic country. The United States and Europe were all developed countries with hundred-year-old democratic systems, and their average income was ten times that of China. At that time, most Chinese already felt the need to go abroad not only to get rid of the autocracy but also to promote their lives.

On September 16, 2007, the people and I discussed the issue of whether the release of these paragraphs of memoirs infringed on the privacy of the related persons. Fortunately, the relevant persons were all scientific workers who had published papers already autonomously exposed to the public and history. Out of curiosity, people at present or in the future may inspect their experiences of study and career, which are conjoint, natural and unrestrictive. In addition, their experiences of study and career could also be mentioned in newspapers, memoirs and television, which was similarly legal as being cited. Accordingly, these paragraphs of memoirs would not infringe on the private issues of the relevant persons.

The airplane landed at the HongQiao airport of Shanghai. My parents had already reached there to pick me up. SuZhou was a tourist attraction, with globally famous HanShan Temple, Humble Administrator's Garden, Tiger Hill, Lion

Grove, North Temple Pagoda and so on. The people in SuZhou spoke SuZhou dialect, very close to Shanghainese. The local SuZhou people were diligent in running businesses and getting rich. The private shops, such as the restaurants, garment shops, etc., were blooming like hundreds of flowers and competing like hundreds of boats in the stream, excellent to survive and inferior to lose. Accordingly, every year, many new restaurants and shops appear, while some old restaurants and shops disappear. There is a very high ratio of turnover. While my parents had both retired, and my family had fewer properties than so many SuZhou bosses and their wives, as I came back from the United States, everybody was courteous and complimentary once meeting with me, while the colleagues and friends were very active in sending the money and gifts to my parents.

After coming back home, I heard that my father had been as upright and diligent as in AnHui, forward in pushing reformation and effective in improving production. Nonetheless, the local workers in SuZhou were different from those in AnHui in admiring the ability and achievements of leaders, whereas instead of being fond of boasting themselves, ardent to establish the image of local SuZhou people, accordingly there emerged some frictions. I also learned that most of our neighbours worked in the thermal and electrical power plant, belonging to the conservative and stubborn faction of Peng Li. They had sometimes hammered throughout the night to interfere with my parents' sleep. My mother was weak in bodily constitution with heart disease and accordingly fell into depression. My parents learned from my Chinese adviser that I studied too much to become psychotic. My parents insisted on sending the literature and books I brought back home to the factory my parents affiliated with to care for and store. I could merely read the chivalrous novels of Yong Jin that my father had borrowed for me and the philosophical books of Freud that I had purchased, being prohibited from reading science books. The managers of the factory considered it normal to read books. However, because of the hypersensitive and depressive reactions of my mother to the factory, they sent my mother to Suzhou Hospital of Psychosis to receive treatment. Mr. Wei in the factory preserved all my pieces of literature and books on science and returned them to me, encouraging me to study and read normally. My father soon recovered and cooperated with GuoCang Xu to actively organize the activities of the JiangSu Society of Printing and Dyeing, not only earning money from outside to back the family, but also maintaining the high level in technology of JiangSu printing and dyeing. His paint coat, with radiant adhesives and wide printing, represented the mainstream level of JiangSu printing and dyeing at that time and stood at the front of national printing and dyeing at that time. Since then, the personality of my father also changed gradually from plant manager to professor, as if from Qi Bai to YuLu Jiao.

The family of my mother was from NanXun, very close to SuZhou. The cause of my mother falling into the disease was the malicious hammering of neighbors to interfere with her sleep. While she was weak in bodily constitution with heart disease, she should be diagnosed with reactive depression caused by sleep deprivation. My mother was treated in the hospital with anti-cholinergic drugs, generally against both depression and schizophrenia. Even though she was cured, the depression was not thoroughly removed as the cause of the disease. Accordingly, my mother relapsed several years later, and after taking the drugs for a long, she fell into dementia.

Besides frequently visiting the hospital to take care of my mother, I continued to read and think of problems. Immediately after the Spring Festival of 1988, my mother recovered and was released from the hospital, and we all started to live harmoniously and happily like before. Due to the lack and deficiency of management at the Shanghai Institute of Biochemistry, even though I was sent by the Institute to the University of Notre Dame to study, I could still use my previous library card of the Institute to borrow books and read literature.

The advantage I had over others was that I learned how to discriminate the significance of achievements, which was not even considered by most common professors. I classified the academics into three levels. On the lowest or most basic level, what was required was real, which was the basic characteristic of science. On the next level, what was required was the achievement to possess novelty, which was hard to realize, to compare the relevant works of all to determine their real novelty, and to determine their progression to this level. The most outstanding scientists in China, such as JingRun Chen, DongCai Liang, LongPing Yuan, etc, usually belonged to this level. On the highest level, there required the discovery of science not only new and novel but also influential and significant, the discovery of a new and significant principle in one field. It was very difficult to realize this point, and it required standing on the shoulders of giants with many scientific achievements. In materialism and the history of development in science, it was treated as a contingency, assuming that, when some subject accumulated to some stage, there would naturally emerge some significant principle, and in accompany there could appear some great scientists such as Newton, Darwin, Watson, Crick, etc. Nonetheless, I adopted the method of scanning many fields along with theoretical integration to solve this problem. There did not seem to be any big problems in biochemistry and molecular biology that I majored in, and hence, I paid attention to the significant theoretical problems in the neural, immune and developmental fields, where there were many unsolved problems. If I was lucky enough to complete one big achievement with the method of integrative theorization, promoting my fame comparable to Newton, Darwin, etc., it was sufficient for my life. If I failed, and there was not any big problem in these biological fields to solve to become a great scientist, it would not be regretful for me to change my major, as I had really scanned all fields in biology and could still change to write novels about Gods in the rest of my life. In addition, in the field of literature and novels, there was no such defect as the substitution of old with new, as in the field of experimental science, where you have more opportunities to become famous.

I carefully read the textbook written cooperatively by Kandel and Schwartz as Principles of Neural Sciences. There, it was stressed that the cellular basis of learning and memory was neuronal plasticity and the biochemical and cellular reactions of neuronal synaptic transmission under repeated electrical stimulation. The book was full of reductionism and intuition, while everything related to nerves and the brain became simple, intuitive, orderly, and easy to understand. Within it, the cerebral cortices of the brain were responsible for the high activities of language and thought, the limbic system was responsible for the emotional reactions, the ascending reticular activating systems were responsible for the arousal and novelty, etc.

I also frequently watched television at home, especially films and television plays from the United States. At that time, Mickey Mouse and Donald Duck were the most popular cartoon figures among the Chinese people. Another film of serial cartoons from the United States that was very impressive to me was "She-Ra-Princess of Power." It educated the people on how to love, as love was both powerful and successful. In addition, there were cop films from the United States and Hong Kong, from which I consolidated the knowledge I learned at the University of Notre Dame that the US police could use violence to shoot. In further, I learned that the Americans humiliated the police as the property of taxpayers.

In the spring of 1988, I generated some ideas on neuroscience, originating from the book of Kandel and Schwartz. I learned there that the memory of humans and mammals is mainly accomplished in a special structure called the hippocampus within the limbic system. Human memory can be divided into short-term and long-term memory, while unstable short-term memory can transform into stable long-term memory via memory consolidation. The hippocampus is just the structure that accomplishes the function of memory consolidation, while some other limbic structures, such as the mammillary bodies, possess a similar function. The limbic system is mainly responsible for emotional regulation in humans and animals. I wondered on my own how the hippocampus distinguishes the two functions and felt that the two functions should be unified. In addition, the mammillary bodies are the important recipient of the hippocampal descending outputs, simple and primitive in structure, and it is merely possible for their functions on emotion and memory to be unified and undistinguished. The event eliciting a human and mammal to respond in emotion should certainly be very important, should be memorized in consolidation, and should be obvious in significance in life science. I considered that emotional reaction can elevate and activate the alertness of a human and mammals, and I naturally wished to see whether the reticular alerting system of the brain possessed a similar function of memory consolidation. If yes, then there could be a simple and easy mechanism to unify them: the important memory activates the limbic emotional system of the brain and further activates the ascending reticular alerting system to accomplish memory consolidation.

I went to the library of the Chinese Academy of Science in Shanghai to look up pieces of literature on this topic. The library of the Chinese Academy of Science in Shanghai collected large quantities of international journals on neural and brain sciences, which are very comprehensive. At the University of Notre Dame in the United States, there were very few scientific journals on neural and brain sciences, and it was difficult to perform research on brain theory. In the library in Shanghai, I discovered a large amount of evidence indicating that the reticular alerting system of the brain goes on biochemical reactions via its terminal neuronal transmitters within the cerebral cortex to accomplish memory consolidation. I also collected a large amount of anatomic and pharmacological evidence on the limbic emotional system of the brain to influence and regulate the ascending reticular alerting system and eventually coupled the two big systems. Nonetheless, there were still some mediodorsal thalamic cases, such as NA, that did not fit the coupling theory at that time. I not only adopted the methods of citing data while removing speculations and dividing memories in more detail but also spent much effort solving the diencephalic difficulties and strictly completing the theory in academics, which was much ahead of time. I screened all kinds of literature in the library but could not find any paper on this thought, which gave me a feeling that my theory was novel and a significant achievement and breakthrough in brain science. Accordingly, I hurried to write this theoretical paper.

Soon, it passed to the early summer of 1988, and I negotiated with my US adviser to return to university. I wrote a letter to him, expressing that I was willing to return to university and finish my Ph.D. My adviser replied no way and did not agree to award me with the Master's degree, which should be made up to me according to the regulations, distinguishing me from other students, without any change in his temperament as psychotic and stubborn. My parents and I eventually felt disgusted with him. We accordingly contacted my Chinese adviser, and he replied that he had run out of measures but was willing to provide further help after coming back to China while I had to prepare myself to apply to other universities in the US. In regret, after my adviser returned to China, the head of Institute of Biochemistry did not realize that it was illegal for the US adviser to use might, stop me from getting my degree, and further dismiss me from the Institute of Biochemistry just because I did not have a degree in compliance with the regulation of the country. The head of Institute of Biochemistry also had no right to dismiss me.

GRE was the indispensable exam for those who applied for graduate studies in the United States, with its mathematics as simple as those in high school and its English words as difficult as those in English literature. It was effective in protecting US students who are weak in mathematics and pushing aside foreign students with English not as their native language, which is not relevant to academic research at all. In the summer of 1988, I spent all the time preparing for the GRE exam, not even watching the Opening Ceremony of the Seoul Olympic Games in 1988. I took the GRE exam in October 1988 and just got a score of 1750. So, I decided to give it another try in February 1989; this time, I got a score of 1880. I got low scores partly because I was not accustomed to it and partly because I happened to make progress in the theory of brain learning and memory, and I was somewhat distracted. It was certainly declined by the US universities I applied for with such low scores.

As soon as I finished the first GRE exam in October 1988, I started to organize and write the paper with the financial assistance of my parents. I finished writing the paper at the end of 1988 and entitled it "The Neural Mechanism of

Declarative Memory Consolidation and Retrieval: A Hypothesis." After completing the paper, I submitted it to the most reputed international scientific journal of that time "Nature." But unfortunately, it was rejected. I was very clear about the significance of the theory and further submitted it to another reputed international scientific journal, "Science", where it was rejected too. In April 1989, I submitted it to the international professional journal on neuroscience, "Neuroscience & Bio-behavioral Reviews", which I liked most on my own, waiting for a long time to review the manuscript. Between the time of submission to "Nature" and "Science", I sat for the GRE exam in February 1989 and got a score of 1880, which was not satisfactory either. Nonetheless, even though I scored low in GRE exams and was not admitted by US universities, I was still indulged in the excitement of great creation in science, not feeling too sad.

Since I was staying at home without doing anything important, I continued to write other theoretical papers with the financial assistance of my parents. Accomplishing one important theoretical achievement may be a fluke, but accomplishing several important theoretical achievements like Newton and Einstein made me an academic giant. One thing that had been troubling me for a long time was the function of sleep. While preparing for the GRE exam in the summer of 1988, I noticed that memorizing English words was harmful to the body and was the manifestation of memories that destroyed physiological health. Accordingly, I adopted sleep to counterbalance and recover. Various pieces of research indicated that sleep possessed multiple functions, such as metabolism, energy conservation, secretion of growth hormone, etc, but these functions were not sufficient to make sleep indispensable to animals. Herbivorous animals were in danger while sleeping in the wild. Research in evolution and experimental research with sleep deprivation also indicated that slow-wave sleep was indispensable. There would be an important but not yet discovered function requiring sleep to accomplish, while the determination of this important function of slow-wave sleep meant to solve another significant problem in biology.

In the textbook of Kandel and Schwartz titled *Principles of Neural Sciences*, many phenomena relevant to slow wave sleep were listed. I had always been paying attention to the relevance of sleep with the depression and emotion in brain. I intuitively felt that the regulation of emotion in slow wave sleep was relevant to life. Nonetheless, what disturbed the emotion to such an extent that it required regulation? On the basis of my deep understanding of memory, I discovered that the emotional memory in the limbic system of the brain transforms into neuronal plasticity. As soon as the natural environments and events in which humans and animals live are random and disordered, the emotional memories also become random and disordered, and their accumulation in the limbic system of the brain breaks the balance of emotion. The brain should readjust the balance, while the slow wave sleep happens to possess this function.

Once more, I went to the library of the Chinese Academy of Science in Shanghai to look up many kinds of literature. As the head of Institute of Biochemistry illegally dismissed me, it was legal and compensatory for me to use the library card to read the books in the Shanghai library. I checked that there was no similar theory about memory accumulation disrupting the emotional balance to require slow wave sleep to adjust. In 1989, once more adopting the method of citing data and removing speculations, I wrote another theoretical article ahead of time, entitled "The Functions of Sleep: Further Analysis." Like the first paper, I also submitted it to the journals "Nature" and "Science," the most famous at that time, and was rejected in a similar manner. I had to submit it in August in 1989 to the international academic journal "Physiology and Behavior," a famous journal on the science of physiology and behavior.

In June 1989 occurred the 4th June incident, which astonished the world and changed the situation in China. In the spring of 1989, the Beijing students were influenced by the death of YaoBang Hu and went to the streets to march to strive for new freedom and elicit powerful suppression from the conservatives headed by Peng Li and backed by eight patriarchs. XiaoPing Deng was forced to yield, and on June 4, 1989, the 27th army belonging to the Beijing military region eventually shot to suppress the movement of students. The public voices in the world severely reprimanded this act. The political situation in China drastically changed as well. After the 4th June incident, the Communist Party of China removed ZiYang Zhao, the leader of reformists, from the position of general secretary. XiaoPing Deng promoted ZeMin Jiang from Shanghai to the post of general secretary of the Communist Party of China. Through political cooperation, he influenced the political situation of China, assured the continuation of reform and opening in China, and achieved the victory of XiaoPing Deng's theory. Since political reformation and democratic progression were grossly suppressed, nobody was allowed to share their opinions freely, films and television were feudal and fatuous, and foreign democratic thoughts were repressed.

During the June 4th incident, I stayed at home in Suzhou and watched television every day. I was very much moved by the brave spirit of the people of Beijing, as they surprisingly dared to fight against the army, confront the gunpoint without fear, and struggle bravely for the future of China. I was greatly moved by them, and several times, my eyes were filled with tears. I also felt sad about the failure of the Beijing people and angry about the brutal and retrogressive behaviour of the army. Nonetheless, I was reluctantly submitting my papers at that time.

Even though I was frustrated with my studies to a degree, my mind was still full of hope and beauty. I believed that I would soon be able to publish my theories in international professional journals. In 1990, my mother was unfortunately diagnosed with cancer. After surgery, I carefully looked after her, fed her with a meatball of Lentinus edodes every day, and insisted for long, not only curing the cancer but also eradicating its recurrence. I was much influenced by the Chinese song "What a Big Tree," sometimes broadcast on television at that time: "*The head props to one sky, the feet stand on one land, you raise your head in a storm, stand up in ice and snow. What a big tree, no matter how the wind roars, with many stories stored in leaves, happy and bitter. Happy you don't laugh, bitter you don't cry, how much green you shade to land, that's the musical note of love. Wind is your song, cloud is your footstep, no matter day and night, you contribute to humans. What a big tree, the blessing of green, your chest in blue sky, your affection in fertile soil."*

Since that time, I have been more fortunate. After a long review and revision, both my two theoretical articles were published. The first theoretical article: "The Neural Mechanism of Declarative Memory Consolidation and Retrieval: A Hypothesis," after being revised in English with the help of Tim Kennedy via my friend Biao Zhao at Columbia University, was successfully published in the international professional journal of neuroscience as "Neuroscience & Bio-behavioral Reviews" in 1990 when I was 25 years old. The second theoretical article: "The Functions of Sleep: Further Analysis," was published in the international professional academic journal "Physiology and Behavior" in 1991 when I was 26 years old. After the publication of two significant theories, I received many letters requesting the reprints of my papers. I was joyous and celebrated my achievements in science with my family.

With the publication of two important theories, my feelings started to change. I felt that I was a famous personage, a very successful scientist. I was really fortunate to be able to publish two important theories whose importance was sufficient to be comparable to the genetic principle of Mendel, the evolutionary theory of Darwin and the double helix of Watson and Crick in biology. They were important works really standing on the shoulders of giants. As email was not so popular at that time, I could not send emails to faculties and students in the university to extend my influence, and I could merely plan to publish books on my brain theories in future to increase my notability. I was relaxed and open in my mental status, radiating youthfulness and brightness all over while gradually emerging totally new, brilliant and attractive characteristics.

Actually, the biological problems I had considered were much more important than these two theories. Simultaneously, in my mind, there were four other problems. One of them was that I had considered at the University of Notre Dame how to explain the problem of immunological self-recognition. I believed that T-cells could play roles, but I did not believe in the deletion of clones of self-immunity in the early period of development. At least there was the presence of adolescence and menopause in humans, and accordingly, the expression of self-proteins in humans was influenced by development and ageing. I was always thinking of this problem in those years and wishing to establish some models, but I was always unsuccessful.

Another problem was with development. At the University of Notre Dame, I had already associated animal development with evolution and realized that different animals had different mechanisms of development due to differences in evolution, and it was impossible to have a unified molecular and cellular mechanism of development. Meanwhile, I also paid attention to the important roles of organogenetic termination in determining developmental formation. After I had returned to China, I wrote an important theoretical article, proposing that organogenetic termination is an intrinsic constraint on animal development and evolution. I submitted this article to some journals in biology, but they all rejected the paper. Finally, in June 2015, the OALib Journal published this paper of mine as "Termination of organogenesis as an intrinsic constraint on animal development and evolution: A theory" (OALib Journal 2, e1646, 2015).

The third problem was the linguistic asymmetry of the cerebral cortex. Prior to 1991, I associated it with stutter and reticular formation, stressing its advantage in mechanism. Unfortunately, my submitted paper was rejected at that time. At the end of April 2015, while constituting the neurolinguistic model of two processes as memory association and cortical coordination, I discovered that the declarative/procedural neurolinguistic model of two neural processes of Pinker/Ullman was not accurate in the classification of memory yet, in which their declarative memory of semantics merely belonged to the remote part of memory but did not require the coordination of reticular formation I felt necessary prior to that time. Accordingly, I adopted a similar episodic memory in brain science to supplement the declarative memory. I also adopted the neurolinguistic model of three processes as semantic meanings, grammatical rule and episodic meanings to supplement and improve the neurolinguistic model of two processes to rise up from the enthusiastic tide of the people in television in various countries highly concerning the neurolinguistic model at that time. In July of that year, the OALib Journal published this neurolinguistic paper of mine as "Semantic Memory Association, Procedural Grammar Syntax and Episodic Modality Coordination as Three Interactive Neural Processes Organizing Language: A Model" (OALib Journal 2, e1718, 2015).

The fourth problem was ageing. I was just curious and had no idea, but since 2008, I have started to determine my aim as the mechanism for the regulation of the time of animal senescence. As people in various countries in television were highly interested, I merely selected the senescent mechanism related to sleep, lest I be involved in suspicion of plagiarism. In December 2015, citing the skin senescence from the wind I felt earlier than the other, I proposed that it could influence the slow wave sleep to result in the senescent degeneration of the hypothalamic suprachiasmatic nucleus (SCN). In 2016, my paper entitled: "A Hypothetic Aging Pathway from Skin to Hypothalamic Suprachiasmatic Nucleus via Slow Wave Sleep" was published in the Brazilian journal "Sleep Science" (9:212-215, 2016). On July 5 of that year, on television, I saw the European people had proposed in their local time one day earlier the male senescent pathway from adipose accumulation to reduction of sperm and to degeneration of the hypothalamic preoptic area (POA), which is very similar. In 2017, I published the paper "The Adipose Cause of Senescence of Male Hypothalamic Preoptic Nucleus: A European View" in "Research & Reviews: Neuroscience, 1(2), 21-26, 2017," reviewing, introducing and supporting the European people and their views.

At that time, another big problem I further considered was that the future artificial intelligence could imitate the neural activities of humans and could invent a humanoid robot like real humans. I learned from the updated literature at that time that British scientists had adopted Very Large-Scale Integrated Circuits to imitate neuronal plasticity as memory. If this method was adopted to imitate the real human brain, both of my two brain theories would be very useful. I noticed that the assembled humanoid robots would acquire the same abilities, wisdom and adaptation as humans. They merely needed to feed energy from an electrical charge, which was sufficient for them. They did not even need water and oxygen and could even survive in very low temperatures. In this regard, they were able to adapt to live in the cosmos more successfully than humans. In future, cosmic civilization will be the cold civilization, where the cold intelligence of humanoid robots will imitate the brains of humans, and the earth of humans can become a greenhouse zoo. In 2006, this subject once more became a hot topic for people on television in various countries around the world.

In the latter half of the year 1991, after publishing two theories, I felt competent to look for a job in research. I applied to join the research work of Shanghai Brain Research Institute of Chinese Academy of Science. With repeated interviews and communication, the Shanghai Brain Research Institute formally informed me to report to work after the Spring Festival in 1992. From returning to China at the end of 1987 to reporting to work at the beginning of 1992, I stayed at home jobless for more than 4 years, relying completely on my parents to live. So, I was quite eager to re-enter the research affiliation to work.

After joining the Brain Research Institute, even though I tried to make my colleagues understand the significance of my theory, there were still many conservative colleagues who opposed my theory as I still did not have a Ph.D. degree, and even though the head of the institute was very good and much international, the institute did not offer me a formal position of research. However, the Brain Research Institute helped me register the Shanghai Hukou, and I became a real Shanghainese. While I was at the Brain Research Institute, I was paid a very low salary, which was merely enough for me, and the apartment in which I temporarily resided was offered by the institute. I was a person somewhat longing for home. So, I returned home to SuZhou every weekend to meet my parents. While I took the train to go forth and back to SuZhou, I felt very happy. I cherished much the days I stayed with my parents, frequently feeling that my mother was suffering from cancer and could leave this world any time soon, while I would as well go abroad once more due to my economic difficulty. Every weekend when I went back home to reunite with my parents, I was very serious and glad, enjoying the happiness of the family reunion.

At that time, there was a significant change in the international situation. Under the leadership of Gorbachev, there was a political reformation in the Soviet Union. In 1990, the conservatives of communists made a coup to lock up Gorbachev, and headed by Yeltsin, the democratic reformists bravely led the people to win over the army and get the victory, disbanding the Communist Party. The Soviet Union was disbanded, the people earned victory and democracy was established. The confrontation and Cold War between the United States and the Soviet Union ended, and the world entered a new era dominated by democracy. This situation totally contrasted with that in China after the June 4th incident in which the conservatives suppressed all with force, forming significant international press toward China.

I was still concerned about the domestic politics. Once at the Shanghai railway station, I instigated the Shanghai people and EastSea Fleet to support ZeMin Jiang while marginalizing Peng Li. As I radiated the characteristics of youthfulness, intelligence, brilliance and attractiveness, I could have some affection and influence on the people around me. I assumed then that, as the country was a winner to the king and a loser to the gangsters, it should belong to the whole people. Accordingly, sooner or later, the country would progress into the people to win and the democracy to succeed, whereas it was required for China to struggle hard, especially since it was difficult to win over the military autocracy. Influenced by the exaggeration of military power in films and television in various countries at that time, with regard to winning over the military autocracy, I had neither any method nor any confidence. I sometimes thought of changing the political commissars of the People's Liberation Army (PLA) into the people's representatives to utilize the gun in reverse to seize territory and support democracy.

In 1992, the important speech of XiaoPing Deng during his tour to the South was announced, and the reform in China was somewhat released. Shanghai also advanced into the new period of PuDong development and comprehensive reformation of the system. The metropolitan appearance was fresh every day and different every month, while the enterprises and metropolises both started to orient to Asia, the Pacific and the international. Going abroad was still a great glory; the whole family of the person who went abroad rose to heaven.

In the early half of the year 1994, I accepted the invitation to attend the international meeting on sleep functions in Italy. The papers in the meeting were compiled in the international academic journal "Behavioral Brain Research" (Vol 69, 1995). With the reformation of the system of Brain Research Institute, all were required to have a Ph.D. degree, and I had to apply and go abroad to have a degree. This time, I went to QianJin Sparetime School to specially prepare for the GRE, and I got a high score of 2180. I was admitted to North-western University in Chicago, which was ranked in integration within the top 15 in the United States at that time. In September 1994, I left for the United States to go to North-western University in Chicago.

In 1994, before leaving China for the United States, I discovered a piece of literature, a paper published by Mishkin and Appenzeller in 1987. The paper also proposed the coupling theory of memory consolidation in the brain, linking the upper parts of the limbic system to the ascending ACH system, similar in part to my theory. However, it was published earlier than mine, and their pathways were half different from mine. They merely adopted one kind of pathway in their ascending activating system, whereas I adopted four kinds and the lower parts of the limbic system instead of the upper parts. The experimental basis of Mishkin was over-simplified, merely adopting one kind of animal as the monkey, whereas I adopted dual evidence from both patients and animals. The biggest defect of their coupling theory was that it was difficult to figure out its conspicuous biological significance. On the other hand, my coupling theory nonetheless linked the descending limbic system responsible for emotional regulation to the ascending reticular activating system responsible for alert regulation, making it visible intuitively so that the important events affecting the emotion of an organism would be consolidated in memory, very conspicuous in the significance of biology.

Nonetheless, their paper was, after all, published earlier than mine, and it was similar to mine in half. Accordingly, it was possible to share my first significant theory from the view of coupling with them. On February 25, 2014, I learned via internet from the papers of the lab of Parvizi on the elicitation of cortical recall with γ frequency modulated by the cholinergic system and associated them with the other clinical results as insufficient to impair memory with lesions to the ventral medial prefrontal cortex, proving my theory and circuits correct in gross.

On September 5, 2008, prior to dawn, prior to falling asleep, to inspect the history, I watched the video of the Opening Ceremony of the Olympic Games held in Seoul on September 17, 1988, as I did not watch it in 1988 because I was preparing for the GRE exam in October in that year. I saw that there were radio waves from satellites to project my new idea of sleep to the stadium, drawing the attention of the whole audience. They knew I already had ideas on the coupling theory of memory. The athletes in the field immediately deduced, according to my carefully chosen reading materials, that the function of sleep was the regulation of emotional disorder caused by the accumulation of random memories and said it should be ascribed as stealing my ideas. They said they deduced without literature and evidence, and it could not be ascribed as science. At that time, personal computers were not so popular, and the commercial internet had not been invented yet. Therefore, I could merely look up literature in the library, which was very arduous. In addition, when I was memorizing GRE words in the summer of 1988, I adopted the Freudian theory of dream-releasing sexual drives to antagonize the hurt from memorizing the GRE words, deeply understanding the correlations among memory, emotion and sleep earlier than they did. Finally, on August 29, 2009, I decided to watch the Spring Festival Gala in 1989. I saw many audiences who mentioned that I had looked up the work of Horne on sleep in Shanghai Library for the Chinese Academy of Science. If this video was real and not modified, it was accordingly demonstrated that I had borrowed and read the book in November or December 1988 between the two GRE exams. At that time, I had directly pointed out that Horne had been wrong in his theory, whereas I had been very successful in my theory. I remembered that I was wearing a shirt to conceive my sleep theory prior to taking a nap after lunch. It could merely be the summer of 1988 when I wrote the paper and submitted it in the summer of 1989. In this regard, the formulation of sleep theory should happen just in September and October during the Olympic Games, and it should be ascribed to the behaviour of satellite operators to project onto the Opening Ceremony of the Olympic Games as divulgence. In April 2014, the people and I proposed that it could not be required in law to compensate for the rejections by scientific journals if the operators of satellites also wrote papers on sleep since it was still possible to publish important theories via writing books.

On August 30, 2009, I once more watched the video of the Spring Festival Gala in 1988 and saw that a few audiences discussed the memory entropy and coupling theory. I remember that I had not felt such content while I had been watching live television. Presumably, I paid more attention to performances than audiences. Even though this video was real and not modified, according to the criteria of science, these scenes could merely be treated as unscientific discussions. The persons on the spot at the 1988 Spring Festival Gala were not able to look up the pieces of literature via internet yet, as internet of business had not appeared until 1995 and personal computers had not been popular yet either. At that time, only in top universities in the United States or Europe and the national libraries of the Academy of Science in big countries comprehensive literature on brain sciences was available, whereas, in most other universities and libraries, little literature on brain sciences was available. Accordingly, the persons on the spot were too far from the international journal in the academy. They did not know the amelioration of depression with total sleep deprivation, were not scientific at all, and more difficult to go beyond the theory of Freud on dream and sex. I adopted the evidence with the most updated observed correlations of some brain activities with slow-wave sleep, such as the metabolism of the limbic system, neuronal activities, local brain lesions, local kindling, etc. I further added the complex clinical correlations between slow-wave sleep and depression, adopting the physiological criteria of heart rate and blood pressure of depression seldom mentioned at that time, and accordingly, I solved the problem. I adopted the ascending reticular system to explain the abnormal phenomenon that total sleep deprivation merely transiently ameliorated depression, which relapsed after a nap. In television, the people were concerned with memory entropy. On the other hand, in science, it was necessary to compare and evaluate it one by one with waking, slow-wave sleep and REM sleep, and it was certainly difficult for them to achieve beyond the scope of Freudian theory on dream and sex.

Likewise, with regard to the coupling theory, without the most updated work on cases JW and BC in 1988, the actors and audiences would be unable not only to exclude the influence of mediodorsal thalamic case NA but also to achieve anything.

In September 2008, the people and I proposed that the Ph.D. degree could be useful in dealing with public and social problems and be a kind of certificate, such as a physician's degree, that is convenient for ignorant people to recognize. Nonetheless, it was unnecessary to deal with problems such as natural science, social science, etc. Science is evaluated with facts and achievements irrelevant to the qualification and experience of the researcher. None of the scientists, such as Newton, Faraday, Mendel, or Einstein, possessed any Ph.D. degree while writing their papers.

In December 2013, I learned via internet that JuTao Chen and others in China had discovered that it was easy to induce LTD in the state of slow-wave sleep, which was useful to support the theory of slow-wave sleep I had published.

End poem of this chapter:

The sage was born while there was heavy rain,
The wonderful child grew up with moistures of dew and rain,
The profound knowledge of aspirant youth shone in wind and rain,
The decent heart looked forward to brightness and rainbow after rain.

Chapter | 2

Satellites Tracing and Reading Brain

Musical Background of Rhythmic Writing: Blue Danube Waltz

Please read the following text sentence-by-sentence to feel the musical background of the rhythmic framework.

Chicago was one of the three biggest cities in the United States (US), while the other two cities were New York and Los Angeles. Chicago was located along Michigan Lake, which is a source of fresh water. Along the lake, there were miles of beaches and rocks linked with highways and beautiful scenery, and further, the lake water was cleaner and more harmless than seawater. The famous sexy journal "Playboy" was just headquartered in Chicago. Chicago had the most number of skyscrapers in the country. At that time, except the World Trade Buildings in New York, which were ranked as the 2nd and 3rd highest buildings in the United States, the 1st, 4th, 5th and 6th highest skyscrapers in the whole country were all located in Chicago, while there were as well nearly 20 buildings of more than 80 floors. The buildings in Chicago were impressive in artistry, and the students majoring in civil engineering could be required to inspect the buildings in Chicago. In politics, the state of Illinois, where Chicago was located, was the hometown of Lincoln and was the more radical place of the Northern side in the Civil War to liberate the black slaves. When I arrived in Chicago, I felt that I was in one of the best places in the United States.

In regard to returning to the United States this time, I was not feeling as happy as I had anticipated. Since my main purpose in going to the United States was to pursue a PhD degree, there was no longer the urgent feeling of going abroad to the United States after returning to China for the first time. Getting off the airplane, I considered how I merged to the society of the United States, and recalled the power of love I learned from Princess She-Ra. I felt that the social sciences were as complex as the brain sciences. Besides being good at dealing with complex phenomena, I could also easily deal with the social sciences.

I shared with Bo Su from WuHan and ShengQing Zhou from NanJing that I would like to rent the base floor of a private house. The house was located in the black area of a small town known as Evanston, where Northwestern University was located. It was somewhat horrible in the environment, but very close to the university. At that time, Northwestern University was ranked in integration above the top 15 in the country. There were two campuses, one located in Evanston in the northern suburb of Chicago, mainly consisting of the colleges of engineering, science and business, while another located in downtown Chicago, consisting of the colleges of law and medicine. Both the campuses, located on Lake Michigan, were very beautiful and claimed to be the most beautiful campuses in the country. North to the Evanston Campus there were tens of kilometers of rich areas, spacious and bright in villas, floral and neat in manors, endless in sight. On the other hand, the Chicago Campus sat close to the main street of Chicago, Michigan Street, with high buildings standing like the forest around, and Navy Pier aside furnishing departure for a lake tour, entertaining and amusing the tourists. In this regard, studying at Northwestern University in the United States was the happiest experience of my life.

I entered into the graduate class at Northwestern University Institute of Neuroscience (NUIN), which was trained in cooperation with many academic departments in both Evanston Campus and Chicago Campus of the university, abundant and diverse in its faculty, and ranked above the top 5 in the country in its integrative level of research on neural sciences. As I just needed to pursue a PhD degree as sufficient, I merely wished to pass all with high grades, and I was accordingly excellent in my grades in most of the courses in the first year of four quarters, nearly always the topper. I was not very fortunate in lab rotation in my first year. The university required every graduate student to perform rotations in one lab each quarter. To match with the teacher well, the student could stay in the lab to finish the PhD degree. I had finished a rotation in three labs, but I did not get admission until I contacted a Japanese teacher, Narahashi, at the Chicago Campus in my 4th quarter. He allowed me to stay in his lab to finish my PhD degree, and I was certainly very grateful to him.

At that time, the Department of Neuroscience at Evanston Campus relied on another Japanese professor to maintain quality, but he did not like too many Chinese in the department, so I stayed away from him. My adviser Narahashi fell in showy sick from senescence. He had previously discovered a neurotoxin and made use of it to facilitate elucidation of the mechanism in the conduction of nerves, and accordingly made important contributions. He showed up with his previous achievements, hoping to repress the Evanston Campus in academics. After all, Narahashi was a Japanese and the American whites beleaguered him for his indiscreet dominance, certainly within the range of academics and mostly in seminars. The old man was naturally not able to resist. In contrast, I considered that he had helped me, while his standing out to dominate was indirectly relevant to me, so I also spoke to help him in seminars.

Coincidentally, there came a new chairman to NUIN in the Chicago Campus. He was an Italian. The young and powerful faculty members of the Evanston Campus were very competent and had the reputation of strongly controlling the whole NUIN. They would certainly not take the new chairman seriously, and it was easy to shock him academically and atmospherically. Whereas, the new chairman was nonetheless as warm and active as other new officers and took advantage of our act of repressing Evanston Campus to profit himself. He made the middle and weak faculty of NUIN join his faction, made the Chicago Campus form one alignment to repress the Evanston Campus in reverse and accordingly made himself the new chairman.

It is always journalistic for the people to struggle with each other. While the two campuses of Northwestern University competed in academics, the people of Chicago and Evanston first acted as an audience and later became participants. I was the center of people's attention, as I had two theories on my hand. Even though I never mentioned them at that time, I accordingly radiated all over young and intelligent, brilliant and attractive, and very impressive in influence. The people staying with me were vigorous and happy, like the phoenix flying toward the sun. I paid attention to the people, discovering that the women in Chicago were legal and nice, whereas the men were relatively unkind and harsh. My roommate ShengQing Zhou from NanJing was very fond of music, having many melodious songs in his collection. I copied one cassette from him with one half containing all the happy songs of love sung by the US female singer Carpenter, and the other half containing the songs of love Carpenter had sung too, including the songs "Thousands of Songs" sung by Chinese HuiXian Chen, and "Regardless of Wind and Rain" sung by the Chinese HuaJian Zhou. These songs were characteristic of associating love with the vigor of progression. I played these songs in my car while driving, and the people in Chicago soon associated the songs from my car with my spirit of justice and philanthropy, giving me the image of a leader and the nickname "Love." The Chicago people lived in an atmosphere of love, vigor, justice, happiness and resonance, accompanied by skyscrapers, beauties and arts of metropolitan Chicago. At that time, Chicago was undoubtedly the most beautiful and great metropolis in the country, the acme and superstar of the country, and the glory and pride of the country.

In the early stage, when I was in the lab of Narahashi, I was bright, and had the opportunity to improve my lab skills further. Nonetheless, Narahashi soon became sick and dismissed me from his lab because of insufficiency in grants. I was sad, and so were the American people. However, I still made efforts to find a professor as influential as my adviser, and I found Professor Siddique at the Chicago Campus of Northwestern University. Professor Siddique was a Pakistani with a black complexion. He recently determined a gene of SOD in ALS patients, and accordingly, his lab was well funded. Professor Siddique was very strict and held many Chinese scholars from Hunan and many Americans and Middle Easterners abundant in talent. I was interested in SOD research, as it was relevant to ageing, which was the direction of research of my dream.

In academics, I at first contended in science with various talents in the lab without referring to my previously published two theories about the brain. The academic standards in the lab were also very high and could be ranked at the top level in the country at that time. In addition, they had already made contributions to ALS pathology, along with the fierce and proud personalities of those from the Middle East and Hunan. Accordingly, we contended more drastically with each other. After a period of mutual contention that did not last very long, I soon resisted the various offences in the lab and got the admiration of most of my colleagues in the lab. After that time, I actively promoted the lab members to join the academic exchanges in the department and got the recognition of most blacks in Chicago. The majority of NUIN also turned toward us, putting half the faculty of Evanston Campus down.

After entering the lab of Professor Siddique, I rented a good room in the silent and beautiful Evanston. The landlord was an old lady who was fond of arts, while the house was very beautiful, with only two people living in it. Every day, I drove past the Evanston Campus of Northwestern University, advanced along the highway, keeping the lake of best sceneries aside, and at last arrived at the Chicago Campus of Northwestern University. On the way, I played the songs of vigor and love, natural and heroic, attractive and prosperous.

As I was attractive and prosperous in popularity, the public activities I attended were more or less political and effective. Once, I attended the activity the graduate school held at Evanston Campus, in which the female Dean of the graduate school joined. Her name was Carol Simpson Stern. She was avant-garde, bright and natural, and was later usually called Pizza by the people on television. I had a good impression of her, thinking of her as able, just and friendly to Chinese. Nonetheless, after the activity, she considered my political influence and helped the Evanston Campus shock us, and we went into opposition. Half of the faculties of NUIN at the Evanston Campus gathered under the flag of Simpson Stern and eventually counterattacked with courage, whereas the NUIN at the Chicago Campus certainly raised the flag of surrender. My adviser, Professor Siddique, who was a black, like other black lab researchers, had to join the academic exchanges of the department; otherwise, they had to face difficulties in the atmosphere. We, at last, rose up to confront. At that time, I was propagating love and philanthropy, attracting a large number of Chicago people wishing for a healthy atmosphere to live in. Meanwhile, the academic ability of Siddique's lab was extraordinarily strong, and we also got support from many blacks. Half of the faculties at Evanston Campus were soon unable to resist, and the Chicago Campus won over once more in reverse. On the other hand, Simpson Stern did not give up while facing difficulties. Despite becoming hysteric and falling sick for a while, she targeted me to struggle without release. Nonetheless, she was still justifiable and nice. Finally, I managed to convince her that I was not malicious to her and she also withdrew from the struggle. At that time, I called myself king, while others called her queen, representing two different campuses, both bright as well.

At that time, another famous personage in Chicago was Jordan, who was a basketball star. In those two years, the Chicago Bulls, led by Jordan, won the championship of the National Basketball Association (NBA). Nonetheless, those matches were broadcast on television, and their instigated opinions were different from mine. Even though I was fairly impressed with Jordan, the effects were really very bad as a whole. Many Americans turned to the side of the Chicago Bulls' team while I was in the lab of Siddique. I still educated the people with "Love", influenced the people with the love songs of Carpenter, and depreciated the Bulls team as a kind of "Play." The people of Chicago soon adjusted their orientation, realized that "Love" was more important while "Play" could be negligible, and turned to support me. In this way, I defeated the Bulls team in Chicago in politics and won the highest prestige there. Surpassing Jordan's popularity, I boasted at that time that, except for Lincoln, I was the greatest in Chicago. The Chicago people called me "Dogcat."

Almost every Chinese in Chicago knew me, too. As I was 30 years old, I sometimes went to church to look for the chance of getting a girlfriend. Having overridden the Bulls team in politics, I was magnificent, like spreading a rainbow in public. Once, I went to the Christian church and helped a girl in Chinatown deal with unfairness. Surprisingly, the church workers dared to unite to oppose me, thinking that they could resist me. Nonetheless, I was like a king in Chicago, and I immediately counterattacked, shouting I was actually the God. Since then, whenever I went to church, I implied appearing as God. However, like others, I also started to face and consider the problem of religion seriously. Early in 1997, I was especially concerned about two paragraphs in the Holy Bible. One was the triunity of the Father, Son and Holy Spirit, while Jesus was just the Son, and the other was the death of Jesus as for the elution of the sins of humans, whereas saving humans would wait until the Holy Spirit to reincarnate to humans. I apprehended the point that salvation of the world from God resorted to the Holy Spirit, and I took upon myself as the Holy Spirit determinedly. At that time, I acted merely as the Holy Spirit on my own, without organizing my churches. In addition, I also took into account that Catholicism and Christianity would both respect Jesus and object to me. Nonetheless, I still insisted on my own way, taking advantage of the Holy Spirit as more modern and advanced, planning to propagandize to defeat the older religion to realize my aims. In this regard, I just acted as the Holy Spirit.

On September 16, 2007, the people and I considered whether these paragraphs of memoirs would infringe on the privacy of relevant persons. These persons were all scientific workers, had published papers and books, and had already been exposed autonomously to the public and history. Out of curiosity, the people at present and in future could inspect their details of life and work at any time, which was conjoint, natural and unrestrictive. It would also be a legal citation in case their lives and works were mentioned further in other books, newspapers and television. In this regard, these paragraphs of memoirs did not infringe on the privacy of relevant persons.

In the spring of 1997, XiaoPing Deng, the General Designer of reformation and opening of China, eventually passed away, with his ashes spread to the sea. In his lifetime, XiaoPing Deng, with his special manner of a black cat, corrected the planned economy as a white cat falling into a dead end and established the theory of marketing economy of socialism. I was greatly influenced by him and respected him much. The demise of XiaoPing Deng saddened me a lot. At that time, I had a great influence and felt that to maintain my good image, I should also kindly take into account the miserable Chinese people under autocracy. On that day, while standing on the street in downtown Chicago, I mumbled to try everything in my power to help my miserable Chinese compatriots. I soon made use of the church and Chinatown, wishing to organize the democratic force in the Chinese church and Chinatown abroad and unite with Hong Kong, Macao and China. I wished that the mainland China would devote to the development of economy, make people rich and strong, and afterwards unite with the democratic forces of Chinese abroad as well as the compatriots in Hong Kong and Macao, following the route of development on the one hand while democratization on the other. I named it "Hong Kong complement," as a complement to the "One country, two systems" that Xiaoping Deng had proposed to execute socialism domestically while allowing Hong Kong and Macao to continue capitalism. My idea got the admiration and support of many people in Chicago, and they were very glad and proud of me.

As I took the position of Holy Spirit on my own, promoted the reformation of religion and further advocated the Hong Kong complement, I became an important personage in the United States (US). In this regard, the US army started to trace me with satellites, gradually understood and clearly heard what I spoke, and eventually read out what I thought in my brain with similar data processing technologies. By reading out a human brain for the first time in history, the satellite operators made a significant breakthrough in technology, while I was possibly the first human whose brain was read out. Prior to 2000, the early warning airplane had already been able to detect 200 kilometers, while the perigee of a spy satellite was about 200 kilometers, which was certainly equipped with sensitive detective radar equipment. The brain was about 20W in energy, far exceeding the reflective waves of radar in energy. In this regard, it was not difficult at all for the satellites to read the brain with the detective equipment. I was very familiar with the academic society at that time, which did not even dare to imagine the problem of reading out the brain. I was also far away from equipment from such military technology as microwave-induced thermoacoustic topography at that time. Reading out the brain with satellites was really a miraculous and leaping breakthrough that would influence human society.

In 2000, after returning to China, I started to collect direct evidence of satellites reading out the brain. At that time, I started to make use of the technology from the satellites tracing me as microwave-induced thermoacoustic topography and direct the satellite operators to follow me and shout aloud to the public with the vibratory energy of satellites, striving for and promoting the progression of democracy in China, and eliciting the attention of the whole world. Satellites to read out the brain were repeatedly perceived and recognized by the people on television. In addition, some of my privacies, such as my privacies in primary school, my opinions on various classmates in university, my experience in the University of Notre Dame, my details in going to see physicians and playing chess, my viewpoints on various politicians and judgments on political situations on television, etc., were all apprehended and comprehended by the people in the whole world. Satellites to read out the brain became the papers written on television. In 2015, a US journal headquartered in India published my report on US satellites in Reading out the Brain, entitled "Advocacy for extension of microwave and infrared to detect the brain activities" (Journal of Medical Diagnostic Methods 4,e188, 2015).

In September 2008, I purchased the videos of the opening ceremony of the Olympic Games from 1984 to 2008 and watched that the US satellites started to trace me from 1988, but I did not know it because they did not project laser rays on me from ranging satellites. There was no such instance in the opening ceremony of the Olympic Games in 1984. The videos of the opening ceremony of the Olympic Games from 1988 to 1996 showed that the athletes and audiences in various countries knew that the people around me and I did not know that the satellites had been tracing me. If these videos were real and not modified, they implied that the US satellites had been secretly tracing me without any purpose from 1988 to 1996.

One day in the spring of 1997, soon after the satellites traced me and read out my brain, while I was in the toilet at home in Evanston, the US ranging satellites projected me with the infrared laser ray and said to me, "Key Chinese Army," meaning that, with the Chinese army as the obstacle, how I could realize democracy in China. They were bad in attitude and conspicuous in their intention to embarrass me. I replied that I had a method and told them about the method I had previously considered. The Chinese army had its own benefit. I realized that democracy did not have much influence on soldiers and most of the military officers. Nonetheless, the political commissars in the Chinese army were offered by the autocrats. As soon as they were changed to become the people's representatives to monitor the army and were allowed to serve the people and democracy, in that way, they could keep their positions, and there would not be any conflict of interest between the Chinese army and democracy, nor could there be any special obstacle in realizing democracy. The US operator confessed it as possibly feasible.

On that night, a strange event occurred for the first time in the history of humans. Very late that night, while I was downstairs to take a midnight snack, the US satellites came again to my room and told me very strangely that, now that I could subdue the Chinese army, I was terrible. They reminded me that I was the Holy Spirit of the Christian religion, while the Christian religion was very influential in the United States. As I possessed the great wisdom to subdue the giant and autocratic Chinese army, the US people would admire me very much, and I would be very influential in the United States. The US army considered that I, as the God of the Holy Spirit, would accordingly influence and command them in future. They did not obey the Chinese because they thought the Chinese had inferior characteristics and asked me to commit suicide to save the United States from my influence. I certainly did not agree. Whereas, out of my anticipation, a US military man shouted in the accent of General Patton: "Ok, break earth." Meanwhile, they presented to me a picture of a military heroine, resembling Simpson Stern, the Dean of Graduate School at Northwestern University at that time, full of the atmosphere of a portion of the US army rebelling to ignite the nuclear war and destroy the whole world. According to the exaggerated understanding of the nuclear striking ability of the United States in the time of 1997, it was possible for the action of "Break Earth" to annihilate or heavily damage humans on land, while the ocean nuclear fusion required the reaction of both deuterium and tritium, both of which were too low in concentration to be ignited.

I had no time to take any measures and was very much scared. I felt that the humans could be extirpated, and the civilization could be terminated. At that time, the method humans used to deal with nuclear war was control instead of war. They would definitely choose to force me to commit suicide. I was extremely nervous, looking like a kidnapped hostage before being killed or decapitated on television. If the event had been propagated to everybody, even though I had committed suicide, I would still have deserved to do so. Nonetheless, if I was required to commit suicide like a psychotic patient without the event known to anybody, even lower than a soldier with discounted payment, I was really unwilling to do so. I anxiously beseeched them and cried aloud: "No, please." The military man in the US satellite repeatedly requested me to commit suicide; otherwise, they would "break earth." However, I again beseeched them, "No, please." How could I agree to suicide? Striving to survive is the instinct of every person. There is merely one life for each person, which will be lost once dead. In addition, their action belonged to military rebels, and accordingly, it was uncertain whether it was real or not. The operator of the US satellite shouted out angrily: "Ok, break earth." I waited silently for a while, watching the reaction of the surrounding people. I felt that it was impossible for the humans to be annihilated in total with one strike. They could possibly be heavily damaged until I was killed by the people surrounding me to appease the event. I was very sad and scared and felt that I was approaching my death.

At that moment, my psychology in anticipation of fortune dramatically increased as well, thinking it was possible that there could be nothing to occur at all; may be the US army fabricated a scenario to hurt my reputation, since after all, the satellite shouts were different from any formal promise and signature. Meanwhile, my psychological terror about nuclear bombing to annihilate all humans somewhat decreased as well, feeling that in trying to do so, the United States could heavily damage the humans and could not exclude that some could leak to survive. Even I, on my own, could also survive the nuclear bombardment since I happened to stay downstairs with good protection. Nonetheless, I also felt that the people around me would still force me to commit suicide or directly kill me since the quantities of deaths were numerous, and I did not have such big merits and virtues as unnecessary to be concerned about the lives or deaths of so many people. I patiently waited for the surrounding reaction and action and soon perceived that nothing had changed. The opponents did not do anything but just shouted out somewhat, which was really boastful. In this regard, I determined that the event belonged to the malicious hurt of my reputation. I relaxed, went to sleep at ease, and believed that I was able to deal with my political and reputational loss. Holy Spirit supervised the greatest religion, and I was certainly not afraid of such hurt to my reputation.

On the second day, after waking up in the morning, I heard many sounds of magpies the US satellites projected into my bedrooms. There were also many friendly voices of military women, blessing me and consoling me to act as the Holy Spirit at ease, to disturb me no more. On the way I went to the lab, carefully acted as the Holy Spirit and experienced the feelings. In the lab, the US satellites made use of the same nuclear terror to threaten me. However, this time, I was no longer offended without prevention. With early experience in mind, I was neither in the appearance of hostage to be decapitated any longer, nor nervous about the surrounding whites to stand out and kill me under the influence of rumor shouts of satellites. Nonetheless, I said with a sense of justice that the military man had been very dangerous with the manner of maligning and vilifying shouts one day earlier and asked the countries of nuclear weapons, such as those in Europe, Russia, China, etc, to prepare for war and target at the United States. Once there occurred this kind of situation, it was emergent to disperse and protect the people, counterattack the United States and annihilate the crime with war. At that time, I considered myself the very famous Holy Spirit, and the various countries would do what I said. Since that time, the US satellites had no longer been threatening and terrifying me with nuclear terror, probably because my calling to war was very dangerous. As per psychology and law, it was the first time I thoughtfully dealt with this event.

According to my later experience, I returned to China to become a major force. The people and I calculated that there were merely about 10 thousand nuclear bombs of different sizes in the United States in 1997. According to the explosive power at that time, they could merely damage a part of China the most. It was not sufficient to destroy the entire civilization on earth. Therefore, the US nuclear bombs were merely targeted at hostile countries, but not at the countries of amity. It was unable to accomplish a nuclear attack on the whole world in one instant. My calling for war preparedness and alarm on the second day was sufficient to assure that the humans would not be annihilated. In 1997, the stock of VX nerve gas in the US and Russia was both within millions of tons. It could cause damage to a total area of hundreds and thousands of square meters, equal to one province or one state. In November 2008, I learned that launching a US nuclear weapon required two staff, separately controlling and matching two commands of codes as the dual keys for safety assurance. Accordingly, the military coup men were not able to launch nuclear weapons to wreak any personal hostility.

On November 8, 2008, I watched the opening ceremony of the Olympic Games in 1996, which I had not watched earlier. If the video was real and not modified, there were many European and American people on the spot mentioning

"Break earth" as the winning force of autocracy and asking the satellite operators to send me to the ocean with the method of requiring me to commit suicide in response to "Break earth." There were also many people on the spot realizing that since the ocean had been difficult to ignite to become sun with big meteorolites, the nuclear bombs could merely damage the lands. Accordingly, in Chicago, the "Break earth" of satellite operators was merely aimed at the humans on land, in compliance with my common knowledge at that time. According to historical facts, it had been difficult for either the US President or Minister of Defense to capture criminal satellite operators for several years. However, it was clear that neither of them could directly reach satellite operators. After 2010, Hillary, the wife of President Clinton, took the opportunity to come to television as the Secretary of State to oppose the apportionment of this event of shouts of "breaking earth" with satellites to her family. In June 2014, Clinton was required to characterize this event as an accident of subordinates. Further, it was also common knowledge that the staff at TV stations found it difficult to operate the laser satellites to shout to me. In this regard, this event was possibly the prank of operators in the controlling center of US NASA, with its method possibly originating from the opening ceremony of the Olympic Games in 1996.

On March 14, 2007, with my kindness of reducing to eating half the amount of meat, I tried to eliminate the negative political influences of this event. On October 10, 2011, the people and I made use of the more real, authoritative and severe missile event of Kennedy and the early ocean nuclear experiments of the USA and USSR to compare and oppress the unreal Chicago event.

Several days after this event in 1997, I just concentrated on acting as the Holy Spirit, while in association with my previous image of "Love," I shouted out the slogan "God is love," similar to most religions. During this period, the US satellites were very friendly. They took the staff from mainland China into the satellite communications and directly transferred me to the party, government and army in mainland China. The mainland of China repeatedly struck me through satellites and required me to go back to China, lest I was inopportune to the situation in China. I replied that I would consider going back to China if there was a formal invitation from China. Afterwards, the Chinese operators of satellites started to say reversely that I was worthless, not very clever, and repeatedly and illegally interfered with my normal life.

Several more days had passed, and I was still afraid of the event. On that day, the satellite shouted, "Break earth," and worried about the malicious US staff requested me once more to commit suicide via making disputes or fabricating pranks. In response, I repeatedly stressed that I was a man and needed to complete merits and virtues to become the Holy Spirit and rise up to heaven. In this way, I felt safer. Actually, as Jesus had been crucified to death, the Holy Spirit could certainly rise up from underground. As I adopted the manner of calling for humans to war to deal with the satellites shouting nuclear war to request me to commit suicide, which was very bad in relation to the people, I felt it could be appropriate for me to withdraw the Holy Spirit not to be threatened by terror once more. Later, I recalled that in Buddhism, a man also became Buddha through meditation and felt that it could be more appropriate for Buddha to act as the Holy Spirit, so I withdrew the Holy Spirit to yield the position to Buddha. At that time, I especially pointed out that there could be many gods in Buddhism, which makes it easier to adapt to social advancement than the religion of a single god. In Buddhism, when important merit and virtue were achieved, it was possible to add a god, but it was impossible to do with the society.

The terrors and hurts from US satellites made it difficult for me to continue acting as the Holy Spirit. Actually, if there had not been such an event as "Break earth you suicide," it would have been possible for me to continue the propagation of philanthropy to become the real Holy Spirit of the Christian religion.

Afterwards, the satellites were hurting me more severely. There were many artistic abstract paintings in the house of the white granny I rented, which looked somewhat like ghosts. I felt scared and moved out, renting a room on the base floor of another apartment in Evanston, hoping to shield satellites. According to my knowledge, microwaves and infrared had neither been lethally harmful to the human body before that time, nor had there been infrared guns. Nonetheless, this time, I encountered the new infrared laser ranging satellites of both China and the United States. The operators from China and the United States utilized these laser satellites to hurt me numerous times. Out of my anticipation, the satellite infrared lasers even penetrated the walls of the room like X-rays and hit me directly, which was really more dangerous and difficult to protect than bullets. I repeatedly appealed to the US army to stop the satellites from hitting me, but there was nobody in response, not at all in effect. Sometimes, I shouted in the subway that the satellite terror had invaded the US territory. Some of the Chicago people were scared, and some supported me. However, the US army was indifferent as it always had been, not having the sense of responsibility to protect the territory at all. Several times, the satellite infrared brutally shocked my heart at night, which was very dangerous. I accordingly felt death was approaching me.

As the satellites read out my brain, with the microwave-induced thermoacoustic vibration, the satellite operators were accordingly able to directly shout out the contents in my mind I wished to shout and propagate to the people. Many female assistants were assigned to me in Chinese satellites. They had very pleasant voices and were specialized in helping shout what I wished in my mind to shout and propagate. Sometimes, when I murmured in a low voice, the contents wished to shout. The satellite operators also accompanied me with a pleasant female voice that could shout not from reading out my brain but from my commands in a low voice.

Even though the satellites sometimes terrified and shocked me at night, they were friendly in the daytime when there were many people. In the daytime, I also discussed the subjects of science and technology with them. The most influential were the investigations about the future. One day in my apartment, I pointed out that the main energy storage on earth, such as petroleum, coal, etc., would soon be used up in future, and we would mainly use solar energy. The shortage of solar energy was caused by the alteration of day and night, and electrical energy was required to be stored after its transformation from light energy. I considered using batteries, but it was inconvenient and unsatisfactory. An American in satellite proposed to utilize photoelectric energy to electrolyze water to make hydrogen and to retransform it into water after being burnt. It had unlimited sources, could be used endlessly and was very convenient in all aspects. We were all excited and felt it would be the era of photoelectric energy that would make hydrogen in the future. I also proposed to make artificial muscles in the future with gene technology, where we would no longer need to kill animals to eat their meats, and the animals and humans would all be protected by the law in similarity, which I named infinity. In that year, I further made use of the solar magnetic field to design a nuclear magnetic spacecraft that could fly in space for a long time. The fans of Unidentified Flying Objects (UFOs) could think of the magnetic spacecraft earlier than I did, which required historians to check videos and whether they had been broadcast on television.

So far to the summer, the Chinese in satellites did not at all consider my investigating future with satellite operators and continued using satellite infrareds at night to hit and hurt me frequently even more and more, making me feel dangerous more and more, and in further making me recall the duty of US police in protecting the people. One night, the Chinese in satellites shouted with a high, tinny sound around my ear with very thin and strong infrared beams from the ranging satellite, making me feel that, if the beams were changed to shock my heart, I could lose my life. I was at last scared very much and got up to call for Evanston police to ask for protection. Out of anticipation, the police did not say anything and just sent me to see the physician, who assumed there was no satellite tracing and sound in the world and sent me into the psychotic hospital with force.

After being hospitalized, I insisted that I was not ill on my own while the satellites were real. In addition, I resorted to the law to protect me. In the hospital, the satellites decreased the intensity of offending me, and I continued discussing science with satellite operators. I proposed that the widely accepted theory of cosmic explosion in physics at that time could not be correct, as the calculated age of the cosmos was merely 20-30 billion years, whereas the cosmos we observed was farther beyond 20-30 billion light years. It was impossible for the cosmos to explode at a speed faster than that of light. I proposed that the central black holes in the Milky Way Galaxy and other galaxies were not dead holes.

On the one hand, they absorbed the light energy in the cosmos, and on the other hand, they spouted out the protons and electrons with some mechanisms, generating the stars in galaxies. Nonetheless, as this was just a preliminary consideration at that time and not mature, and as I could not figure out why the black holes spouted out matters in reverse, I had to temporarily put them all aside. In the hospital, another event occurred that grieved me. As I was hospitalized, I could not continue my Ph.D. study and once again missed the Ph.D. degree. After being hospitalized for several weeks, I eventually won the lawsuit and was released from the hospital.

As soon as I had left the hospital, the satellite operators strengthened their offences and terrors toward me, whereas this time, I adopted international action in response. I thought that satellite terror was merely the cooperation between the two countries of the United States and China, and if I left the United States and went to a third country, I could acquire the protection of law in that country if it was still traced by satellites any longer. In this way, I was able to make use of the law in the third country against the satellites and able to acquire safety. I applied for a visa to travel to Canada for the tour. While I was waiting for its visa, I struggled against the terror with satellite slogans in Chicago, directing satellites to shout in Chinese: "惩恶扬善是法律 (Punishing evil and promoting kindness are law)."

I waited and eventually got a travelling visa to Canada. I took the train at the Chicago railway station, the biggest in the United States, to leave for Toronto, a Metropolis in Canada. The US operators in satellites were very angry at my going to Canada, considering it somewhat harmful to their reputation. On the way to Canada, the satellite operators beamed my chest and abdomen with infrared rays and continually projected pictures of terror, exerting big psychological pressure on me. After arriving in Toronto, the Chinese and US satellite operators, desperate to trace me and ferocious in shocking me, did not care about the boundary of the country at all and shocked and stretched me nearly to death with a kind of infrared laser satellite of very high energy. A US female at last released beams and saved my life. Nonetheless, the Chinese satellites also learned to control this kind of satellite of very high energy, repeatedly shocking me and making it very dangerous. I had to escape to the hospital, asking physicians to help me, but they did not rescue me from danger. Instead, they locked me in the hospital of psychosis to allow the satellites to shock me at their will. In the hospital of psychosis, the satellites once again decreased the strength of shocking and terrifying me. I repeated the same tactic, resorting to the law to defend that I did not fall ill due to psychosis. At last, the hospital was angry with me and accordingly discharged me away from the hospital. During my stay in the Canadian hospital, I compiled the scientific achievements in communication with satellites into a booklet for propagation.

After leaving the hospital, I tried to propagate the danger of satellites through newspapers, motivating people to control satellites, but I was unsuccessful. As Canada could not protect me, I had no other choice but to return to the United States. I wished to go to such political centers as the United Nations in New York or the US Congress in Washington, using the sounds of satellites to make annoyance, and mobilizing the people to struggle against the terror of satellites, and finally winning back the safety. In this regard, I took the train to return to Chicago from Toronto. On the way back to the United States, I thought that the United States was the leader of world democracy and also had nice, high-quality people and I would definitely be able to take advantage of the spirit of democracy to promote the opinions of people in the country, controlling the satellites and protecting my safety. On the way, I sang songs aloud to praise the United States.

After I arrived in Chicago, my relative Kathy picked me up at the airport and arranged for me to live in her home in Evanston. At night, the Chinese in satellites repeatedly annoyed me, agitating the whole night. Kathy was intolerant and wanted to report to the police the second morning. I told them it was useless to report to the police. The police would definitely be indifferent and would say the satellites were illusions and send me once more to the hospital for psychosis. Kathy assured me not to worry. She was a lawyer, and her family was willing to witness the satellites as terror and crime, believing in the US system to protect the people. At last, she, her husband and I went together to report to the police. Nonetheless, the police still repeated the same tactic, taking the chance of checking my health to directly transfer me to the hospital of psychosis, while extruding away the family of Kathy, not listening to their explanation of satellites at all. In the hospital, I still insisted on going out, whereas the hospital replied that unless I was repatriated back to China, I would be forced to take medicine. I objected, but soon, I had to give up. I had satellites tracing me, was in much danger and would definitely be killed. In this regard, I would rather return to China and meet my parents for the last family union. At last, I decided to go back to China and asked my good friend Bo Su to help me receive the Diploma of Master's Degree and mail it back to me.

In November 1997, after being traced by the satellites for more than half a year, I was eventually forced to leave the United States due to the malfeasance and incompetence of Chicago police. On the way back home, my pessimistic thoughts of inevitable death disappeared. On the airplane, I directed the satellites to accompany the sound and sing the song: "Praise God superior to all things, the world of all things praise the Lord," indicating that it was me as the real God to come back home, and it was as well the important thing of humans. I was not only happy but also excited. I was ambitious and thoughtful, determined to grow up once more, full of confidence. I was famous worldwide with abundant scientific and religious backgrounds and a degree from a famous US university. Further, I also had the satellites trace and shout on my behalf. As soon as I got a good job, I would be prosperous in future. When the airplane landed at the Beijing airport, my father and a relative from Beijing came to pick me up. I returned to my own country, and my life turned over into a new chapter.

End poem of this chapter:

Love and salvation emerged to the Holy Spirit as cause and chance.
The novel creation of reading brain with satellites added to miracles.
The declaration of war struggled against the nuclear request of suicide as a response.
The lights of satellites with terrific infringe were difficult to overcome with a sad voice.

Chapter | 3

Democracy Calling for Law Execution,

New Theory of Army and Police

Musical Background of Rhythmic Writing: The Theme Song "The Blood of Steel and Heart of Faith" in "The Legend of the Condor Heroes"

Please read the following text sentence-by-sentence to feel the musical background of the rhythmic framework.

After getting off the airplane, my father and I stayed just for one day at the home of my relative in Beijing and returned to SuZhou. At that time, Beijing looked rather dirty, with dust everywhere, and it lagged much more than the United States. SuZhou did not change at all; it was the same as it was in 1994 when I had gone abroad. However, the city was tidier and more hygienic. Shortly after, I returned to SuZhou and BoSu mailed me the Diploma of Master's Degree from Northwestern University. From the end of 1997 to the Spring Festival of 1998, I mainly looked for a job in SuZhou and contacted several universities. Nonetheless, they all prevaricated to think for a while. Finally, I decided to go to Shanghai while working as a salesman in the Stanford Property Agency. During this period, while reading books at the SuZhou Library, I happened to find a Chinese book for the popularization of science and technology, introducing both the utilization and storage of solar energy, including storage by batteries, redox of metals, making hydrogen fuels, etc., while using electrolysis to make hydrogen by solar energy was just one method of making fuels, earlier than the satellite operator.

Shortly after the Spring Festival of 1998, I went to Shanghai to work and started living in a single room at ZhuHang. I worked at Shanghai Stanford Property Agency, where the boss was Chen, a quite able young man who always encouraged me. I worked rather diligently, mainly dealing with the property rent for expatriates of foreign companies. I was also allowed to learn all aspects and details of Shanghai as a modern and international metropolis. Shanghai had changed dramatically over the past few years. It had abundant high buildings, was beautiful and clean in decorations, and had further been constructed with subways. The metropolis had then already been internationalized totally, with foreign companies and representative offices everywhere, while the European and US advertisements were dominant in business, promoting their products and culture. The Shanghai people were nice, modern and aspirant previously. After being internationalized, they were neater in clothes, more various in colors, and more civil in demeanors. English was popularized quickly, becoming the 2nd working language of many companies.

I worked at the Stanford Company for several months. Nonetheless, due to my inability to register my residence, I had to leave them. I changed to ZhongXi Pharmaceutical Co., Ltd., a big nationally owned pharmaceutical plant which mainly works on international trading. The company supplied me with a dormitory and helped me register my residence in

Shanghai. In the autumn of 1998, the ZhongXi Pharmaceutical Company sent me to Guangzhou to attend the Guangzhou Fair of China Export Commodities. For the first time, I toured GuangZhou and the ZhuJiang River. GuangZhou was also quite internationalized, and abundant in high buildings. The people in Guangzhou were rather fair, modern, sexy and Westernized in decoration, while the English were not as popular as in Shanghai. The atmosphere in GuangZhou was hotter and more active than that in Shanghai, hot and red in restaurants, dauntless and sexy in Kala OK, with the ZhuJiang River rather splendid and beautiful. These were my primary impressions of Guangzhou at that time: beautiful and opening.

In regard to the methods of struggling against satellites, I learned from the lesson of failure in reporting to the police in the United States. In the account of China as an autocratic country, the Chinese satellites just represented the autocratic Party, government and army. If I objected to them in public, I would definitely earn nothing. Hence, I no longer shouted to catch them publicly or mentioned the satellites to the surrounding supervisors and colleagues. The satellites terrified and harassed me continually while they were repressed by the international atmosphere in Shanghai. Hence, the Chinese satellites were ameliorated much in their terrifying atmosphere, often beginning to hurt me in the evening and quite lower in the energy of beams. The hurt from satellites extended my comprehension of the protective function of the police, and I began to realize that the police were different from the law. The law helped the victim to fairly get revenge after the case, while the police were further able to prevent the crimes before their occurrence and stop crimes by their violence on the spot. The police might actively utilize their forces firstly by law!

At the end of 1998, since the ZhongXi Pharmaceutical Company was not high in income, the departmental manager suggested I find a better job. I was lucky enough to find a job in a big US electronic company, Seagate, in WuXi in the post of senior supervisor of human resources. I assisted the Singaporean human resource director, helping him run errands and recruit senior employees, and also fit my speciality as a US Master of Psychology. I started working in WuXi in January 1999 and received a total of about 5500RMB/month (salary + allowance for errands), which was quite a high salary in the area southern to the Yangtze River. In Wuxi, I lived in QingYang New Village, a famous civil and clean Village in Wuxi. I shared an apartment with two bedrooms and one dining room with an engineer named Zhang from HuBei. He was honest and active but somewhat cautious and parsimonious in personality. While talking about politics, he would speak against his own will. We often went outside to enjoy food or to watch videos of sex. He often helped me inquire where there were videos of sex and where there were women, fairly flattery.

At Seagate Company, I recruited senior talents throughout the country. Hence, I often ran errands to Shanghai, Beijing, Tianjin, Shenzhen, etc. and lived in international hotels above four stars. I had been to Beijing twice, once in TianJin and once in ShenZhen. My impression of Beijing at that time was rapidly an internationalization of the metropolis, quite Westernized in the dress of the people, somewhat hot in cultural atmosphere, nonetheless a little drier and fiercer than

Shanghai and Guangzhou. When the night came and the weather became cold, the market turned cool and quiet. Nonetheless, the erotic places were still hot. My impression of ShenZhen at that time was that it was quite modern in the metropolis, abundant in high buildings, wide and straight streets, and full of graded separation of highways. The people of Shen Zhen came from all over the country, and hence, it was not as Westernized as Guangzhou and more domestic than Guang Zhou.

In Seagate Company, besides learning human resources, I also learned the concept of law execution, which further intensified my impression of the mandatory and violent characteristics of police and law. Due to the illegal harassment of satellites and the international atmosphere of China, I enjoyed the advantages of police more while gradually throwing away the shadows in the United States. I believed that the police were obliged to protect the people, so if I relied on the police and the internationalized society of law, I would finally acquire the chance to defeat the terrors of satellites.

Prior to October 1999, I occasionally relied on the US satellites to protect me from being hurt by the Chinese satellites. One day, when I was at home in Suzhou at night, for the sake of escaping from the satellite beams, I slept in the big bedroom of my parents. I asked the US satellites to protect me on the spot. The US satellites projected a picture of one female police with blonde hair and a white suit, sitting on the satellite orbit and saying World Police. I was rather happy, often using this term later. I could not accurately recall when it happened, either in 1998 or 1999. From the video of the inspection of military troops on National Day on October 1, 1999, it could be seen that Beijing was deeply influenced by our thoughts of world-armed police.

Through Seagate Company, I set up a model for foreign companies. I promoted foreign companies to enter China while advocating for them to engulf nationally owned companies. It liberated the Chinese people from the autocratic control of government, thereby setting up a bright flag for the Chinese people, advancing toward the world of democracy. In October 1999, since Seagate Company was planning to downsize on a large scale, and I was paid high, I was actively asked to quit the job and leave, returning to Shanghai. I was quite happy in the several months I stayed at Seagate Company.

I found a job as the human resources manager at Shanghai Trayton Furniture Company. I was asked to report to work that October. I rented a single room in the noblest HongQiao District in Shanghai. Although it was expensive, it fit my status as a senior manager in a foreign company. From my struggle against the terrors of satellites, the Shanghai people comprehended more about the responsibility of the police to protect the common people. Hence, the police would finally become good people. The world police had a more vivid and deep impression on the minds of the Shanghai people.

At the end of 1999 and the beginning of 2000, the Chinese operators of satellites did not yet deduct their harassment and terror from me. One day, I said, "In this way, I might lose my life." Nonetheless, the satellite operators continued fighting against me. Hence, I was angry and said the accommodations to me were even below that of Dan Wang, the leader of students, on June 4th. The Chinese operators of satellites thought I deserved the service in this way. I replied that I would promote democracy for retaliation while they were all the igniters. The Chinese operators of satellites did not mind and set me free, by my way. Previously, since there were satellites tracing me, I was thereby exposed. Hence, it was not appropriate for me to promote democracy. Nonetheless, the terrors and crimes of satellites against me even exceeded the abuse against the democratic personages, so I would certainly rise up vigorously, resisting the terrors and promoting democracy. The next day, sitting in the office of Trayton Furniture Company, I told the operators of satellites that I upheld ZiYang Zhao. The laser-ranging satellite projected an image of a man from the People's Liberation Army (PLA) and said, in quite an emotional voice, that by my help, Ziyang Zhao might acquire help as if from God; hence, all things in China would improve. The Chinese and American satellites were both excited and quite happy. They finally had a good task that was compatible with their own hopes, while the job of satellite operator was a good one!

One day later, I felt that important psychological obstacles to the democracy of China were the old revolutionists of YanAn and the People's Liberation Army (PLA), as both accounted for the country as owned by themselves, whilst most people also consented to this point. Democracy should partly usurp their country, just as they usurp their properties. Hence, the old revolutionists of YanAn and the People's Liberation Army (PLA) both objected to democracy from their hearts. Nonetheless, the people were not so cruel as to usurp the properties of theirs. It was necessary to overcome this difficulty. At that time, on the street in the HongQiao District of Shanghai, the atmosphere of internationalization and properties was strong and salient in the philosophical belief of private property. They stood along with me to resist the properties of the country owned by YanAn and the People's Liberation Army (PLA). The confrontation made me think that the country was supplied by developed areas such as Shanghai and so on, and hence, should be the property of paid taxes from areas such as Shanghai and so on. I immediately recalled and cited the term "Property of paid taxes" and learned from the television play that previously, it was the term the US people used to disparage the police and is seldom heard in Chinese society. When I cited the term "Property of paid taxes," I immediately generated strong emotional and novel feelings about the country belonging to the people, grasping the key point and thereby keeping it permanent in memory. Then, I admired the old American concept of "Property of paid taxes," which was really wise and correct. It was short of an input of voice or letter from satellites for "Property of paid taxes" then. Even though there might be an input of pictures to uphold my consideration, they were neither important nor mature and were far from the surrounding environment and atmosphere in affection. Whether there was anybody on television thinking in the same way as I did required further investigation; nonetheless, I was sure there should be quite a few while not being able to form a political influence. Within the later three years, from television, the people also generally recognized that "Property of paid taxes" was my thought and slogan at that time, and the satellite operators differed in opinion.

"Property of paid taxes" was the intuitive slogan from the

principle of law that the country belonged to the people. At that moment, I directed the satellites to shout loudly in Chinese, “纳税财产 (Property of paid taxes),” and the Shanghai people around also heard me, comprehended its significance and became relieved. At that time, China was still in the period of repressing democracy, so if anybody propagated or promoted democracy, they might be arrested and punished severely. Since the appearance of this slogan, it has been possible for the people to acquire protection as masters and owners by law while realizing democracy formally and publicly. If the YanAn conservatives and People's Liberation Army (PLA) objected more, they might fall into the unfavorable situation of being gangsters and repressed.

Several weeks later, I also recalled that China was still a country of democratic dictatorship nominally. Hence, I felt it would be easier to use the slogan of democratic dictatorship. From television news, I saw ZeMin Jiang had also thought of this point earlier than I, and further, he had felt I was also able to recall it and use it to act. I really made use of it and propagated democracy vigorously. I also directed the satellite operators to shout loudly in Chinese in Shanghai, SuZhou and on the train: “纳税财产，民主专政 (Property of paid taxes, Democratic dictatorship).” Since then, the word “democracy” has appeared in the slogans of satellites. As a result, the Chinese people, who dared not mention the word “democracy” previously, began to talk about “democracy” publicly. It broke through the oppressive situation in China after the June 4th incident of 1989, by which the Chinese people might be arrested and punished severely if they tried to propagate or shout for democracy. By the law of China and the world, the

Chinese people were allowed to shout for democracy!

I used the newest method of directing the Chinese and US satellites to shout; hence, it was an advantage in propagation. I was rather fortunate to establish my brand and lead the advancement of Chinese democracy. I sometimes directed the satellites to shout by brain directly, while sometimes directed them to shout by throat murmurs. Hence, I corresponded with the anchorperson and leader. At home, I directed the satellites to shout either on the balcony or on the bed while sleeping. On the way, I directed the satellites to shout on the bus, taxi, or while walking. In the office, I directed the satellites to shout in the office and aisle. For the sake of awarding the satellite voices following me to shout democracy, I also said it was necessary to especially award the police badges to the voices from satellites following my direction and helping my shouts of democracy. It was possible to sweep across several countries for the shouts of satellites from a horizontal direction, huge in power of propagation.

At that time, for the promotion of democracy, I thought it necessary to attract many people to uphold and favor. Hence, I found a nickname for myself as "哪吒 (Nezha)." "Nezha" was recorded mainly in the stories of "Investiture of Gods" and "The Journey to the West." He was the god of a little boy who stepped on the windy flaming wheels and whom everybody was fond of. He was also a good God of kindness and justice. The Chinese people were mostly fond of the nickname then. Additionally, I also often utilized the computer to sing the song "The Blood of Steel and Heart of Faith" in "The Legend of the Condor Heroes," courageous and heroic, vigorous and aspirant. In 2007, the Beijing sound from satellite protested and said I was too risky in future. Hence, they were not fond of me to be Nezha. Therefore, I resigned Nezha just as I had resigned the Holy Spirit previously, lest some Chinese might find trouble.

In April 2000, due to the difference in working style from the Danish boss, I quit the job and transferred to an investment company in Shanghai. I also served as a human resource manager from July 2000 to October 2000. In these three months, in Shanghai, in SuZhou and on the train, I directed the satellites to shout in Chinese: "纳税财产，民主专政 (Property of paid taxes, Democratic dictatorship)." The Shanghai people shook off their shackles and spirited aspiringly and vigorously while the thought of democracy spread widely. The sky of Shanghai turned nearly red!

In October 2000, I quit the job in Shanghai and registered my own company in SuZhou. I named it "SuZhou CaiFortune Investment and Information Consulting Co., Ltd." I initially hoped to set up the company for the convenience of my patents to attract investments while also running the company to serve for meetings. Nonetheless, I did not earn enough from the business meeting by the end of the year; hence, I was nervous. Then, a PLA (People's Liberation Army) man of satellite said it might be rather profitable to do headhunting business. Following his suggestion, I began to do headhunting business, which was a fortunate business for several years until the global economic crisis in 2008.

On September 16, 2007, people and I accounted whether these paragraphs of memoirs infringed on the privacy of relevant companies illegally. Fortunately, the companies I had worked with had all been advertised in newspapers or on television; hence, they had been partially exposed to the public and history. However, the internal technological and commercial secrets of these companies were not mentioned in my memoirs. Hence, these paragraphs of memoirs did not infringe on the privacy of relevant companies illegally.

Additionally, after entering Trayton Company in 1999, I began directing the satellites to shout, promoting the democracy of China. The satellites and I became one of the main political centers of the whole China, and even the whole world. Since my relatives and the persons around me were all exposed to the audience of television, just as the relatives and persons around Yat-Sen Sun and Lincoln, they did not have privacy. Hence, in compliance with the conventions, they should all belong to natural, legal and conjoint characteristics.

By the end of 2000, while "纳税财产，民主专政 (Property of paid taxes, Democratic dictatorship)" was shouted by me sufficiently, I thought more about welfare. I suggested that if the welfare of society was increased, the money held by the poor people and the purchasing ability of people would increase, and the economic level would thereby rise. Nonetheless, the main economic thoughts in the world then were the policies of low welfare and high competition in the United States, causing poverty in large populations in Latin America. The speciality of my thoughts then was different from that of the communist and socialist parties. They advocated high welfare from the insight of humanity of society, while I advocated high welfare from the insight of increasing the market and improving the economy. Hence, I was directly shocked by the economic policies of capitalism as low in welfare and high in competition. From television news,

I saw that, in the New Year of 2001, the people in various countries accepted my thoughts and objected to the economic policies of low welfare and high competition in the United States while upholding the increment of welfare.

In the presidential election in the United States, George Bush won over the previous US Vice President Gore. At the beginning of 2001, he was formally inaugurated as the new US President. Nonetheless, the Chinese satellites still offended me repeatedly. I told the satellites that, if they annoyed me more, I would go to Beijing to shout, where there were many activists of June 4th incident who hoped to kill all of them. The satellites were still indifferent and continued offending me. I was irritated, especially when going to Beijing. On the TianAnMen Square, I directed the satellites to shout loudly in Chinese: "纳税财产，民主专政 (Property of paid taxes, Democratic dictatorship)." The satellite operators projected to me a picture of a relative of XiaoPing Deng and said I was rather brilliant on that day.

At that time, ZeMin Jiang took over the mantle of Xiaoping Deng, actively promoting the reforming and opening up of China, which was rather fruitful. Nonetheless, out of expectation, he stood out to object democracy while relocating KuangDi Xu to Beijing, the mayor of Shanghai who sympathized with democracy. I thought that the people were the owners of the country and should have the right to democracy. If the Party and government insisted on an illegal option, the people should have the right to execute by law against the illegal party and government. In this way, I changed how Europe and the United States were encouraged previously to strive for democracy by non-violent measures while adopting the legal execution by law to remove the autocratic rule, hence acquiring historical significance. I carefully chose slogans and directed the satellites to shout in Chinese: "纳税财产，民主专政，人民法执 (Property of paid taxes, Democratic dictatorship, People execution by law)." For the first time, I created the term "Democracy calling for law execution," which is different from the revolution previously.

Shortly afterwards, I further pointed out that the army was not horrible. The army, large in scale in films and television, was exaggerated by the arts, while mobilization of the army of the whole country might solely suppress Beijing. If the whole country fought against the army, the army might not be able to win. The satellites quickly transferred my ideas to the whole country. In response, the Chinese people shouted for war actively, and execution by law. Shortly afterwards, the people and I thought of many methods for the people to win over the army. The earliest was certainly the use of cars to directly bump against the army, by which the Americans often shouted. A driver might crush many soldiers to death. Later, we changed to motorcycles, which could also bump the soldiers to death once speeding up. Then, I further found the key reason why the people were afraid of the army. It was because the army had guns. However, the gun was actually not big enough to hold power. Hence, it was possible to shield against bullets with bulletproof clothes while also potentially allowing the thick armor to work without bulletproof clothes. The Chinese people greatly thrived in spirits while reprimanding the armies of the United States, England and Western Europe as stupid and idiots who should have earlier used armors and flamethrowers rather than allowing the guns to threaten the people, resulting in terrors in the whole world and infestations of autocracy. All these might be inspected and proved by television videos in such public situations as news, arts, sports, etc. The Chinese people and I thoroughly threw away the false effects of films and televisions in exaggerating the military abilities. For the first time, it showed the whole world the colossal force owned by democracy calling for law execution, influencing significantly and greatly and shocking the whole world!

At that time, the people all over the country hoped that Beijing would execute by law and that China would realize democracy as quickly as possible. Nonetheless, this time, the Beijing people behaved selfishly. Since Beijing was lagging compared to the South, it hoped to delay in time and get rich earlier. In the meantime, the Central Committee headed by Jiang and Li, along with the military army, also threatened Beijing to continue autocracy. I felt that it was impossible to win over the whole army by relying solely on Beijing as one metropolis. Hence, I gave up Beijing and resorted to the South to influence the whole country, which allowed democracy to acquire the winning force. The Beijing people were certainly unhappy, less active and less cooperative. Hence, there grew emotions against the South, and the northern opposing faction centred on Beijing, suppressed and destroyed the intention of democracy from Southern China, shouting for the kill and clamoring for desolation, characterized by yellow perils. In July 2001, when Beijing successfully bid for the Olympic Games, the North and South had already opposed it. For the sake of overwhelming the North, the Southern people and I put forward the possibility of changing the capital in future to a more southern place from Beijing.

It was dramatic in significance for the democracy calling for law execution in China at that time. At that time, the United States and Western Europe both advocated non-violence, requesting the army and police not to be concerned with politics while resorting to democratic countries to propagate and contrast their achievements to promote democracy. Democracy had previously been achieved by non-violent, peaceful marches and strikes in India, Thailand, Korea, the Philippines, etc. However, in the case of big countries, such as the United States, it needs to be upheld directly. Sometimes, violent revolutions or coups were carried out in France, Russia, Romania, etc. The slogans they utilized were human rights and freedom, democracy and advancement, and putting down and overthrowing reactionary rulers, while law and order were usually the slogans often utilized by the autocrats. It was not the concept of juristic theory that the country belonged to the people was novel, but the people did not make use of it to promote democracy in practice previously. It was the first time in the world for me to lead the democracy calling for law execution in China. It was not only limited to the slogan I raised first but also to the practical performances with determined aims and repeated accumulations to overcome the defect of revolution and war by relying on temporary eruptive forces. It was the first time in practice for the law force to formally help the people strive for democracy, influencing and changing the people of the whole world. Hence, it was scientific in characteristics. Since then, humans have acquired the huge force of law execution while striving for democracy, and the contrast between the forces of democracy and autocracy has changed qualitatively. From television, the world people began advancing all the way, manifesting aspirant and vigorous spirits, and rising high in self-confidence. Hence, it was one of the historical turning points for the democratic forces to achieve significant dominance. Comparing the videos of human history before and after this event made it easy to find its significance in history.

In September 2007, the satellite operators and I adopted the Government and Police (GP) principles to confine the contents I directed the satellites to shout. The satellite operators further pointed out that the United States (US) was able to operate the satellites and read out the brain, but China was not able to do so. Hence, it was necessary to contain the principles of the US government and police. In regard to my directing the satellites of both China and the United States to shout and promote the democracy of China, it was fortunate not only for the democracy and law control of the world but also for catching a part of operators of satellites who terrified and harassed me. Hence, it was compatible with the US principles of police and law.

In 2001, another quite important historical breakthrough was achieved. "纳税财产，民主专政，人民法执 (Property of paid taxes, Democratic dictatorship, People execution by law)" was the satellite slogan then for me to encourage the people to strive for democracy. Nonetheless, prior to 2000, I had already often adopted the internationalization and world police to protect the people in Shanghai, corresponding to the international law salvage. Hence, the world police had been popular there for several years. Since 2001, the Chinese people and I just associated them with the democracy calling for law execution, while I directed the satellites to shout in Chinese: "纳税财产，民主专政，人民法执，警察国际 (Property of paid taxes, Democratic dictatorship, People execution by law, World police)." One day in 2001, after I had directed the satellites to loudly shout this slogan in the daytime and the evening, through the window of my bedroom, the Chinese operators of satellites projected many pictures of tanks of the People's Liberation Army, hoping to occupy the cities, and asked me how I could deal with them. I thought the world police could not defeat the tanks presently. Hence, I had to resort to the people in large quantities in cities to execute by law. Nonetheless, I was unsatisfactory and argued that the police could act earlier and shoot once the opponent initiated any illegal action. But the army had to wait for command before action, which was rather clumsy and slow. Even though the police were not competent to defeat the army presently, they, after all, both stayed in a peaceful time. The police could monitor the army from time to time, especially the military officers. If anything illegal happened, they could arrest and kill the officers early on time, making them as compliant as the eunuchs. On the second day, from television, I found that the Chinese people were quite concerned about this subject as many were talking about police and eunuchs and hoping to put pressure on the officers of the People's Liberation Army. Historians could find out when this happened from the videos on television about various public situations.

This was an important initiation. Since then, the satellite operators and I, the people of China and the whole world all began letting the police fight against the army while naturally thinking it necessary to equip the heavy weapons to the police. I was simple at the beginning, thinking that the police could directly control the air force, navy and strategic nuclear troops, while the land army left was just targeted with nuclear bombs, which was sufficient. A man from the People's Liberation Army projected a picture to me while saying it was appropriate for the land missile troops to join the police. I added the rocket artilleries, while the US operator of satellite reminded me that the police often utilized helicopters. Several days later, I suggested transferring the budget of the army to that of the police, combining the two budgets into one while directly improving the efficiency of using budgets for armed troops. I also pointed out that the logistics of armed police might be dispersed and socialized, while the logistics of the army were liable to attack in war. Further, the missiles and rockets of armed police were competent in concealment, possessing a tactical advantage.

This was quite significant. It had already been witnessed early that the police joined the war. However, they only played the assistant role, while the army was the main force of war. This time, it was comprehensively and formally suggested that the armed police would substitute and defeat an army, changing the structure of armed troops and the manners of war of human society, thereby impacting broad social influences while possessing profound historical significance.

In the latter half of the year 2001, I motivated the SuZhou people to actively promote democracy. From television, in the game of women's volleyball, the Russians were also thinking why democracy was required. They explained that, in this way, it was possible to make the highest officer resign while ensuring the term of service was fixed and limited on time; hence, it was possible to constrain the highest officer by law. XiaoPing Deng abolished the lifelong tenure system for leaders in China. Therefore, it was also possible to investigate the legal liability of leaders. At that time, China was deeply influenced by the reforming and opening up of Xiaoping Deng. Hence, I also followed to propagate the successful experience of the Party and government in SuZhou for attraction of investment and internationalization. I directed the satellites to shout for the democratic election of the mayors of cities. Competing with each other, the superiors won, and the inferiors lost. Without democracy, it would be impossible for the city to achieve success!

Several weeks later, I further realized that the needs of the people had to be raised in the country, while democracy should solve the various needs of people and balance the various benefits of people. Hence, it was the market channel through which the country could serve the people. In this way, the parliamentary system, composed of multiple parties, seemed more democratic than the deputy system, electing mayors directly. It was also compatible with the system of the People's Congress of China. On the contrary, the United States, recognized then by the world as the democratic leader, had wrongly accounted for the direct election of mayors and president as the most democratic. Hence, it was nonetheless not as democratic as the system in China. The parliamentary system of multiple parties was the more democratic system. Therefore, I named it a demo decision. At that time, it happened to meet the holiday; the Chinese people were so happy and cheerful as to jump and bloom, so glad and joyful as to touch the sky and earth, rejoicing at their own country having a good system.

Then, why wasn't China, with the system of the People's Congress of multiple parties, accounted for as democratic? The key was not that the national system of China was not democratic, but that the Party and government illegally nominated and arranged the people's representatives, apportioned in quantity, deprived the people of the right of election, and hence caused the autocracy of one single Party.

For the shouts for eunuchs, it was generated by the armed police, and then it was aware of the system of the People's Congress in China. Hence, I changed the Chinese slogans of the satellites I directed from "纳税财产，民主专政，人民法执，警察国际 (Property of paid taxes, Democratic dictatorship, People execution by law, World police)" to "世警武装，民主执政 (World police, Demo decision)." The latter slogan of satellite showed the beautiful future to the people. Hence, the satellite operators shouted it vigorously while the Chinese people listened to it cheerfully.

Since 2002, my influence and the strength of my counterstriking against satellite terrors had been increasing continually. As long as I shouted more about the satellite terrors, people could hear and know. In this way, I began to acquire the ability to legally get revenge against the terrors of satellites.

Nonetheless, it was quite possible for JinTao Hu, who had been benefited from the June 4th event, to replace ZeMin Jiang while becoming the general secretary of the Central Committee of the Communist Party of China and the president of the nation. JinTao Hu had once led Tibet. He was smart and agile, reactionary and clangorous in personality. His chest was like that of a chick, and he walked like a goose in the image. Among his followers, there were many brutal and cruel rogues and villains upholding the military government. Hence, China might become more cruel and brutal, while the Chinese operators of satellites might also become irresponsible, killing them first and then reporting. In the latter half of the year 2002, I was concerned about the terrors and dangers of satellites, hence promoting democracy against Hu. After all, for the sake of becoming the general secretary, it was necessary for JinTao Hu to resort to the election by the Communist Party. So long as the various local places strengthened the law execution onto the Communist Party while prohibiting the representatives of the 16th National Congress of the Communist Party from voting and electing JinTao Hu, it was possible to prevent the possible catastrophe. Nonetheless, the northern Chinese people headed by Beijing were then complaining about the economic strength of southeastern China, while the southwestern Chinese people were also rather lagged, with nothing unsatisfactory to JinTao Hu especially, nor supportive of democracy enthusiastically. Hence, I relied mainly on the people around the Yangtze River, Yellow River, and so on to resist JinTao Hu.

In November 2002, the 16th National Congress of the Communist Party of China was held, by which both ZeMin Jiang and Peng Li retired. Nonetheless, the meeting still violated the intention of most members of the Party in the country, electing JinTao Hu as the general secretary and ZeMin Jiang as the chairman of the Military Committee. The people were rather unhappy. Hence, it broke down the hope for the democracy in China to make instant achievement and quick success, while the movement for democracy also transformed from the original vigor and vitality into opposition and stalemate.

Several months after the winter of 2002, when JinTao Hu took over at the Spring Festival of 2003, the Chinese operators of satellites strengthened the terrors and threats against me. The People's Liberation Army of satellites even said to send murderers on the ground to assassinate me. I replied that if anybody would try to kill people by the tool of the country, all his relatives and colleagues would be counted as complicities. The Chinese operators of satellites said again to employ murderers abroad and assassinate me. I replied that, in that way, the chief instigator of the murderer should be punished severely, while the country and police of China would be counted as complicities and be punished similarly. Since I was a famous leader of democracy and had satellites tracing me, the country should send police to protect me in a normal situation. Hence, by the charge of disrupting the nation and police, I implicated the family of JinTao Hu. Finally, the sounds of threats from satellites of the People's Liberation Army gradually lost the support of JinTao Hu and the Central Committee, and the terrific expressions and actions of Chinese satellites declined gradually.

In 2003, I continually directed the satellites to shout in Chinese: "世警武装，民主执政 (World police, Demo decision)." The armored police vehicles and armored missile vehicles were the main images of armed police then, creating the big social tide for establishing the armed police publicly.

In the summer of 2003, I went to GuangZhou to open a branch for the company. When the airplane was landing at the GuangZhou airport from the high sky, I overlooked the familiar and beautiful night scene of GuangZhou, while directing the satellites to shout loudly in Chinese: "特区警导，民主执政 (Missile police special zone, Demo decision)." I went to GuangZhou two to three times that summer. Several times, I took the train to go forth and back there, while on the way, I observed the zeal and support from the people in western ZheJiang and eastern JiangXi.

In the early half of the year 2004, from television, I saw that the northern Chinese hoped to make use of autocrats to make rumours, changing the attribution of achievement for the theory of armed police. I, hence, decided to write a book summarizing the achievements of armed police. The title of the book in Chinese was "武器、武装与战争—警察武装战胜军 (Weapons, Armed Troops and War—The Armed Police Winning over the Army)." While writing the book, I further found that, since most local armed police were supervised by local congress, it was difficult for the reverse situation upholding the autocracy to occur. Hence, because of its compatibility with the democratic system, the armed police were much better than the present army.

In May 2004, I formally finished writing the book in Chinese "武器、武装与战争—警察武装战胜军 (Weapons, Armed Troops and War—The Armed Police Winning over the Army)." After applying for and acquiring its copyright, I printed 1000 copies and distributed about 500 copies to the people in Shanghai, Jiangsu and so on till June 2006. Additionally, I sent it by email in the form of a gift to the email accounts of thousands of people. While writing the book, the satellite operators provided me with many supportive sounds, pictures and suggestions. A few of them were good enough to be incorporated into the book.

The book was composed of nine chapters, which are as follows:

- The Brief Situation of Weapon Development Up to Now.
- The Critical Properties of Weapons and the Trends of Their Improvement.
- Weapons Can Be Similarly Equipped to the Police to War.
- The Strategic Predominance of Armed Police—Budget, Equipment and Training.
- The Structure of Command and Measures of Communication of Armed Police.
- The Defensive Tactics of Armed Police in War.
- The Offensive Tactics of Armed Police in War.
- The Strategy and Tactics of Strategic Long-Distant Strike and Revenge.
- The Appearance of Armed Police Would Affect All Countries in the World.

In the book, I suggested in chapter 4 that the armed police could use the budgets more efficiently, while the civil police could freely accumulate large quantities of weapons such as missiles, rocket artilleries, helicopters, etc. Hence, the country could win the strategic predominance by quantity, which was more advantageous than the military reserves. In chapter 9, I discussed the armed police affecting the society and politics, demonstrating the armed police appropriate for the provincial and municipal parliamentary democracy. The book ended with a short poem: "世间风雨多，谁言永太平。警察武装出，孰能与争风 (World has many storms, who can say peace forever? When armed police step ever since, who can compete for the keen rays?)"

In 2004, JinTao Hu promised not to make terror against me on the ground any more. Hence, his relationship with people improved a little. Nonetheless, under the influence of the Central Committee of Hu, the bureaucrats of the Communist Party were afraid of themselves, abnormal and anomalous, gradually turning into defending the Central Committee and opposing the people, inactive to democratic progression and opposite in opinion to economic construction. In September 2004, on the 4th Plenary Session of the 16th Central Committee held then, the bureaucrats of the Communist Party did not at all account that the traditional Yanan faction yielded to democracy while hoping to normalize the country, thoroughly hostile to the people and tolerant to the army. LiangYu Chen, the secretary of the Shanghai Municipal Committee of the Party, was courageous in upholding the YanAn faction and admired my promotion of democracy in China. Unfortunately, he was dismissed and arrested for trivial reasons by the Central Committee for Discipline Inspection of the Communist Party of China, eliciting resentfulness from the people. All these were manifested on television. On August 24, 2015, I just found that joining Christian could rebuild the historical reputation of LiangYu Chen.

In December 2004, I made an adjustment to the forces in southern China. I had always relied on the Yellow River to defend southern China. Nonetheless, back then, the several provinces along the Yellow River were rather poor and insensitive to the destructive policy of the Central Committee. I recognized that the people in AnHui strove for fame and pursued richness, and hence, should be guided and helped appropriately. Therefore, I began guiding the people in JiangSu and ZheJiang and attracting and helping the people in AnHui. The southern people in AnHui seized the opportunity, while the people in the whole province also responded gradually; hence, AnHui began merging into the developed areas in east China of JiangSu and ZheJiang.

On January 26, 2005, I began maintaining diaries. I noted down the important things every day, improving the accuracy of writing the memoirs. I could almost make accuracy to the exact date for everything happening after then, with the deviation mostly up to 3 days. Prior to then, I had nonetheless been unable to accurately calculate the date and month, with the deviation even up to half a year. The contents of television I witnessed and noted down in my diaries reflected the real situations I saw by myself. I was unable to see most of the contents on television then; hence, it was necessary for historians to make up the losses.

On August 22, 2005, I introspected that the struggle for democracy was always difficult and arduous, while the rampage of autocracy was nonetheless audacious and murderous. The difficulty for the progression of democracy lay in the insufficiency of revenge after the victory of democracy, hence culturing the audacity of autocratic restoration. I could live today since I creatively adopted the complicities of revenge, making the opponent not dare to kill me blindly. This was significant for democracy in acquiring the overwhelming force of law. I directed the satellites to shout in Chinese: “民主报复要加倍 (Revenge from democracy would double).” From television, I saw that Chinese people had similar views.

On September 14, 2005, on television, I saw the Chinese people were concerned about the inevitability of the country belonging to the people, which was the premise of democracy calling for law execution. I discussed the issue with the operators of satellites, and both presented many suggestions, while those from mine accounted for about 50%. Finally, I decided to use “人民所有，独裁强盗 (People owners, Autocrats robbers)” to demonstrate the principle while directing the satellites to shout in Chinese. Several days later, on television, I saw the Chinese people expressing satisfaction, which also happened to correspond to an ancient Chinese proverb: “胜者为王，败者为寇 (Winner to king, Loser to gangster).” It was a significant supplement to the principle of law for democracy from the democratic movement of China at that time and was significant in theory.

In March 2006, I learned from the internet that some small countries, such as San Marino, Mauritius, Costa Rica, etc, did not have a formal army and, hence, might have realized the armed police earlier. It was necessary to further investigate and compare.

On July 25, 2006, I spent two whole days scanning all countries on the internet globally. I then further categorized the small countries not having an army and police concurrently as the following:

- Countries such as Liechtenstein, Andorra, Iceland,

Solomon Islands, Vanuatu, Kiribati, Nauru, Marshall Islands, Tuvalu, Samoa, Belau, Cook Islands, Haiti, Panama, Grenada, St Vincent, Grenadines, etc that do not have an army but have the police, and due to not having their own national defence, rely on other countries for defence.

- Countries, such as the Maldives, that do not have the police but have an army, or the army engulfs the police.
- Countries, such as Costa Rica and Mauritius, that do not have an army but have the police and armed police to take on national defence.

The countries from (1) and (2) categories were short of function in the national defence of the police and, hence, were conspicuously different from our theory of armed police. The countries from the third category, or the two countries, namely Costa Rica and Mauritius, might be accounted to share our theory of armed police.

After 2007, I began frequently watching the large vocal concert of songs and dances "The Same Song" of China Central Television (CCTV), directed by Xin Meng. Every week, "The Same Song" went around making performances in various places in China. Every time, it chose a large scene for performance and the most excellent stars from Hong Kong, Taiwan and China to sing and dance, with those on stage and under stage merging into one entity, cheering and applauding as if thunders by a wave. While listening to the theme song, "The Same Song," I felt I was leading the Chinese people to contend for democracy. Later, many audiences just put me as the object of praise of "The Same Song" directly. All these could be checked and proved from the videos of the vocal concert of "The Same Song," with many people on the spot thinking of me and talking to me.

In September 2008, from the video of the opening ceremony of the Olympic Games of 2000, I saw the Australian people shout that they suggested the foundation of troops for armed police on the spot and further mentioned it was necessary to account for the small countries for the armed police. These were not the formal theories for armed police, while the reputation for the foundation of troops of armed police should be attributed to Mauritius and Costa Rica, which had already established the armed police. Our theory of armed police originated from that: under the direction of thought of police protecting the legal people while the army did not have the role, I led the Chinese people to use the international police to confront the illegal tide of thoughts from a portion of People's Liberation Army and elicited the thought of armed police to replace the US army as the main image of world police then. Up to 2004, I summarized them into a book and added factors such as command, maintenance, tactics, society, etc., that were less mentioned on television, and accomplished the formal theory systematically, scientifically and representatively. The Chinese people and I adopted "世警武装 (World police)" and "特区警导 (Missile police special zone)" to promote the propagation of armed police, demonstrating the practice of democracy calling for law execution led by me for the first time to increase the courage, and its significant influence on establishing the theory of armed police, not afraid of the police to cause the professional autocracy by their becoming too strong and too many. These were the historical backgrounds of force and critical points of our scientific creation of the theory of armed police by the premise of guaranteeing democracy.

It was different from the historical backgrounds of Mauritius and Costa Rica, with a population of fewer than 5 million people. Nonetheless, it could be conjectured that, from the 1980s, when television was popularized, to the early 21st century, when the democracy calling for law execution appeared, the people in many small countries such as Mauritius, Costa Rica, etc, might sometimes also compare the advantages between the armed police and army in different social backgrounds on television. In regret, it saw neither their presentation of formal theory nor the historical background of force as the practice of democracy calling for law execution, which increased the courage and guaranteed democracy. The rational arrangement should be that the theory of armed police was led by me, with the satellite operators, China as a big country, and many small countries such as Mauritius, Costa Rica, etc, jointly sharing it.

In July 2009, for the first time, the Chinese people and I applied the theory of armed police successfully, directing the democracy calling for law execution in China and creating a new situation of the Chinese army calling for humans.

On January 30, 2012, I pointed out that it was necessary to use a heavy missile to break the tank, while a single soldier of militia could carry a maximum of 30 kilograms of TNT within the range of resistance of the tank. Hence, the militia did not work, while the armed police were indispensable. On December 23, 2013, the Chinese army and I pointed out that the armed police were more trained in running and fighting, while the militias were less competent. Earlier in the book on armed police, I had already pointed out that the armed police were more advantageous than militias in terms of training and weapons.

On August 24, 2012, the people and I pointed out that the revolution was to oppose the police and elicit suppression from the police. It was tremendously destructive and unfortunate for the economy and culture. Moreover, the various factions of spontaneous revolution might even conflict with one another, reducing the number of weapons, even incompetent to the centralized eunuch of the airforce under the surveillance of the police. In this regard, the theory of armed police would adopt the democracy calling for law execution, rather than revolution, as its social force to prevent the police from becoming autocrats. I directed the satellites to shout in Chinese: "革命破坏警不用 (Revolution and destruction police no)." On September 2, 2015, I also pointed out that the democracy calling for law execution might comprise the force of people without any weapon, different from the war necessarily using armed troops. The people and I further pointed out that the democracy calling for law execution overcame the defect of revolution and war by relying on temporary eruptive forces.

On March 17, 2013, people in various countries pointed out that the theory of armed police was established on the basis of ease of achieving success by law to execute in some provinces and cities; hence, they were more democratic and stronger than the army. It was not necessary for the democracy calling for law execution to achieve victory completely, nor did it require the people to win over the army and police totally. Hence, the earliest practice in history, by which I led the democracy calling for law execution in China, was just the social foundation of the theory of armed police.

On July 8, 2016, I, along with people in various countries, found that the law from the agreement was not the foundation of democracy calling for law execution; rather, it might even result in autocracy by party or religion. Both the law from the agreement and the law from the king were just the forms of legislation of the country. It was the deduction of hurts and compensation for losses that was instead the purpose and truth of law science! I directed the satellites to shout in Chinese: "科学法律治伤损 (Scientific laws to treat hurts and losses)."

End poem of the chapter:

It was feasible to contend for democracy by execution lawfully.
It was like the winding and firing balls for the people spiritually.
It was advantageous in democracy and law for the police and army.
It was resonant for the armed police to the world wholly.

Chapter | 4

Winning over Nuclear Crisis on Earth

Musical Background of Rhythmic Writing: The Theme Song "The Blood of Steel and Heart of Faith" in "The Legend of the Condor Heroes"

Please read the following text sentence-by-sentence to feel the musical background of the rhythmic framework.

In 2001, there was a drastic change in the international situation. The United States and Western Europe had been the leaders of world democracy for a long time. Nonetheless, in the latter half of the year 2001, when democracy was calling for law execution in China, the French in Shanghai first expressed intolerance, while the French in Europe said that once China realized democracy, Chinese women might no longer marry the men on the middle and low level in Europe, shouting to object to and interfere with the democracy of China! Then, other European countries also began objecting to and interfering with the democracy in China, and the United States also took part in the European list. These might all be checked and proved in television videos in public situations at that time.

Since the European and American whites struck the democracy of China, I tried to change the anchor of democracy of China from the United States and Western Europe to Latin America and then to Russia, while neither Latin America nor

Russia could possibly stand and offend the strong United States and Western Europe solely for protecting China. Hence, I finally led China to India. I thought that, even though the Hindus were a little selfish, knowing that other countries hampered the democracy of its neighbor China, the people of India could stand up and object to them. After reconciliation for one to two years, the people of China and India finally took over the responsibility of leading the Southern world hand-by-hand and shoulder-by-shoulder and were later joined by the countries of Asia, Africa and the Middle East. These could all be checked and proved in television videos in public situations, such as news, art performances, sports, etc., of various countries in the world from 2002 to 2004.

In 2002, it could be seen on television that the white racists in Europe and the United States continually instigated the racial hostile emotions, objecting to and interfering with the democracy in China. In 1997, in the United States, I experienced the US satellites shouting to break the civilization on earth. Therefore, I worried that when the democracy of China was befalling, the United States might threaten to bomb and destroy China while it was propagated everywhere in the world by satellites. Shortly, on television, the white racists in Europe and the United States became more and more violent, shouting to take advantage of white dominance in the population in the United States, making the United States declare war on democracy, using nuclear bombs to totally destroy China and annihilate the Chinese people.

While confronting the adverse international situation, I adopted the "World police" to prohibit them in the early times. If they had committed the crime of genocide against China, the

Chinese abroad might resort to the world police while motivating the world people to take revenge, at least kill the whole family of senators and the president who committed the execution of the genocide. Since the democratic system in the United States had already been realized, the senators and president must all step down for certainly being subjected to the punishment of the law. This method affected them. On television, US President George Bush had always been indifferent and disregardful to the white genocidal shouts. Hence, the white shouts of nuclear threats in Europe and the United States were nonetheless unable to rise up to the formal US governmental organizations.

Being stimulated at that time, the Chinese people strove for democracy more actively, determined to control China by democracy and control the nuclear revenging force of China. On television, it was shown that the soldiers of the People's Liberation Army (PLA) expressed their opinions actively, hoping to be normal and responsible and protect the Chinese people. In the latter half of the year 2002 or so, I thought that there were mountains in China, while ZheJiang and GuangDong both happened to be mountainous. Affected by the hills and mountains, the power and the damaging ability of the nuclear weapons were drastically decreased. The people in plain might also dig tunnels to hide, further decreasing the annihilating power of nuclear weapons. I made an estimation that there might be about ten thousand nuclear weapons in the United States, and due to a decrease in their power, the average damaging radius for each nuclear bomb was 3-5 kilometers, which could destroy and bleach a total area 300 hundred thousand square kilometres, comprising two provinces of ZheJiang and GuangDong, and occupying only 3% of the national land of China. The Chinese people were relieved immediately. At that time, in mountainous provinces such as Sichuan, ShanXi, etc., the people might resort to many mountains to think that they were unnecessarily afraid of nuclear threats earlier, while the television did not broadcast them. The VX nerve gas of the United States and Russia were not more than millions of tons in storage at that time, with a total damaging area of around one hundred thousand square kilometres, equivalent to one province or state, and solely the oddment of the damaging area of nuclear weapons. Hence, it might be less concerned. It was a dramatic irony to the US satellites for their shouts of breaking earth in Chicago!

The military officers in the US Defence Department should have previously known about the power of nuclear bombs and their threats. In this regard, who should be attributed to the historical achievement of winning over the nuclear war? I led the Chinese people to win over the nuclear war this time, correcting the comprehension of nuclear war seriously and scientifically in the whole world by pointing out that the nuclear war was much smaller in power than imagined previously. Hence, for the first time, humans acquired the confidence to win over nuclear weapons, which is significant for the strategic instruction to deal with nuclear war. Since then, the people began to consider increasing the quantity of nuclear weapons the country held reasonably. It was a turning point in history and hence significant; it should occupy the dominant status necessarily. When the United States and the Soviet Union confronted the Cold War, the popular comprehension of humans was that nuclear war could damage humanity severely and even annihilate the race and, hence, should be deducted and destructed resolutely. I directed the satellites to shout in Chinese: "战胜核武器圣转折 (Winning over nuclear weapons San turning)."

It was necessary to point out that, during the Cultural Revolution, ZeDong Mao also requested the people to dig tunnels and protect themselves against both atomic attacks and hegemonism. Nonetheless, at that time, the Soviet Union had not threatened to kill all Chinese people with nuclear weapons, nor had China calculated how many Chinese the Soviet Union could kill if they used all nuclear force to strike. Hence, it did not affect the strategic attitude of humans toward nuclear weapons at all, and certainly, it was not the strategic turning point of humans to win over nuclear weapons.

In 2002, there was also the crisis of damaging the earth on science theoretically. At that time, I thought of the accelerators to accelerate the particles to collide, while the energy was artificial and huge supernaturally. Therefore, the particle collision might generate the particle of a black hole of high density, destroying the earth. I was rather nervous, feeling the earth might really be destroyed in this way. Hence, I hurriedly sent emails to many universities in Europe and the United States, calling for prohibition from developing the accelerators. However, they were mostly turned down. Finally, from some replied emails, I found that some particles in cosmic rays possessed higher energy than the particles in accelerators. Now that they collided with the earth without generating the black holes, the earth could not be destroyed and was safe.

In 2003, under the leadership of US President Bush, the United States invaded Iraq and caught President Saddam.

In 2003, there was another crisis damaging the earth. It was the crisis of ocean nuclear fusion that was finally solved by me. One day, I thought by incident that if the ocean rich in deuterium and tritium was ignited by a hydrogen bomb, it was possible to explore and destroy the whole earth. In my office in TaiHua Business Building, the US operators of satellites further supplied many other situations to uphold my idea. For instance, if a bomber or a submarine capable of carrying hundreds of nuclear bombs explored, it could release huge amounts of energy and ignite the ocean's nuclear fusion. I saw on television that the people of the whole world then were mostly influenced by such an idea of mine and became extraordinarily nervous. Nonetheless, a few white politicians in Western Europe and bureaucrats of the Party and government in China gloated on the misfortune. They shouted that if they fell out of power, they would explore the earth. This time, somebody really intended to adopt the method of exploring the earth to realize autocracy. Fortunately, neither Chinese President JinTao Hu nor US President Bush was interested in ocean nuclear fusion. I did not see any relevant speech or talk of theirs on this problem on television. If they had imitated the nuclear coercion in Chicago, requesting me to commit suicide, I would have been required to account for it for a few days. The people in most countries, including me, all upheld to establish the strong leadership of the United Nations to overcome nuclear terror. Some operators of satellites suggested that the terrorists unsatisfactory with the reality could still bypass the United Nations to explore the earth.

One or two days later, I generated other thoughts. I thought of the ancient asteroid with tens of thousands of times more energy than the present megaton hydrogen bomb colliding with the ocean, just as the comet collided with Jupiter in 1994 by energy. There should certainly be some mechanisms preventing the ocean from being ignited totally by the local nuclear fusion. I looked for the reason following this thought. Firstly, I thought nuclear fusion gasified the surrounding seawater, and then the nuclear reaction diffused further. Shortly, I walked into the aisle of the TaiHua Business Building while continuing to imagine the explosion of the hydrogen bomb in the ocean. The center was the region of the nuclear fusion reaction, while the surroundings were the seawater gasified by super-high temperature, waiting for the further occurrence of nuclear fusion. In synchrony, the satellites amplified the picture of my imagination to support me. I stared and fixed on the seawater gasified by the super-high temperature and found that the center possessed the higher temperature and would move upward naturally. In this regard, due to the high temperature, the whole center of the nuclear reaction should leave the liquid sea water, and be pushed to the high sky, separated from the ocean. Without the region of high temperature capable of igniting the nuclear reaction, nuclear fusion could no longer continue to happen in the ocean. Hence, the earth should thereby acquire safety. I was quite excited at that time, solving the crisis of ocean nuclear fusion on the earth while directing the satellites to shout. I saw on television that, after learning it, people in various countries became relieved and happy. Likewise, following the analogous thought, it could also solve the problem of the accelerator in generating the particle of a black hole.

On November 15, 2008, the bank staff in the United States and I further pointed to light to cause gasification, demonstrating that the elevation mechanism was correct. The next morning, the satellite operators and I transformed the cross-section of the reaction into concentration. Hence, the rate of reaction of deuterium to deuterium was half that of deuterium to tritium, while the rate of reaction of deuterium to hydrogen was half that of deuterium to deuterium. The complete nuclear fusion of 1 kilogram of deuterium was equivalent to the energy generated by burning 10 thousand tons of petroleum, while the complete nuclear fusion of deuterium contained in 1-liter seawater was equivalent to the energy generated by burning 300 liters of petroleum. Hence, I estimated that the concentration of deuterium was around 0.00003 in the ocean, while the rate of reaction of deuterium to hydrogen in the ocean should be around $1/2\times0.00003\times 99.99\%=0.000015$ that of a deuterium bomb. The complete nuclear fusion of 1 ton of ideal deuterium bomb was almost equivalent to the energy generated by burning $10000\times1000 =1\times10^7$ tons of fuels. By the rate of reaction of ocean water, nuclear fusion of 1 ton of or 1 cubic meter of seawater was equivalent to the energy generated by burning $(1\times10^7)\times 0.000015=150$ tons of fuels each time unit, which was certainly unable to propagate the nuclear fusion and compatible with the popular explanation of concentration. At that time, I creatively changed the unit of seawater to a cube of 10-meters each side, within which the nuclear fusion of seawater was equivalent to the energy generated by burning $150 \times 10^3 = 150000$ tons of fuels each time unit, comparable to that of the atomic bomb. Additionally, with time passing, it could continuously accumulate and superimpose up to 200000 tons equivalent, 300000 tons equivalent and so on. Hence, the mechanism of explosion and rise was thereby the key solution to the ocean nuclear crisis.

On November 21, 2008, in a video on the internet on the experiments of undersea nuclear explosion （http://v.youku.com/v_show/id_XODQwMzIwNA==.html,http://v.youku.com/v_show/id_co00XOTIwODA0.html）, I saw that the US military experimental staff were also worried about the possible ignition of ocean, while they relied more on the calculation of physics, thinking it insufficient to ignite the ocean, and hence igniting the hydrogen bomb on the bottom of sea resolutely. While rising up into the air, the explosion of the hydrogen bomb brought up a lot of water vapour and water liquid, forming a mushroom cloud in the high sky. Even though the army in various countries, before 1990, had carried out the experiments of a nuclear explosion of hydrogen bombs on the bottom of the sea, it was in 2003, by my guidance, that, for the first time, humans began caring about the safety of both ocean and earth.

It was quite salient in significance to win over the ocean nuclear crisis on a long-term basis. If the ocean could be ignited by a big hydrogen bomb, the force of autocracy could acquire absolute predominance on the earth. If the available hydrogen bombs were not able to ignite the ocean presently, the autocrats could further make the super-huge hydrogen bomb, quite bigger than the hydrogen bomb presently available and try to ignite the ocean continually to seize the might of absolute autocracy. Additionally, on February 2, 2012, I further pointed out that it was common military knowledge that, once the war broke out, any part of the participants would try all the way to sink the opposite submarine carrying the nuclear missiles. Solely by the mechanism of explosion and rise, it was possible to suppress the fantasies of autocrats and warmongers. Hence, it was possible for the ocean and earth to remain safe forever.

Some white politicians in Western Europe were rather unsatisfactory. On television in 2003, it could be seen that they shouted publicly that they would rather kill me earlier so that I would not be able to solve the crisis of ocean nuclear fusion, and they would take advantage of nuclear destruction of the earth to threaten and rule the world. These television videos were also the historical evidence that I solved the crisis of ocean nuclear fusion. The shouts of white politicians in Western Europe on television influenced the US operators of satellites. One day at midnight, European and American white satellite operators utilized the infrared laser satellite of quite big energy, hoping to shock me to death. Nonetheless, they failed and then withdrew immediately. The white operator of the satellite at that time could speak English with a strong German accent. This event further impelled me to consider making an infrared-proof sleeping cabinet, preventing the raids of satellites at night.

Finally, came the year 2004. I spent the holidays in the Spring Festival making the infrared-proof protective cabinet of a multi-layered alternative structure against the satellites.

Out of my expectation, the effect of light transmittance of this structure was not the direct product of their luminousness. On account of the reflection back and forth between layers, the minimal luminousness of this structure was the luminousness of a single structure divided by e. In this regard, the net luminousness of my multi-layered infrared-proof sleeping cabinet was around 30%. Even though it protected the satellite beams, it was ineffective when the satellite operators shocked me with several satellites. Later, I gradually learned to use the walls of multi-layers of buildings to protect myself by the effect of light transmittance, which was the direct product of their luminousness.

In the summer of 2004, when the Olympic Games were held, the satellites made criminals outrageously. They shocked the athletes everywhere with infrared beams, and especially when the athletes were lifting weights, it was quite dangerous to shock their hearts and blood vessels with infrareds. The live telecasts and video rebroadcasts made all humans watch the illegal intentions and behaviors of satellites to hurt the athletes by infrareds, without considering the repeated protests of people and masses in big public situations. Nonetheless, neither the US president and Congress nor the Chinese president and People's Congress were concerned at all. The United Nations (UN), too, remained silent. So decadent the world on rationality, so angry the hair to erect!

End poem of the chapter:

The Chinese stood up to win the nuclear war triumphantly.
The annihilation by nuclear weapons was crashed illusively.

It was impossible to elevate the nuclear ignition of the ocean to the sky clearly.
The autocracy by nuclear power was muted away arrogantly.

Chapter | 5

Laureate as San Force

Musical Background of the Rhythmic Writing: The Theme Song "The Blood of Steel and Heart of Faith" in "The Legend of the Condor Heroes"

Please read the following text sentence-by-sentence to feel the musical background of the rhythmic framework.

In early 2005, satellite operators took advantage of satellites to spread rumors, which caught my attention. Now that there were satellite rumors, I thought of a name for myself: "San Force King," representing the dominant personage in a historical period while increasing the historical perception and public attention.

On December 14, 2005, I hoped the descendants would discern my status more accurately. I was an eminent person who was quite influential among people for methods of activities such as propaganda by shouts and guidance of the public, but without the might of administration or the obligation to compassionate the people as king; hence, I changed the name from San Force King to San Force. I directed the satellites to shout in Chinese: "名称正确武圣人 (Name correct San Force)," "武圣王改成武圣人 (San Force King changed to San Force)." On that day, I saw on television that people in China and abroad had all had this thought, while they had all taken "World Police, Demo Decision" to represent the achievements and symbol of the democratic movement of China at that time.

On December 16, 2005, I thought that the nuclear crisis was a big event on the earth and was equivalent to the potential impact of the "World Police, Demo Decision." The next day, on December 17 of that year, the GuangDong sound from a satellite said that the nuclear crisis on the earth was rather unfortunate and suggested changing it to humans winning over nuclear weapons. I was delighted and directed the satellites to shout in Chinese: "武圣人时代，人类战胜核 (San Force Era, Humans winning over nuclear weapons)."

On December 18, 2005, in the news, I saw many people in Eastern Europe point out that, even though in 1997, the United States had really possessed the ability and executed it to destroy all humans, the other animals on earth might still take the place of humans to continue evolution. They thought of monkeys, mice and so on. At least, the mice lived underground and, hence, could certainly survive in portion while continuing to evolve and become as intelligent as or even more intelligent than humans.

In the atmosphere of happiness, the Chinese people greeted the Spring Festival of 2006. On the first day of the lunar year, on January 29, 2006, I recognized that I had just won the nuclear war on the earth solely, while the nuclear war in the solar system had not been conquered. Hence, I changed the Chinese slogan from "人类战胜核 (Humans winning over nuclear weapons)" to "战胜地球核 (Winning over earth nuclear weapons)."

On March 30, 2006, the people and I pointed out that

there were three symbols for me as San Force:

- Led the democracy calling for law execution in China; hence, for the first time, the promotion of democracy acquired the support of the law force.
- Led the Chinese people and the people worldwide to establish the theory of armed police.
- Led humans to acquire the confidence and method to win over the nuclear war on the earth and the war and terror of extremely high energy, ensuring the confidence and power of justice and law in the future on the earth.

On June 16, 2006, my roommate Xiao Ning introduced two Christian friends of SuZhou natives to me. One of them was called Xiao Jiang, who was comfortable chatting with me. He brought with him the Chinese Koran of Islamism. I read it thoroughly and found that there was no rule forcing women to wear the veil or masking their faces. Rather, there was a rule strictly prohibiting the eating of the pork. I directed the satellites to shout in Chinese: "古兰经无须戴面纱 (Koran unnecessary to wear veils)."

On October 8, 2006, I felt it appropriate to give more respect to the Earth God. I had been the Holy Spirit, highest in rank like Jesus. Then, I immediately imagined that if God had adjusted from the lesson that the humans had committed the crime of killing Jesus, it would have been possible to excuse my story in Chicago not committing suicide to save humans. I directed the satellites to shout: "Chicago, Jesus no longer." On television, I saw that somebody abroad had already thought of this sentence earlier than I had.

On October 13, 2006, I found that in Chicago, when US

satellites were shouting to break the earth, I was taking charge of the Holy Spirit of Christianity. In reference to the Holy Bible, it was necessary for the Holy Spirit to save the followers believing in Christianity. However, it was not necessary to save all the humans. Hence, the fact that I had not committed suicide was compatible with my status as Holy Spirit at that time. I directed the satellites to shout: "Religion human irrelevant."

I was also aware that the family name in Chinese 蔡 (Cai) (human above god) had been explained as showing respect to the water god Ji in ancient times. Nonetheless, since I had acted as the Holy Spirit in 1997, this name could be explained as the fact that I became the god in heaven from an ordinary person by practice.

On October 15, 2006, I pointed out that, in 1997, a few US satellite operators requesting me to commit suicide certainly did not confess to me as their Holy Spirit, while they believed in Jesus, different from me in the religious denomination.

On the morning of October 16, 2006, I said that the Earth God was rather powerful. Hence, it was necessary to create such a powerful god in the future. Religions should accommodate such content as democracy, law, sex, and so on in the future, but they do not do so presently.

The Earth God occasionally appeared in artistic works previously. However, they were very few in number and had never become a religion. In 2006, there appeared the shouts for creating the religion of Earth God.

Various big religions believed in the heaven gods presently, while all reprimanded the land in their books for being miserable. These situations happened in Christianity,

Islam, Buddhism and Taoism.

On November 9, 2006, I thought that it was quite often illegal in humans. It was necessary for many religious organizations of Earth Gods to compete and win the Earth God in the future, while there might even be several Earth Gods present to compete, far from being pure and beautiful as hoped by the people. Hence, I should comply with the hope of people, attributing the achievements to the earth while making me, San Force, become the Earth God I by myself. I directed the satellites to shout in Chinese: "地球神一世斗卫星 (Earth God I struggling satellites)."

On December 31, 2006, the Chinese people pointed out that the images and stories of female Earth God could solely be determined after popularizing the religious organizations of Earth God later than my era. Hence, I should become the Ancestor of Earth God, resigning from the post of the Earth God I. It was not necessary for the Ancestor of Earth God to do missionary work, but it was for the Earth God.

On March 7, 2007, I said that I, like heaven god Nezha, was also a real god. He returned his bones and flesh body to humans, fitting the Chicago event in 1997. On that day, a Chinese satellite operator suggested that Nezha could become the Infant Earth God, eliciting my interest.

On March 14, 2007, a satellite operator reminded me whether I accepted if the Christians respected me as their Holy Spirit. After consideration, I said that they would be inappropriate if they did so. The reason was that I had once been forced to resign from the post of Holy Spirit, being accommodated as Jesus. In this regard, if I was respected to be the Holy Spirit, it was unfavorable to the image of Christianity while staying along with Jesus.

Since I represented one era in history, for the sake of deducting the disgust against me from the vegetarian descendants while recognizing the reality of the success of humans eating meat presently, I decided to deduct the amount of meat I ate to half.

In April 2007, since the achievements of ancient humans in the invention of languages, tools and so on might exceed my glories, the humans no longer cared whether I was the Infant Earth God. On April 17 of that year, on television, I saw that the people pointed out that, since I had adopted the name of the heaven god Nezha in the critical period of democracy calling for law execution in China, it was not appropriate for me to represent the Earth God, while it was better for me to return to become the heaven god Nezha. Hence, I decided no longer to be the Earth God.

In August 2007, the Beijing sound from satellite protested and said that since I was too risky in future, they were not fond of me to be Nezha. In contrast, other operators of satellites advised me to resign from the post of the heaven God Nezha, just as I had resigned from the post of the Holy Spirit previously, lest some Chinese could find trouble. I consented to resign from the post of Nezha. I was San Force by myself and was no longer in the same image as Nezha. I might still be his new teacher or good friend, but not necessarily Nezha himself.

On September 21, 2007, I thought that now that the United States were not able to annihilate humans, it should be impossible for humans to become extinct. So, why should they require me to commit suicide? I directed the satellites to shout in Chinese: "人类不会死，干吗要我死 (Humans not extinct, why should I die?)" On September 15, 2008, before dawn, I pointed out that, in regard to the Chicago event in 1997, it was possible for me to request the US Army to compensate my reputation. I directed the satellites to shout: "Chicago reputation compensation."

On March 13, 2008, the satellite operators and I pointed out that, when in Chicago, the US operators of satellites requested me to commit suicide by "breaking earth", and I rejected it on the first day, I watched outside the surroundings, indicating that I doubted the synchrony of nuclear explosions to annihilate the humans, equal to requiring the humans to die in half and then suicide. I directed the satellites to shout in Chinese: "死掉一半再自杀 (Suicide after dying in half)." On September 23 of that year, the people and I further pointed out that when the US satellites were requesting me to commit suicide by breaking earth, it was implicated that the people were not able to learn about the real situation; otherwise, I could certainly have required to set up a monument at first, and then commit suicide. It was not accurate to comment that I did not want to commit suicide because I was afraid of death since the democracy calling for law execution was more dangerous! It was necessary to add that they requested me to commit suicide like a psychotic person, lower than a soldier with payment discounted, certainly intolerable for me to accept. I directed the satellites to shout in Chinese: "芝加哥自杀少立碑 (Suicide in Chicago short of monument)."

On August 14, 2008, in the light of Washington resigning to help establish the United States as the first big democratic country without king, demonstrating the operation and success of democratic system to the whole world, I hoped to respect him as San Intellectual King. Nonetheless, Great Britain had already realized democracy through a constitutional monarchy, and since America had been a colony of Great Britain, it had also realized that the election had occurred prior to its War of Independence, while the American War of Independence, led by Washington, was not aimed at realizing democracy. On November 3, 2008, I learned from internet that the democratic system had operated in ancient Greece and Rome for hundreds of years as the earliest democratic system in human history, earlier than the constitutional monarchy of Great Britain. On October 19, 2014, the people and I pointed out that Washington and Jefferson shared the achievement of establishing the first democratic system without a king in history, belonging to one of the San Intellectuals. I learned from internet that, in the earlier republic of Holland, the people did not have the right to election. Hence, it was not considered a contributor to the achievement.

On August 31, 2008, I pointed out that the French Revolution had virtually been the spontaneous huge riot of residents in the capital, surging in the emotion of livelihood against tax. They arrested the King in the big mess. Finally, they swallowed the pain of mess and failure. I picked out the wise philosophers and intellectuals struggling for democracy in those years in France, respecting those individuals as San Intellectuals of democracy.

On October 14, 2008, I learned from internet that the control center of the US National Aeronautics and Space Administration (NASA) was located in either the Goddard

Space Flight Center in Maryland or Johnson Space Center in Houston, Texas, while the launch center in Florida was under the direct control of that in Texas, responsible for assembly and launch solely. In 1997, when the US satellites were shouting to break earth, the Chinese part had not participated yet, meaning that there were only the US satellites. Additionally, the US Presidents and Defense Ministers had not been able to capture the operators of satellites these years. Hence, it was possible that the Chicago event was just a prank by NASA. After 2010, Hillary, the wife of President Clinton, as Secretary of State, objected many times on television for her family to share the event of satellites shouting for breaking earth. Clinton was also required to characterize this event as an accident caused by subordinates. On May 20, 2013, people in various countries pointed out that tracing me and presidents by satellites was one of the routine duties of information collection. Hence, they determined its location at the Goddard Space Flight Center in Maryland, while the Johnson Space Center in Houston, Texas, was solely responsible for space navigation rather than information collection and management.

On November 9, 2008, I pointed out that, in the event of Chicago in 1997, my comprehension of ocean nuclear fusion had been its impossibility to be ignited. The attitude and effect on the second day of my shouting for war also demonstrated that the satellite operators and I had all thought it impossible to ignite the nuclear fusion of the ocean that year. It was common knowledge at that time that, on the bottom of the sea, the big countries had already tested nuclear explosions. I directed the satellites to shout in Chinese: "芝加

哥地球不含海洋 (Chicago earth did not contain ocean)." Several days later, I changed to direct the satellites to shout: "Chicago ocean safe 2nd day." On January 2, 2015, from the news I saw, the Latin people pointed out that if I had recognized that there could have happened the nuclear fusion of the ocean, it would have been impossible to wait until 2003 to solve this problem.

On November 12, 2008, the people in JiangSu and I noticed that, in regard to the comprehension of mine and the operators of satellites on breaking earth in 1997, they had hoped to annihilate or heavily damage the entire human race while not being able to destroy the ocean or annihilate animals such as mice, with the boundaries of species conspicuous. Then, for the first time, I happened to lead the humans to practise the democracy calling for law execution, establish the theory of armed police and win over the nuclear war on earth; hence, I was just the leader of democratic law of all the humans. On the 17th of that month, I pointed out that, for the democracy calling for law execution, it often resorted to foreign forces, while it was fond of colonization. If I accepted the name of the race leader of humans, the intelligent robots and dolphins would often colonize humans in the future; hence, it was not appropriate for me to take the name. I directed the satellites to shout in Chinese: "人种领袖 colony (Leader of human race colony)." In 2012, in regard to my shouting for war to deal with the satellite operators constantly requesting me to commit suicide by "Breaking earth" in 1997 in Chicago, the people defined me as one belonging to the subspecies of humans and local police, but not the race leader of humans.

On November 21, 2008, from the videos on internet on the nuclear explosion under the sea (http://v.youku.com/v_show/id_XODQwMzIwNA==.html, http://v.youku.com/v_show/id_co00XOTIwODA0.html and so on), I saw that, prior to 1997, the armies of the Europe and United States had already carried out experiments of nuclear explosion of hydrogen bomb on the bottom of the sea. I directed the satellites to shout in Chinese: "海底核爆炸 97 前 (Nuclear explosion on the bottom of the sea prior to 1997)." On February 2, 2012, I pointed out that once the war broke out, any participant in the war would strive all the way to sink the opposite nuclear submarine, resulting in the explosion of the submarine. This was the common military knowledge. I directed the satellites to shout in Chinese: "战争击沉核潜艇 (War sinks submarine)."

On November 24, 2008, I learned from internet that while using nuclear weapon, the US army strictly followed the dual control system, requiring two officers to cooperate and then make the execution possible. After receiving the command of launch, the two officers should input their own codes of nuclear control separately. After the combination, it was then possible to enter the launch program. I directed the satellites to shout: "Atom dual code key." After comprehending the dual control for the launch of US nuclear missiles, it was understandable that, even if it had happened to be the military mutiny in Chicago event in 1997, it would still have been impossible to crazily command all military officers, launch all nuclear weapons, and annihilate all the humans by using nuclear weapons.

On August 23, 2009, I compared the relationship between

me and humans with the relationship between the Indians and other natives. Not only could I marry a human for reproduction, but also my parents could join my family and share with me the glories of my family, just as the whites and blacks could live within one family! The next day, on August 24 of that year, I directed the satellites to shout in Chinese: "圣比土著印第安 (San analogous to natives and Indians)."

On August 29, 2009, before dawn, the US operator from a satellite said that they might collaborate with the laser satellite and kill me. In the afternoon of that day, I thought that if the laser weapon of the satellite was separate in command for targeting and shooting, it would be safer, just as the nuclear submarine adopted dual codes to ensure safety. I directed the satellites to shout: "Sate-laser dual codes." In the evening, from the news, I saw that many people in China and abroad had already thought to this point earlier than I had. Dual codes for laser satellites might effectively prevent the event of terror in outer space in the future and ensure the safety of the satellite weapons there.

It was necessary to point out that, although it was expensive to launch and maintain the satellite weapons, it was still the most effective measure to fight down the terror of satellites by the laser on the ground in future. Dual coding for laser satellites and national fighting down satellites against terror both might prevent and strike satellite terrors in future, possessing some significance in history.

On October 9, 2009, I requested the descendants not to use my name to set up any prize, lest awarding eminent persons in a mess like the Nobel Prize. It was more rational to let famous persons affect society and history naturally rather than nominate and promote them with prizes. On the next day, October 10 of that year, I directed the satellites to shout in Chinese: "武圣人名义不设奖 (No prize set up by the name of San Force)."

On October 10, 2011, on television I saw many GuangDong people saying, while dealing with the Cuban Missile Crisis, the action of Kennedy was more real and serious, exceeding the military coup on organization and rigor. Since there were many evil persons among the people on quantity, deleting or prohibiting the scandalous event of Chicago might cause the rumors to reversely surge. In this regard, the people and I made use of the more real, more authoritative and more severe missile event of Kennedy, as well as the early ocean nuclear experiments of the United States and Europe, to compare and oppress the unreal Chicago event.

On December 2, 2011, the US sound from satellite said that the Christian Bible claimed that the end of world would be more severe than their shouting to break earth. Hence, this event had no influence on Christianity.

On April 22, 2012, I, along with people in various countries, analogized my behavior in 1997 in Chicago, having refused to commit suicide but called for war to the military mutiny for law and counter strike by the defence, corresponding to the local provincial and municipal police in armed police, while I became the subspecies of humans.

On May 20, 2012, one satellite operator said that, in the Chicago event in 1997, the shouts to annihilate the humans had been insufficient in both organization and force. It was certainly impossible for humans to be extinct. Hence, it was incompatible with the standard for me to become a subspecies of humans. On the evening of May 22 of that year, I pointed out that my call for the war then was just the legal counter-strike against the benefits of all humans, corresponding to the legal insurrection of provincial and municipal police for defence, and hence certainly belonging to the subspecies of humans. The key to determining the subspecies was the legal insurrection for defence against the benefits of the whole humans, rather than the scale and power of the illegal strike.

On September 13, 2012, I pointed out that the Holy Spirit could give birth to children, corresponding to God on his giving birth to Jesus. Resigning from the post of Holy Spirit should certainly not result in termination of reproduction. It was the trend of religion to eliminate ignorance and brutality. It would definitely be consented by religions for the monks and priests to reproduce in future. On September 9, 2013, I learned from internet that HongZhi Li, the King God of FaLun Gong, had likewise married and given birth to at least one daughter, while a GuangDong sound from a satellite said that XiuQuan Hong had also reproduced children.

After 2012, the people and I regarded that, for my accomplishment of both democracy calling for law execution and theory of armed police, the assistance from US satellites was their compensation to me for the denigration and isolation of me from the Chicago event in 1997. On March 24, 2013, I pointed out that to compensate for my positive impacts on robots as Holy Spirit, it was necessary to combine the two parts altogether. I directed the satellites to shout: "Good robots to God."

On February 10, 2015, before dawn, I pointed out that it was usually impossible for a subspecies to join the army and police in all. Hence, it was impossible to become extinct from war. The European and American people pointed out that the municipal police mostly gave birth to progeny in peaceful times. Hence, even if I partially represented the municipal police on behalf of a single subspecies, it was impossible to become the excuse for extinction.

On February 28, 2017, the people and I classified the social sciences into six categories: democracy, economy, war, law, independence and welfare. My theory of democracy calling for law execution belonged to democracy and law, while both the theories of armed police and winning over the nuclear weapons on the earth belonged to war.

End poem of the chapter:

By the elegant talent of aspirant youth, the salvation yearning,
By the democracy calling for law execution, the police and army strengthening,
By the victory over the nuclear weapons, the spirit and courage rising,
By the decade of winds and fires, the San Force resounding.

Chapter | 6

Great Unification for Physics

Musical Background of Rhythmic Writing: The Same Song

Please read the following text sentence-by-sentence to feel the musical background of the rhythmic framework.

During the second half of the year 2004, I began to think of the physics before and considered the problems of transformation between mass and energy together with the essence of mass. Finally, I achieved a conjecture that the essence of mass was the localization of electromagnetic waves, which was capable of accounting for the fact that the γ photon of high energy might transform into the electron of stationary mass.

On September 1, 2005, to finally unify the electromagnetic and gravitational forces, I investigated the essence of physics with the string of electromagnetic energy. The operators of satellites were occasionally interested in the problem but did not have any valuable opinions. During the long holidays of National Day in October 2005, I began organizing the satellite operators to think of the physics comprehensively and named the satellite operators joining the activity as "Sate-commune Group," manifesting the cooperation between them to make the achievements altogether. I was the host of "Sate-commune Group" and tried my best to maintain fairness and make sure that the contributions from satellite operators were recognized. While encountering the situation of discussion altogether, I made use of "I and the operators of satellites" to manifest that my contribution dominated in proportion and made use of "the operators of satellites and I" to manifest the reverse. I directed the operators of satellites to shout to directly announce our achievements with satellites and also propagate them with microwaves and infrared to the whole world. This method was propagated to the television news and live public telecasts in the whole world. The people in various countries of the world participated enthusiastically, and all believed that, in synchrony with us, it was possible to harvest scientific achievements for the first time while making use of television for the live telecast of scientific news. We made use of the internet, which had developed after the 1990s, as the major measure for searching the literature, discussing the problems in physics, and altogether accomplishing the great unification and leap of physics.

In September 2007, I, along with the operators of satellites, began making use of the principles of Government and Police (GP) in China and the United States to formalize the contents. I directed the satellites to shout. The operators of satellites and I led the people of the whole world together to realize the great unification and leap of physics, directly in compliance with the principle of supporting the human civil progression among the GP principles of China and the United States.

❖ Mass and Photon

The situations of physics during that time were approximately that humans had already found that there were four kinds of forces in nature: electromagnetic force, gravitational force, strong force and weak force. Scientists, despite trying to unify these four forces, did not achieve satisfactory results. It was already known that the matter was all composed of atoms, while the atom was composed of the atomic nucleus and the electrons around the nucleus. The electromagnetic force bound the atomic nucleus and electrons together. Within the atomic nucleus, there were the protons and neutrons. In the recent high-energy physics of particles, it had further been supposed that the protons and neutrons were both composed of quarks. Between the quarks and between the proton and neutron, there was the strong force that bound them together.

There were concurrently two significant and influential theories in physics during that time. One was the quantum mechanics, supposing that there must be the duality of wave and particle for all matters. Therefore, with regard to the photon of frequency as ν, the lowest unit of energy should be $E=h\nu$, where h was Planck's quantum constant. Quantum mechanics was mainly applicable to the fields of microscopic particle physics. Another significant theory of physics was Einstein's theory of relativity, which emphasized the relativity of time and space. In other words, for the time and space, it was not absolutely the same between the reference systems in movement and at a standstill, which was capable of being correlated with the Lorenz transformation. In the special theory of relativity of Einstein, there were adopted the following two important axioms on the basis of considering the presence of relativity for time and space:

- The axiom of special relativity that the corresponding principles of physics for matter were identical among each inertial reference system;
- The principle that the speed of light was identical for all inertial reference systems. In accordance with these, Einstein deduced not only the relativity of time and space of Lorenz transformation but also the famous equation of mass and energy: $E=mc^2$, where E was the energy, m was the mass and C was the light speed.

In the general theory of relativity, Einstein further correlated the relativity of time and space with the gravitational force. The axioms of Einstein's theory of relativity were as follows:

- The gravitational force was equivalent to the inertial force, or the gravitational mass was equivalent to the inertial mass;
- The axiom of general relativity that the forms of corresponding principles of physics were all identical among all reference systems.

From these two axioms, Einstein deduced that the gravitational force should cause the curvature of time and space. The theories of relativity were mainly applicable to matters of huge mass or high velocity, such as the celestial bodies in the cosmos and so on.

During that time, physicists were also trying to establish new theories and unify the four natural forces. The most famous of these theories was the theory of the superstring. However, they were very far from real unification and great success. Therefore, it was an opportunity for me and the satellite operators to lead the people in the whole world to achieve breakthroughs in physics and unify the four natural forces altogether.

During the long holidays of National Day in October 2005, I called together the satellite operators to discuss the physics. Since the frequency of light was the energy capable of being directly assayed, it was intuitively advantageous to unify the four forces with the electromagnetic force. On the morning of October 5, 2005, I pointed out that although the frequencies and wavelengths of light of different colors were different, they travelled at almost the same speed in the vacuum. At that moment, a ZheJiang sound from a satellite said that the speed of the electrical field was constant, so the light as the electromagnetic wave should also travel at a constant speed along the direction of the electrical field or magnetic field. A female in Beijing from a satellite found that the light was the rolling bead with E-H rotation. I pointed out that in that situation, the travelling speed of light would be correlated with the rate and frequency of rotation of the bead. The satellites sent me a photograph of Darwin and a picture of a bead and said in English, "It's E." I comprehended his meaning. The light was indeed the rolling bead. Its travelling speed along the direction of E or H was just that of E or H, while its rate and frequency of rotation was the changing speed of E and H, but not the travelling speed. The operators of satellites and I easily considered that the mass was certainly also the electromagnetic rotation or electromagnetic twist, supporting my conjecture before that time. Therefore, the conclusions on that day were "Sate-commune Group, 质量旋转光滚动 (Mass rotation light roll)," while I directed the satellites to shout and announce. During the evening on the same day, in accordance with the model of mass rotation and light roll, a ZheJiang sound from a satellite said that the electron might generate its charge from its own rotation or spin. Later on television, I saw somebody likewise say mass rotation and light roll during a European football game, which might even be several days earlier than we did it. Mass rotation and light roll played key guiding roles in the great unification of physics at that time.

On October 7, 2005, I considered that in the case of directly adding the Two Partial Differential Equations of Schrödinger to the Maxwell Equations, it must be negative in character or subtract the quantum term, enabling it to maintain the conservation of energy. I supposed that the electrical field E would correspond to the spatial x, while the magnetic field H would correspond to the temporal t. At that moment, a Beijing female operator of a satellite said, "This time, the Party supports. It is square." I comprehended her meaning. The electrical field E and magnetic field H were the same and unified, but they were only different on the second-order differentials. The satellite operators and I quickly supposed that H should be like the wineglass in shape while E should be like the granule in shape. I directed satellites to shout in Chinese: "Sate-commune Group, 磁场酒杯电场米 (Magnetic field wineglass and electrical field granule)."

In the afternoon on October 9, 2005, I went to the bookstore to purchase a book on physics. In the evening, I read the book and learnt that the electrical to magnetic transformation was positive in character on the linear differential item in the equation and negative in reverse transformation. Similarly, it was left-handed in one equation and right-handed in another. In accordance, we recognized that it was difficult to unify and account for the electrical field E and the magnetic field H, with the magnetic field resembling wineglass and the electrical field resembling granule, because of their difficulty in compliance with the difference in the linear differential items in equations of positive and negative character.

On October 10, 2005, after getting up in the morning, I comprehended that, for the purpose of unifying the electrical field E and the magnetic field H, the linear terms in electromagnetic equations required to be the same in positive and negative character, but not for the added non-linear terms. The US satellite members were supposed to use only one high partial differential equation of H against space to unify the electrical to magnetic transformation and magnetic to electrical transformation, with the shape of field H resembling a saddle. In that situation, relative to the electrical-to-magnetic transformation, the magnetic-to-electrical transformation was no longer -90 degrees but +270 degrees. Here, the linear differential term manifested the direct electromagnetic transformation with energy conservation, while the two partial differential terms were no longer linear and clear on their origins. I directed the satellites to shout in Chinese: "Sate-commune Group, 电磁统一大 H (Electromagnetic unification with big H)." In the evening, on television, I saw that there were likewise many considerations elsewhere in China about both H unification and 270 degrees on magnetic to electrical transformation.

❖ Relativity and the Universal Gravitational Force

On the morning of October 6, 2005, the satellite operators and I continued considering the structure of electrons. We imagined that the negative electrical field of electronic charge was homogeneous in all directions, so we inferred that the electron might also concurrently rotate and become homogeneous in all directions. In accordance, we imagined H like a spittoon and E like a reverse cone above, with the two transforming with each other, strong and weak from time to time. I also added such a change as overturn so that realized homogeneous could be in all directions, while the electrical field of the electron could scintillate from time to time. At that moment, the satellite projected to me a photograph of a young American female wearing a white uniform. She told me that the electrical field of electrons was changing and that energy should be generated. Then, the satellite projected to me another photograph of a fat American male, who said to me, "It's energy." I immediately comprehended that he meant the gravitational energy G. I was very happy then and directed the satellites to shout and announce in Chinese: "Sate-commune Group, 电子闪烁是引力 (Electronic scintillation is gravity)."

On October 11, 2005, at noon, while having lunch in the dining room, I found that the gravitational force manifested as order, while the thermodynamic increment of entropy manifested as chaos. It was required to add the characteristics of order and anti-entropy to the gravitational force. After returning to the office, I emphasized that one term of electromagnetic attractive force was added to the interactions among the atoms and molecules while the rest were compliant with thermodynamics. I directed the satellites to shout in Chinese: "电磁半吸是引力 (Electromagnetic semi-attraction gravity)." In the afternoon, the satellite sent me a sound of a white male saying 3k, meaning the background radiation at 3 degrees universally and homogeneously existing in the cosmos. The gravitational force might be considered as the flow of 3k. After 5 o'clock in the afternoon, a Beijing male from a satellite reminded me to consider the electromagnetic waves directly as flows so that, in this way, it was possible to include and substitute the 3k. Interactions of electromagnetic waves generated flows, with big vortexes having big gravitational force and small vortexes having small gravitational force.

After returning home in the evening, a sound from the satellite with a heavy SuZhou accent, calling himself ZheJiang, said that electromagnetic waves should draw closer to each other during the attraction, increased in stability and longer in interactive time, and should bounce off rapidly during repulsion, shorter in interactive time. In accordance, they were asymmetrical, which might possibly be the major component of gravitational force. This was better than the explanation for gravity from the electromagnetic half attraction. At that moment, an American from a satellite said that, in case there is the universal and homogeneous G, it should be possible that there existed a pure gravitational force independent from the interactions of electromagnetic waves.

On October 12, 2005, I specifically named the phenomenon of electromagnetic waves longer during attraction and shorter in repulsion found by ZheJiang satellite operators as the polarizing force of electromagnetic waves or the electromagnetic polarizing force. After 2008, I once more changed it to the name of the orienting force of electromagnetic waves or the electromagnetic orienting force, which is more correct in meaning.

On the morning of October 13, 2005, while waiting for a bus at the bus station to go to work, I strongly felt uncomfortable about relativity. I perceived that there must be another solution in mathematics because space in relativity was becoming shorter. After boarding the bus, I considered whether the movement in the reverse direction was capable of making the time longer, but I also recalled that the space was homogeneous in all directions, so everything should be the same. However, I felt uncomfortable because v and –v were different after all, so that everything should be opposite.

At that moment, I found that there needed to be a third reference system to observe the difference. The operators of the satellites dared not say anything, and nor did they have any idea. They were only sending me pictures of 3 reference systems to support me, letting me consider the problem.

Then, I continued considering this problem. With regard to the stationary reference system O, the reference system A moved at v on constant velocity, while the reference system B moved at –v on constant velocity. With regard to the reference system B, the reference system A moved at 2v on velocity. Observed from the reference system O, A moved at v on relative velocity, with its relative time changed as t, and B moved at -v on relative velocity, with its relative time also changed as t in the same. Therefore, as observed from the reference system O, the reference systems A and B were the same on time, with the difference of relative time between them as 0 and as t with regard to the reference system O. Again, observed from the reference system B, A moved at 2v on relative velocity, with its relative time changed approximately as 2t. This situation was different from the physical processes observed from the reference system O. These two states were concurrent but contradictory, so it was impossible to happen. After getting off the bus and arriving at the office, I assumed that the only explanation was t=0, or there was no relativity for time. During the whole process, the satellite operators did not say a word, nor did anybody on the bus perceive any idea from the satellite operators. Now that the relativity of time was wrong, the special relativity should also be wrong. Since Einstein's theory of relativity was very great and famous, I resorted to my reputation and influence, mustered up my courage, made a decision to say that special relativity might be wrong, and further directed the satellites to shout and announce.

For the purpose of investigating why there appeared the real experimental phenomena of different time and space discussed in special relativity, the American satellite operator gave me a picture of 3k, believing that the electromagnetic movement might make friction or electromagnetic orientation with the 3k background that might cause instability and change, manifesting as a change in time. In the afternoon, I found that they analogously caused contradiction to become incapable of solving the problem. The details were as follows:

With the same 3 reference systems as above, the reference system 0 was stationary, the reference system A moved at v on constant velocity, and the reference system B moved at -v on constant velocity. Particle X moved at v on constant velocity, while Particle Y moved at -v on constant velocity. Both of them made friction or electromagnetic orientation with the 3k background, and both changed in their longevity as t in the same, so that there was no change in relative longevity for Particle X relative to Particle Y. These were the results observed from the reference system 0. Observed from the reference system B, Particle Y moved at 0 on velocity, and Particle X moved at 2v on velocity. Particle Y did not change in longevity, while Particle X changed in longevity roughly as 2t because of its friction or electromagnetic orientation with the 3k background, different from Particle Y. This was different from the results observed from the reference system 0 that both Particle X and Particle Y changed in their longevity in the same as t, manifesting the concurrent and contradictory phenomena on physics, which was impossible. Therefore, explaining friction or electromagnetic orientation with the 3k background likewise became difficult.

Then, we shifted to consider other models and explanations. An American sound from a satellite said there was a need to simulate the interactions with the relatively fixed electrical field. We made a concise comparison and found it a successful explanation, with the following details:

The same 3 reference systems as above were adopted. The reference system 0 was stationary, the reference system A moved at v on constant velocity, and the reference system B moved at -v on constant velocity. Particle X moved at v on constant velocity, while Particle Y moved at –v on constant velocity. At the center of the reference system O, there was a spherical electrical field E. In this situation, both Particle X and Particle Y made electromagnetic orientation with the spherical electrical field E, and both their wavelength decreased in the same as x. Therefore, there was no change in relative wavelength for Particle X relative to Particle Y. These were the results observed from the reference system O. Observed from the reference system B, Particle Y moved at 0 on velocity, while Particle X moved at 2v on velocity. At this moment, the spherical electrical field E acquired v as its relative velocity of movement. Particle X moved at v on velocity relative to the spherical electrical field E. Movement made its electromagnetic orientation with E shift to blue, and therefore made its wavelength reduce as x. Particle Y moved at -v on velocity relative to the spherical electrical field E. Movement likewise made its electromagnetic orientation with E shift to blue, and therefore likewise made its wavelength reduce as x. Both the two particles, X and Y, changed the same in their wavelength as x. This was compatible with the results observed from the reference system O without any contradiction. Therefore, the experimental phenomena of relative reduction in length of space were capable of being explained with such an electromagnetic method. An American in a satellite made a preliminary and rather prospective explanation of the phenomena of special relativity. I directed the satellites to help him shout and announce in time.

In the afternoon of October 14, 2005, I considered that, since there existed electromagnetic scintillation, the kinetic energy of the earth moving around the sun should likewise also transform into the infrared rays and dissipate away so that the earth would no longer have sufficient energy to move around the sun, and would finally stop. An American in a satellite said that there were many forces pushing the earth forward and projected a picture of the sun to me. I considered it and comprehended what he meant to say, that is, the sun rotated by itself to affect the electromagnetic fields of the earth, pushing the earth to move around it. Although the energy of self-rotation of the sun might also be consumed because there were nuclear reactions within the sun for maintaining its vortices at high temperatures, the energy for the rotation of the sun should be supplemented continuously. I directed the satellites to shout in Chinese: "Satecommmune Group, 太阳自转拉地球 (Sun rotates to draw earth)."

In the evening on the same day, the satellite operators and I recognized that the electromagnetic force was capable of causing the difference in the distribution of components of planets. Mercury, Venus, Earth and Mars are the inner planets. They are close to the sun and rich in elements such as iron, silicates, carbonates, etc. They are sensitive to electromagnetic interaction, are big in the electromagnetic force and revolve fast around the sun. In contrast, Jupiter and Saturn are the outer planets. They are farther from the sun and rich in elements such as hydrogen. Since they are in a gaseous state, they are not very sensitive to electromagnetic force and revolve slowly around the sun. The outermost planets were difficult to account for and might possibly be apprehended from the cosmos. The other stars were analogous to the sun in characteristics such as gravitational force and electromagnetic force so that their planets might also distribute in the same pattern as those in the solar system. I directed the satellites to shout in Chinese: "Satecommmune Group, 恒星都像太阳系 (Stars all resemble solar system)."

In the evening, while coming back home, I watched on television that there were many Chinese directly adding the planets rich in iron to the inner circles during that daytime. Their purpose was also wonderful, expecting to turn all the stars into the solar system. This model affected and inspired humans for a whole day. However, I believed that the astrophysicists had earlier established the same models.

In the evening on the same day, I once again watched on the television that the Russians were specifically emphasizing that the mutual gravitational forces among matters of different components were capable of being assayed very accurately, proving the universal and homogeneous existence of gravitational force, different from the explanation with electromagnetic orienting force. Several years later, I solved this problem by concentrating the gravitational masses on the positive and negative quarks in the atomic nuclei.

On the morning of October 16, 2005, I read a book at SuZhou Library entitled "Dynamics of Astronomy and Earth," edited by ShuHua Ye and Cheng Huang. There were data indicating that the deviations calculated with the general relativity and only with the Newton dynamics differed at 10^{-9} as an exponent on the surface of the earth and at 10^{-6} as an exponent on the surface of the sun. The satellite sent me a picture of an American woman who reminded me that the calculation of gravitational force with general relativity was very accurate; hence, the experimental effects of general relativity should manifest the gravitational force.

In the afternoon on the same day, I realized on the bus why the high partial differential term of H did not transform into infrared and microwaves to dissipate. At that moment, I believed that the high partial differential term of H might not emit energy but attract energy, manifesting as gravity. I apprehended this point, pointing out that they released large amounts of energy while the objects were flying toward black holes or the satellites returning to Earth. Therefore, I recognized that the attractive energy was negative. I directed the satellites to shout in Chinese: "旋转吸能是引力 (Rotation and energy attraction is gravity)." The people on the same bus recognized my effort and consented to the slogan I directed the satellites to shout.

Then, I began to consider how to emit outside the high partial differential term of H and how to attract the gravitational receptor. I imagined the cone attracting the objects. A ZheJiang sound from a satellite said that it must be rectified to the parabolic shape or the parabolic cone. In three dimensions, they were very close to the gravitational field, such as most planets moving on elliptical orbits, while some comets moving on parabolic curves and never returning. A European from a satellite said that it must be rectified to the shape of a saddle. Hearing about them, I consented to all of them. The operators of satellites began to simulate the gravitational force and did not intend to calculate anymore. Watching athletic games on television, I saw that the Chinese people complained that we were too slow in progression. In those days, the ShenZhou 6 Spacecraft was carrying and sending Chinese astronauts to space. So, people learned to partly adopt a calculation in aeronautical engineering and shift to simulation in case they encountered any difficulty with calculation. Therefore, the people were inspired, intending to simulate the gravitational force of H. The satellite operators and I imagined various possible shapes for the high partial differential term of H, such as the nail, rolling wheel, rolling cross, etc, while the people on television also concurrently imagined all of them.

On October 17, 2005, in the office, the satellite operators reminded me to consider the black hole, supposing that the energy should not be capable of emitting from it. The rolling wheel of a high partial differential term of H also belonged to the mutual electromagnetic transformation, certainly possessing energy, to be attracted back to the black hole and be incapable of reaching outside of a black hole. However, it was contemporarily observed that the gravity outside the black hole was huge and, hence, difficult to account for.

I then considered the 3k background radiation universally existing in the cosmos. The well of the negative potential energy of the black hole attracted the 3k radiation in the cosmos around the black hole, bringing about the 3k energy flows, attracting the matters outside and generating the gravitational force. At that moment, an American satellite operator pointed out that the 3k radiation acquiring the energy of gravity from a black hole should emit rather strong light, incompatible with many observations. A ZheJiang from a satellite said that the light generated as such should lose energy again and transform back to the 3k radiation after escaping from the gravitational field of the black hole. The light would even possibly be lower in energy to solve the problem.

On October 18, 2005, I resorted to internet and saw how to make use of the gravitational curvature of time and space of Einstein to account for the black hole. When the gravitational force was big enough, the light rays emitting from some angles would return. Since it was adopted with the Riemannian space but not Euclidean space when the gravity was sufficiently big and exceeded the Schwartz constant, even though the light ray emitted at 90 degrees, it would still return. I rectified that the black hole wobbled and rotated so that the space of the black hole could always change. Therefore, the light rays might be affected by the wobble and rotation of the black hole when they are curved back to the black hole, while a small portion of them might just escape away from the gravitational field of a black hole. The black hole leaked a little light. I read the writings about black holes on internet and found that there were two types of black holes. One was the small black hole with a mass smaller than that of ten suns. It was generated from the star. Another was the huge black hole located at the center of a galaxy with a mass equivalent to billions of suns. The most recent news in the United States reported that they observed the huge black hole directly emitting matters of very high energy. We immediately categorized the X-ray of a black hole as the energy released from the matter falling down to the black hole and the eruption of extremely high energy as the direct emission of the latter type of the huge black hole, via which the protons and electrons were generated, and finally fulfilled the whole galaxy.

On the evening of the same day, on television, I saw that

many people in China, the United States and Latin America had reached the new conclusion that black holes had leaked light earlier than we had. This was the common progression made altogether by the people of the whole world.

On the morning of October 19, 2005, I recognized that once there happened the electromagnetic interaction between the high partial differential term of H and receptor, no matter the positive charge or negative charge, so long as they changed with each other and generated new changes, then the receptor would take over the change in momentum in accordance with the momentum conservation. Therefore, the gravitational force was transferred to the receptor. In the evening, while watching television, I saw that some Shanghainese and Latinos had already recognized the use of momentum to transfer gravity, with the Latinos doing it earlier on time.

On December 18, 2007, in the afternoon, the satellite operators and I discussed the mechanism that the electrical field and the magnetic field transmitted infinitely in space. The ZheJiang from satellites mentioned to polarize or orient the space. I believed the ether flows and found that the electromagnetic waves were the ether. Therefore, it was easy to work out the mechanism that the electrical field and the magnetic field were capable of transmitting in space.

In the evening of the same day, while watching television, I saw that many Americans in the United States had considered directly using the theory of electromagnetic friction or electromagnetic orientation of American satellite operators before to explain the phenomena of relativity and further explain the gravitational force earlier than we did.

On December 23, 2007, I found on internet that many conclusions of Einstein's special relativity were relative to the clock of physics. Many skills were also adopted involving the movement in affecting the clock of physics, different from ours in the angle of insight on considering the problem so that the two were not directly contradictory for the moment.

On the evening of December 28, 2007, I found that it was necessary to rectify the contemporary gravitational theory to the effects of general relativity mediated through the orienting force of electromagnetic waves. I directed the satellites to shout in Chinese: "电磁波相对性是引力，武圣人喊叫 (Relativity of electromagnetic wave is gravity, San Force shouts)." On television, I saw that a few Beijing people had achieved the same ideas several hours earlier than I did.

On the morning of January 20, 2008, I found that the effect of the increment in mass from the condensation of quarks was capable of disproving that time and space themselves possessed general relativity, so it was obligatory to rectify and explain gravity with the effects of general relativity from the electromagnetic wavelength of matter.

On the evening of February 29, 2008, a Beijing sound from a satellite replaced the time and space with the wavelengths of two particles, disturbing my non-relativity of ideal time and space. I insisted on my own opinion, supposing that time and space should be different from the interactions of physics. On the evening of March 2, 2008, I found that I observed the time for the first when I disproved relativity, which was the easiest to generate the paradox. The paradox of the relativity of time made it easy to distinguish time and space from the interactions of physics. I directed the satellites to shout: "Time early easier." On the next day, on television, there were many people, including Kun Jiang in the advertisement, disproving the relativity through methods such as calling with handphones, taking photos, etc.

On the evening of March 3, 2008, I found that if the electromagnetic orientation between the electromagnetic mass and electromagnetic waves was formed, and the electromagnetic wave got rid of such orienting interaction and returned to the original status, there consumed energy and released heat, with its own wavelength becoming longer, which might be the cause for the redshift in general relativity. I directed the satellites to shout in Chinese: "引力红移放热量，武圣人喊叫 (Gravitational redshift releases heat, San Force shouts)." In the evening, while watching television, I saw that when NanJing leaders were interviewing the US visitors, both of them might have considered the gravitational redshift causing the release of heat energy earlier than I did. On April 25 of the same year, the Shanghai sound from a satellite pointed out that the relative redshift of electromagnetic waves only changed in wavelength, while it was incapable of transmitting among them. In accordance with this, I rectified the gravitational field so that the relative curvature plus redshift of electromagnetic waves mediated gravity. Both curvature in the gravitational field and manifestation of refraction of light supported this explanation.

On April 21, 2008, I defined special relativity as the influence of movement on the electromagnetic orienting effects between matters. Since it was different from and not dependent on general relativity, it improved the electromagnetic theory of special relativity from the American satellites. On January 23, 2009, the satellite sent a photo of a Wuxi woman who pointed out that, after acquiring the velocity of movement, the particle itself transformed into more orderly in the direction of movement, strengthening the electromagnetic orienting effect. Therefore, she solved the problem of movement causing shorter lengths and slower times in special relativity. I directed the satellites to shout in Chinese: "运动有序化相对性，卫星无锡喊 (Order from movement is relativity, Sate-commune Wuxi shouts)." On television, I saw that the people in the United Kingdom and Brazil had already considered the movement causing the order for relativity one day earlier than we did.

On the evening of September 25, 2008, I analogized the medium of vacuum to glass while fixing the speed of light so that I could explain that the photon emitted from the moving light source was constant in light speed while shifting to red or blue. The next day, I watched on television that some persons in Yangzhou had also considered the redshift in the evening one day before, about one hour earlier than I did.

On October 31, 2009, before falling asleep, I pointed out that the time of moving axis corresponded to the frequency of sound perceived within the moving train, the same as the stationary frequency of sound perceived in the external stationary reference system. In other words, the moving train did not change the time itself. In the morning on the same day, I directed the satellites to shout in Chinese: "时间火车内部频率 (Time in train is internal frequency)." In the evening, I watched on television that two children in the United States had considered that the time corresponded to the internal frequency of the train close to me on time.

On October 7, 2015, I found on internet that the neutrino sometimes manifested movement at a speed not slower than that of light while possessing mass, which is unfavorable to Einstein's theory of relativity.

On February 12, 2016, I watched on television that the United States had already declared the discovery of a gravitational wave. In concurrence, I pointed out that this did not contradict our explanation of the gravitational force mediated through electromagnetic waves.

- Quark and Strong Interaction

After solving the problem of gravity, we began paying attention to the problem of quark and strong interaction. In the contemporary theory of quark, the baryons, including protons and neutrons, were composed of 3 quarks, while the mesons were composed of 2 quarks. The proton was composed of one d quark (of -1/3e as charge) and two u quarks (of 2/3e as charge), while the neutron was composed of one u quark (of 2/3e as charge) and two d quarks (of -1/3e as charge).

On October 20, 2005, I looked up the internet, finding the strong interaction 100 times stronger than the electromagnetic interaction. I also found a big difficulty for the theory of quark, that was no matter how huge the accelerator to bombard or how high in energy the cosmic particle, it was nonetheless incapable of finding any single quark, while it was very easy to find the fundamental particles composed of 2 to 3 quarks. The satellite operators and I considered that the quark and electron were both the same in manifesting the spatially localized electromagnetic mass entity.

On the evening of October 23, 2005, at my home, I emphasized the stability of the proton and imagined together with the satellite operators the multiple pairing structures like nets, but it did not solve the problem. I told them that the structure of the proton was just analogous to the DNA in life science, which is very important. For a moment, a male Hindu sound from a satellite said: "It's DNA." I comprehended his meaning. He considered the quarks constituting the proton just the same as DNA in life science, possessing the helical chain structure of multiple pairs while only composed of the electromagnetic entities of positive and negative charges. The electromagnetic helical quarks stabilized the proton through multiple pairing. It was very important. On the next day, I directed the satellites to shout in Chinese: "Satecommmune India, 电磁螺旋是夸克 (Electromagnetic helix is quark)."

On October 24, 2005, I found a Japanese paper on the internet about the phenomenon of quark condensation and learnt that the three quarks in the proton or neutron only accounted for 2% of the mass of the proton or neutron, while the remaining 98% of the mass was generated from the mutual interactions of quarks.

In the evening of the same day, on television, I watched that the Africans and Polish people had consented to the electromagnetic helix, while the American, Latin and Moscow people had shouted for the electromagnetic 8 shape, claiming that it was more suitable than the helix. I immediately objected to the electromagnetic 8 shape, saying that the 8 shape missed the essence of electromagnetic helical pairs of satellite Hindu. The electromagnetic helical pairs might form multiple pairs, which are very stable. At that moment, I thought that there must be concurrently existing many electrical fields E and magnetic fields B with regard to the electromagnetic helix of quark. I further imagined the process of mutual generation of B and E in photons. I found that while a changing B generated a changing E, the newly generated changing E could immediately generate a changing B. At that moment, the original B had changed only a little. In this way, they accumulated until the earliest changing B vanished, and the photon acquired many small electromagnetic hairs composed of B and E and the electromagnetic helical structure.

On the morning of October 25, 2005, I pointed out that if the centre of electromagnetic rotation of the quark was located at the original point of O, the quark should resemble the electromagnetic ball rather than the electromagnetic helix. That morning in the office, the operators of satellites and I altogether rectified it to the elliptic or pea shape, full of small electromagnetic hairs on the surface, so it could also form a hybrid on multiple points.

In the evening of the same day, on television, I saw that some staff of the United Nations (UN) had considered that the strong interaction might also be the well of negative potential energy from high partial differential term of H, related to frequency. So long as the frequency was sufficiently high, the strong interaction might be very big, probably far exceeding the electromagnetic force.

On October 26, 2005, after getting up in the morning, I looked up the book of physics I bought, estimated and calculated out the highest frequency for proton as the following:

$\nu=mC^2/h=(1.67\times10^{-27})(3\times10^8)^2/6.6\times10^{-34}=10^{22}\text{-}10^{24}$

In contrast, the ratio of the strength of the strong force to that of the gravitational force was about 10^{39}, about 10^{15}-10^{17} times higher than the highest frequency of the proton. I perceived that the difference was too drastic, so it was not successful to account for the strong interaction with the high partial differential term of H.

I considered B and E and further considered the proposal of Zhejiang, the operator of the satellite, that the positive and negative attraction should be longer and more stable than the repulsion from the same charge. Since the hybrid of electromagnetic hairy peas supported and stabilized the positive and negative attraction, the generated Δt should certainly be much bigger than Δt between the electromagnetic waves. Besides, with many hybrid points, the summation of Δt from their product of multiplication should exceed a hundred or thousand times the electromagnetic interaction in strength, compatible with the characteristics of the strong interaction. In the evening, on television, I saw that the staff of the United Nations (UN) had also considered Δt one day earlier than we did.

On December 21, 2005, at noon, the Hindu sound from a satellite reminded me that the structure of a quark was the electromagnetic helical ball rather than the electromagnetic hairy pea. The reasons were that the electromagnetic hairy pea was neither continuous with regard to B and E on the surface nor equal in their intervals, while the electromagnetic helical ball was equal in the interval. Although there might be spatial invaginations, they might be capable of generating the stable electromagnetic helix through the stereoscopic hybridization between the adjacent quarks of the same frequency. I consented and directed the satellites to shout in Chinese: “Satecommmune Group, 夸克电磁螺旋球 (Quark electromagnetic helical ball).”

On the morning of December 22, 2005, I considered that although the quark and frequencies of protons were different from those of electrons, the electrical charge of protons happened to be equal to that of electrons. God should not be so much coincident! It was possible that the quarks in proton were just the positron and electron, which in turn hybridized to gain mass, namely the effect of condensation of quarks. Therefore, there were 2 quarks as positron and 1 quark as electron within the proton, and 2 quarks as positron and 2 quarks as electron within the neutron. In the evening, on television, I saw that some Beijing people had also thought from the electrical charge that the quarks were just the positron and electron.

On December 24, 2005, while having lunch, I considered that the combination of positron and electron should generate photons so that the particle composed of two quarks as positron and electron should not be stable. Meanwhile, two positrons are repelled because they have the same characteristic in charge, so neither should form a strong interaction. When the proton was composed of 3 quarks as 2 positrons and 1 electron, the 2 positron quarks and 1 electron quark were capable of generating stable structure through the electromagnetic hybridization, while it was required to overcome a big barrier of energy for the positrons and electron to neutralize and give out photons, so that the proton was rather stable. I directed the satellites to shout in Chinese: "正负夸克两个光，武圣人喊叫 (Positive and negative two quarks turn into photons, San Force shouts)." In the evening, while watching television, I saw that the players and audiences of US NBA (National Basketball Association) games had reached the same conclusion a little earlier than I did on time.

Before falling asleep in the evening of the same day, I considered that the π meson and μ particle were only different a little in mass, while the μ particle had decayed from the π meson and was even capable of further decaying and becoming the positron and electron. However, the π meson was capable of forming strong interaction with the atomic nucleus, while the μ particle was not. Therefore, if the strong interaction happened only between the positron and electron within the proton, the μ particle containing the positron and electron should likewise be capable of forming a strong interaction with the positron and electron in the atomic nucleus. In accordance with this, except for the positron and electron as the components of the proton, there must be some quarks of bigger mass. Considering the equal quantity of charges for the atomic nucleus and electrons, the other quarks should contribute 0 in summation to the electrical charge of a proton. Otherwise, the electrical charges within and outside the atomic nucleus were not capable of being neutralized. Just as the annihilation of positron and electron, 2 quarks of opposite charges were also capable of transforming into and giving out photons and, therefore, were not stable. In contrast, 2 quarks of the same charges and 1 quark of opposite charge were not capable of realizing a net charge of 0 and, therefore, were not correct. Only with 4 quarks of big mass, 2 carrying a positive charge and 2 carrying a negative charge, it was possible to generate the mass of proton from hybridization with a net charge from quarks as 0. The electrical charge of a proton came from the contribution of a positron outside the 4 quarks, while that of a neutron came from the combination of a proton with one more electron. I directed the satellites to shout in Chinese: "质子质量 4 夸克，武圣人喊叫 (Proton mass from 4 quarks, San Force shouts)."

On the morning of September 15, 2006, while praising more the polarizing (orienting) force of electromagnetic waves, I considered that the strong interaction was one hundred times stronger in energy than the electromagnetic interaction, so I required resorting to other energy to further explain the strong interaction with the electromagnetic helices. I immediately thought that the electromagnetic helices should anneal and separate as DNA so that they can immediately anneal again in case they separate. Here appeared the transformational energy between order and randomness, which was exactly the energy of entropy in thermodynamics. I believed that this energy of entropy was exactly the strong interaction. To simplify the matter, an American from a satellite said that, after annealing, the electromagnetic helices fell into freezing like ice and should give out the melting energy, making the strong interaction more intuitive. I directed the satellites to shout in Chinese: "强相互作用是熵能，武圣人喊叫 (Strong interaction is entropy energy, San Force shouts)," "强相互作用像结冰 (Strong interaction likes freezing ice), Sate-commune Group."

In the evening of the same day, I watched on television that in the scene of a US congressman going off work, there was the background of analogous meaning, without the relevant shape of the mouth.

On December 20, 2007, I found on the internet that if a photon was higher than 1.02MeV in energy, it might suddenly disappear while passing through the vicinity of the atomic nucleus while generating a pair of particles as the positron and electron. When the positron and electron annihilated, they conventionally generated 2 photons opposite in direction, each with 0.511MeV in energy. I believed that there should be an orienting interaction between the single photon of high energy and the quark of electrical charge in the atomic nucleus, generating a hybrid of every other electromagnetic hair and, therefore, separating the positive and negative electrical vectors in photons. At that moment, the electrical vectors without hybridization but with opposite electrical charges generated the changing magnetic field by themselves. Again, they changed back from the generated and changing magnetic field in the conservation of electrical vectors. In accordance, many new hairs were formed, splitting away as an independent half. These electromagnetic hairs splitting away were the same in the direction of their electrical vectors and repelled because they had the same electrical characteristic of charge, forming the spherical structure with the electromagnetic hairs protruding outward, which was exactly the positron we assayed. I directed the satellites to shout in Chinese: "电磁毛同性是齿轮，武圣人喊叫 (Electromagnetic hairs same in charge are gear, San Force shouts)." I watched on television that some Shanghainese had also considered this point during that daytime, earlier than I did on time.

On December 22, 2007, I watched on television that, in accordance with the model of electromagnetic hairy spherical gear, some Beijing people pointed out that if the quarks were not the positron and electron, the frequency was required to form the mass of quark to be the integral times of that of electron, and to make it feasible to hybridize with the positron and compose the proton. Since this situation was rather low in probability, it was also rather low in probability for my model of proton with four quarks hybridizing with the positron to be correct. It was almost certain that the quarks were just the positron and electron.

On March 4, 2008, while watching television, I saw that many members of the Chinese People's Political Consultative Conference in Beijing had considered that for each period of photon, its electrical field E and magnetic field B might only move forward in distance as one interval of wavelength. On the next day of the same year, in the evening, before falling asleep, I believed that, under the condition of light speed, the process of physics was still capable of being investigated as cause and consequence, supporting the structure of electromagnetic multiple hairs of the photon. I directed the satellites to shout in Chinese: "原因结果再光速 (Cause consequence then light speed)." On the evening of March 6, resorting to the existence of photons of higher frequency, I proved that the speed of electrical to magnetic and magnetic to electrical transformation was capable of exceeding the light speed, generating the electromagnetic multiple hairy structures. On television, I saw that some Chinese had already considered the relationship between frequency and electromagnetic transformation during that daytime earlier than I did on time.

On March 5, 2008, when I was supposed to use the electromagnetic hairs to solve the problem of particles, the ZheJiang sound from the satellite reminded me to use the electron. I associated the frequency with the mass of the electron and further included the external electrical field of the electron to deduce that the electron was the hairy ball of gear. I directed the satellites to shout in Chinese: "电子多毛已完成 (Multiple hairs finished in electron), Sate-commune together." In the evening, while watching television, I saw that many people in Europe, South America, and Beijing had considered electronic electromagnetic hairs earlier than I did. On May 16 of the same year, I found that it was likewise possible that the centric radial electrical field of the electron was generated through the rotation of the electromagnetic nail without the electromagnetic multiple hairs. Therefore, the electromagnetic multiple hairs of the electrons must be generated in the same manner as the multiple hairs of the photons.

From March 23 to 25, 2008, a Beijing sound from a satellite resorted to the fact that the collision of positron or electron was capable of making particles containing quarks such as the proton, neutron, meson, etc. so that he could prove that the quarks were transformed from and composed of electromagnetic matter.

During these three days, we further considered that the particle merging from the fusion of the positron and electron was smaller in curvature and bigger in radius, while the fusion of several positrons caused summation of their electrical fields, bigger in curvature and smaller in radius. Therefore, we determined that the strong interaction was accomplished not through the fusion but through the electromagnetic hybridization. On March 27 of the same year, I supplemented the rough linear correlation of increment in atomic number and radii and further ascertained that the strong interaction was not accomplished through fusion.

On the evening of March 28, 2008, a PLA man from a satellite said that, in comparison of π meson and μ particle, they were different in electromagnetic frequency and in the characteristic of the strong interaction, which was capable of supporting the mechanism of strong interaction from the electromagnetic hybridization. On television, I saw that the Koreans had also considered the difference between π meson and μ particle in the strong interaction earlier than I did on time.

On the evening of December 28, 2008, I pointed out that the effect of condensation of quarks might exclude the possibility of the strong interaction originating from the drastic increase in strength of the varying electrical field of quarks itself within the range of distance of the strong interaction.

❖ Weak Interaction

On October 27, 2005, after getting up in the morning, I found in the book of physics that if the strong interaction was relatively 1 in strength, 10^{-15} meter in interactive distance and 10^{-23} seconds in interactive time, the weak interaction was relatively 10^{-5}-10^{-11} in strength, 10^{-17} meter in interactive distance and 10^{-10}-10^{-16} second in interactive time, while the electromagnetic interaction was relatively 10^{-2} in strength, infinite in interactive distance and 10^{-16}-10^{-20} second in interactive time. The operators of satellites and I concurrently paid attention to the fact that the interactive distance of the weak interaction was much shorter than that of the strong interaction, while its interactive time was nonetheless even longer than that of the electromagnetic interaction, which was somewhat strange.

In the afternoon of the same day, I looked up on internet for some common knowledge on weak interaction and found that there was no charge for neutrinos but a tiny mass smaller than that of the electron. There were three types of neutrinos existing in nature, capable of transforming with each other. In accordance with our model for mass as rotation and light as roll, the satellite operators and I perceived that the neutrino should originate from the shift of the rotational axis of photons of X-ray or visible light. An American from a satellite said that energy should be required to shift the rotational axis so that there should exist a value of threshold. In the evening on television, I saw that the people in Shanghai and ZheJiang had all considered the weak interaction, and all laughed at the physics before that time in using the Z and W meson of very big mass to explain the weak interaction.

On October 28, 2005, while having supper, we preliminarily selected the decay of π meson as the simple model for the weak interaction. The process for decay of the π meson was as follows:

One π meson decayed to generate one μ particle and one

neutrino, while one μ particle decayed again to generate one positron or electron and other neutrinos.

After the supper, the satellite operators and I perceived that since the μ particle was big in mass, almost the same as that of the π meson, while it was, in addition, decayed from the π meson, it should contain the heavy quark of the π meson. However, it was strange that the π meson was capable of taking part in the strong interaction while the μ particle was not. It was very faint in interaction with the atomic nucleus. A ZheJiang sound from a satellite answered this question, supposing that, during the decay of π meson, its heavy quark should lose a part of its energy because of the shift of the rotational axis of the photon to generate the neutrino, making it lower in frequency. In accordance with geometry, it was no longer capable of hybridizing with the original π heavy quark, so the μ particle did not manifest interaction with the atomic nucleus. I directed the satellites to shout in Chinese: "卫星浙江喊，移轴就是弱作用 (Sate-commune ZheJiang shouts, Axial shift is weak interaction)." In the evening on television, I saw that the players and audiences of US NBA (National Basketball Association) games had already apprehended the decay of the π meson one day before on their local time and concurrently considered the problem of a shift in axis and a decrease in frequency the same as the explanation of ZheJiang from satellite 8 hours earlier than we did on time.

In the evening of the same day, the satellite operators and I further imitated the reaction of the axial shift of photons. The Beijing sound from a satellite said that the collision of an extrinsic photon with quarks might generate a weak interaction. A Hindu female from a satellite asked how to shift the axis of such a big photon. A GuangDong sound from a satellite reminded that only if every small hair of B and E of photon shifted in axis, then the whole B and E shifted in axis, which was rather difficult. Before going to bed, the satellite operators and I added the electrical field of photons. I imagined that there was an electromagnetic interaction between the electromagnetic quark and the external electrical field of the photon. The external electrical field should, therefore, scintillate and give out infrared. I further imagined the effects of the external electrical field exerting on the electromagnetic hairs of the quark. The satellite showed a picture of infrared emission. I corrected it and pointed out that it should be the electromagnetic rotation of neutrino; hence, it was acquiring the mass. In accordance with this, I explained the weak interaction. I directed the satellites to shout in Chinese: "电磁毛旋转中微子 (Rotation of electromagnetic hairs is neutrino)." On October 30 of the same year, while watching the replay of the competition on Latin dance on China Central Television, full of ShenZhen audiences, I saw that they had likewise believed the neutrino to be the same as the electromagnetic quark in possession of rotation and mass, even 2 hours earlier than I did on time.

On December 24, 2005, at noon, a ZheJiang sound from a satellite said that the electromagnetic rotation of the neutrino was long in wavelength and caused diffraction of the neutrino. Moving in the electrical field, there was disturbance and rectification from such diffraction, resulting in no electrical charge assayed for the neutrino.

On January 18, 2008, I found that the electronic neutrino might be the energy released from the electronic quark transforming from the pea shape to the ball shape. The Beijing sound from a satellite found that the negative μ-type neutrino might be the energy released from the electronic quark transforming from the cubic shape to the ball shape. I directed the satellites to shout in Chinese: "豌豆方圆中微子，武圣人北京一起喊 (Pea or square to round is neutrino, San Force and Beijing shout together)."

On March 4, 2008, in the afternoon, the satellite operators and I believed that the neutrino might be the region of an electromagnetic hybrid without charge, while the Hindu sound from the satellite pointed out that it was compatible with the short distance of weak interaction. Before supper, I pointed out that since the π meson was too big in the region of electromagnetic hybrid that it carried, it was roughly close to the shape of a square. In accordance with that, it decayed to decrease its region of electromagnetic hybrid and transformed into the μ particle closer to the spherical shape while giving out one neutrino. I directed the satellites to shout in Chinese: "中微子肯定是杂交区 (Neutrino is certainly the region of hybrid)." In the evening, while watching television, I saw that many Chinese had considered the problem regarding the drop of the hybrid region in the morning on the same day, several hours earlier than we did.

On the morning of March 6, 2008, a Taiwan sound from a satellite pointed out that if the neutrino was the dropped region of a hybrid, there should be difficulty in tension. A Beijing male from a satellite pointed out that there was tension for the π meson in a square shape. So, it is implied that the neutrino might be the extrinsic electrical field pairing with the region of a hybrid. A Beijing female from a satellite said that there might be several neutrinos of different sources orienting and pairing in the same direction with one hybrid region and inferred that different neutrinos might originate from different electrical fields. Herein, the neutrino structure was rectified to the extrinsic electrical field capable of forming a pair with the hybrid region, while after dropped, it was further bound with another extrinsic electrical field and formed the oscillatory structure of positive and negative electrical fields.

On April 1, 2008, while watching television, I saw that some Europeans said that the neutrino was capable of reacting reversely in the weak interaction, and therefore, the weak interaction should not be unreasonably explained with the decrease in energy and frequency through the release of neutrino; otherwise, there should not be the reverse reaction.

At noon on the same day, I recalled that the neutrino possessed the helical characteristic, which had been assayed in experiments. Therefore, it was possible that the neutrino was the region of the hybrid in structure. I directed the satellites to shout in Chinese: "中微子螺旋性 π μ (Neutrino helix πμ)." In the evening, while watching television, I saw that some people in NanJing had said the helix of the neutrino one day earlier than I did.

At noon on April 3, 2008, the Beijing sound from a satellite said that if the π meson was in a square and crumpled shape, there should not be a nuclear reaction; therefore, the π meson must be square in shape. I said that in that case, the μ particle should also be in the shape between square and round or in the elliptical shape. I directed the satellites to shout in Chinese: "μ 子方圆形 (μ particle in shape between square and round)."

At noon on the same day, I found that when the helix of neutrino decreased in frequency, it should be asymmetrical in its two positive and negative chains, incapable of forming the hybrid after a reduction in frequency. So, it was determined that the helical structure of neutrino was wrong. I directed the satellites to shout in Chinese: "杂交区减频不同步 (Asynchronous reduction in the frequency of hybrid)." In the evening, while watching television, I saw that some persons in NanJing had considered the asynchrony in the reduction of frequency of hybrid region that morning, several hours earlier than I did.

On the afternoon of April 9, 2008, the satellite operators and I found that the hybrid of quarks made many electromagnetic hairs orient in the same direction, causing a change in electromagnetic orienting force and generating a bigger gravitational force. We found that, although the structure of the crystal was periodic and orderly, its intrinsic atomic nuclei were in the same way as those in the liquid and gas. On May 1 of the same year, I found that the positive and negative π meson of square conformation might cause a much bigger change in the curvature of electromagnetic wave than the positron and electron of spherical conformation, while in further, there was coordination in the orienting change for the electromagnetic hairs in square conformation. Therefore, there should be a rather big difference in gravity and mass to account for the manifestation that their mass differed more than 200 times.

On the afternoon of April 26, 2008, in accordance with the β+ and β- decays, I believed that the external electrical fields forming the neutrino in the weak interaction might just be the electrical fields from the movement of positive and negative quarks themselves in the atomic nucleus, and might have been existing beforehand in the atomic nucleus as the positive and negative oscillation. Meanwhile, the Beijing sound from the satellite ascertained that it was impossible to explain the β+ decay with the helical structure of neutrino. In the evening, while watching television, I saw that many people in China and Europe had considered the problem of electrical fields within and outside the atomic nucleus earlier than we did.

On September 28, 2008, I considered the problem of spin of particles. The spins of electron, quark, proton and neutron were all 1/2, while the spin of meson was 0 or 1. I found from internet that the spin of the neutrino was 1/2, that of the μ particle was 1/2, and that of the π meson was 0. I believed that the spin of π meson might be analogized to the mutual neutralization of positive and negative charges. If the π meson was composed of a positron or electron and three semi-neutrinos of opposite charge in our model, since the energy of spin of the semi-neutrino was lower than that of the positron or electron, after combining with 3 semi-neutrinos of opposite charge, the spin of the π meson was 0, equivalent to freezing. Whereas after combining with 2 semi-neutrinos of opposite charge, the spin of the μ particle was 1/2, compatible with the experimental observations. I directed the satellites to shout in Chinese: "介子自旋是加和 (Spin of meson is summation), Sate-commune Group." In the evening of the same day, while watching television, I saw that many people said that the shouts on spin on television were all sorts of data from the internet, while they needed to wait for me to direct the satellites to shout.

On June 22, 2016, I found on internet that the physicists considered that the big masses of W/Z bosons corresponded to the shortest distance of the weak interaction; therefore, their wavelengths should correspond to the interval between the positive and negative entity of electromagnetic hybrid.

On the same day, I pointed out that the τ type neutrino might just be composed of the external electrical field capable of adjusting the angle of the neighboring flat hybrid planes of the π meson. On the evening of December 6 of the same year, many female volleyball players from various provinces in China pointed out that the sharp electrical field was capable of protruding an angle outward, while the blunt electrical field was capable of pressing a plane to a flat.

On March 17, 2017, while watching television, I saw that people in various countries pointed out that the oscillation of neutrino among three different statuses demonstrated that its electromagnetic shape was subjected to oscillation and transformation correspondingly, supporting the electro-magnetic structure of the mass.

❖ Rectification and Substantiation

On December 22, 2005, after waking up in the morning, we considered the absorption of the photon with atoms and molecules. The ZheJiang sound from a satellite said that the photon might collide with the electron to generate momentum, manifesting absorption. I, along with other satellite operators, considered that the probability of such collision with the axis of photon to electron was too low. It was reasonable that there was an electromagnetic interaction between the lateral hairs of both photon and electron. The electron was affected to move and, as a result, absorbed the energy.

On March 17, 2008, I found that the frequency of an electron was very low, so its wavelength was longer than the radius of the atomic nucleus. Therefore, it was problematic to explain the interactions within the nucleus with the electron. On March 22 of the same year, a ZheJiang sound from a satellite pointed out that the negative electrical line of electrons was transformed from the magnetic field so that the radii of electrons and protons might be very small, in fact, smaller than their average wavelength of energy wave. Therefore, it was not appropriate to comprehend the correlation between the electromagnetic interval and frequency of proton and electron with that of photon because they were their average value. I directed the satellites to shout in Chinese: "电子波长平均的 (Electronic wavelength is average)." In the evening, on television, I saw that many domestic and foreign people had said "average" earlier than we did.

On March 24, 2008, a ZheJiang sound from a satellite pointed out that the interval for the hybrid of positron and electron might penetrate deep within their average radii, explaining the problem that the radius of the atomic nucleus was smaller than that of the electron.

On April 19, 2008, a ZheJiang sound from a satellite said that the energy needed for the explosion of the middle-sized black hole might not definitely be bigger than the high energy needed for γ burst in the cosmos.

On May 10, 2008, I required the group to consider the atom of Helium. The Beijing sound from a satellite pointed out that in accordance with the atomic weight of Helium from the linear summation of the proton and neutron, it might be deduced that the mass of the proton should also be the linear summation of that of quarks if they did not change in conformation while constituting the proton. Therefore, it might be deduced that the proton was made of 7-9 π mesons. I directed the satellites to shout in Chinese: "质子质量氦原子，卫星北京喊 (Proton mass like Helium atom, Sate-commune Beijing shouts)."

On September 1, 2008, when I was watching the video of the opening ceremony of the Olympic Games held in Athens in 2004, I found that many athletes had talked about physics during the parade for entrance. They had already approximately realized the twin paradox of relativity and the electromagnetic helix, while it was mentioned that the non-relativity of time and space should wait for the passage of time and the leading politician to promote it. On relativity, they neither treated the problem of the constancy of light speed nor concurrently reestablished the electromagnetic special relativity for replacement as we did. Therefore, they were not capable of affecting Einstein's theory of relativity with the axiom of constancy in light speed and on the basis of measurable time and space of physics. On the electromagnetic helix, without the electromagnetic orienting force and release of entropy energy, they could neither solve the most fundamental problem of repulsion among positive charges within the atomic nucleus nor account for the strong interaction, which is far from ours. The electromagnetic helix supported by the Indian satellite operators was founded on the basis of my spatially localized electromagnetic structure of the mass, which is certainly more scientific. In 2004, although I did not watch the opening ceremony of the Olympic Games, I paid attention to the news related to the Olympic Games. I remembered that many terrible rays of satellites had interfered with the athletes then at the Olympic Games, writing down the crimes of terror from the satellite rays into history. People in various countries watching the Olympic Games on television were mainly concerned about the safety of the games. On the next day, September 2, while watching the video of the opening ceremony of the Olympic Games held in 2000, I found that some people had already realized the explosion of the black hole earlier than I did.

Although the opening ceremonies of both the 2000 and 2004 Olympic Games were broadcast to the whole world, they did not have much influence on the people in various countries. In 2005, when we started the movement of unification of physics, it was directly manifested from television that people worldwide did not know that there had been analogous ideas as ours before. Due to limited time, lack of systematization and their lack of ability to look up the literature from the internet, it was impossible to accept their viewpoints on the opening ceremony of the Olympic Games as scientific. However, considering that these videos of the opening ceremony of the Olympic Games might be real and unmodified, I introduced their names as the irresponsible second or third authors to be concurrently collected into the papers in the colloquia of physics I compiled, altogether sharing the reputation of promoting the progression of science.

On the morning of September 4, 2009, I found that with the conformation of the quark changed into a planar hybrid, there was a possible difference of a hundred times in strength compared to the spherical electromagnetic interaction with the same distance. I believed that, with the multiplication of the strong interaction above the electromagnetic interaction compared to the multiplication in mass from the effect of condensation of quarks, it was possible to estimate the proportion of contribution to the strong interaction from both the electromagnetic multiple hairy hybrids and the thermodynamics. Since the strong interaction was the summation rather than the product of the two, it was estimated that the thermodynamics contributed more to the strong interaction. I directed the satellites to shout in Chinese: "强作用增倍比凝聚 (Comparison with multiplication of strong interaction to condensation)." At the vocal concert "The Same Song" at the end of August 2009, there were many performers and audiences who considered this problem earlier than I did.

On October 21, 2009, I found that the great breakthrough in physics I led at that time was the global movement, huge in scale. There were many international cultural and athletic spots that verified with one another and directly became history. I directed the satellites to shout: "Physics movement." On that evening, while watching television, I saw that many people in China and abroad recognized this physics movement earlier than I did. On April 25, 2010, I pointed out that the whole process of our movement of unification of physics itself demonstrated that the problem of unification of physics had never been scientifically and comprehensively considered on television in the whole world before. I directed the satellites to shout: "Physics process novelty." On television, I found that many European people had already considered this point one day earlier than I did.

On November 4, 2009, I pointed out that the diffraction of neutrons was the pattern of diffraction from the wave of the hybrid of the electromagnetic hairs within the neutron, which is much higher in frequency than that of the electron.

On January 29, 2012, believing that in the black hole of huge mass, the positrons and electrons were pressed by gravity to become round disks flatter than the quarks, I explained the source of the huge mass of the black hole of such huge mass. I directed the satellites to shout in Chinese: "黑洞圆饼引力大 (Round disks in black holes are big in gravity)."

On June 8, 2012, I hypothesized that the mouth of the eruption of the black hole and neutron star might be analogous to the mouth of a volcano, extending toward the internal region of high temperature. I thought that the black hole continuously erupted matters, which continuously collided in the same direction to overcome gravity. Therefore, the neutrons collided with the heaven of the cosmos and then decayed to become hydrogen. I directed the satellites to shout in Chinese: "黑洞火山口连续撞 (Continuous collision at the mouth of the volcano on the black hole)." On July 23, 2016, I found on the internet that there was evidence of the existence of dark matter in the cosmos because the mass of the galaxy was smaller, explaining its speed of rotation. Therefore, the dark matter might just be the materials emitted by the black hole at the center of the galaxy before the formation of stars. I directed the satellites to shout in Chinese: "黑洞喷射暗物质 (Black hole emits dark matter)." On December 1, 2017, I pointed out that gravity and movement in the solar system did not require the use of dark matter to explain.

On October 6, 2015, the European people pointed out that the quarks of high mass generated in the accelerator were analogous in structure to those within the black hole. I directed the satellites to shout in Chinese: "加速器夸克黑洞多 (Accelerator quarks more in a black hole)." On March 31, 2016, while watching television, I found the Brazilian people shouting that without external force to push, the dented area of a particle should automatically transform into flat while increasing the frequency.

On the morning of November 25, 2015, I pointed out that the electron only absorbed or released the photon with its average electrical strength identical to its individual electrical hairs and further only absorbed or released one photon at a time. Therefore, it was capable of explaining the effect of quantum on the electronic transition around the atomic nucleus. With the same strength in the electrical field of individual electromagnetic hairs, the energy of the photon should only be proportional to its frequency. I directed the satellites to shout in Chinese: "电子场强，量子常数 (Field strength of electron, Constant of quantum)." At the end of March 2016, while writing a review paper in accordance with the fact that there was only one type of photon in physics rather than two types of photons separately from the electron and quark, I proved that the positive and negative quarks were just the respective positron and electron with one flat hybrid plane.

On January 1, 2016, I made use of the deviation from the original point for the return of the electromagnetic wave of an electron to successfully explain the quantum tunnelling effect.

On August 27, 2016, people in various countries, including the foreign ministers of the United States and Russia, pointed out that since the physical time and space of Einstein were correspondingly the change in wavelength, the general relativity was correct, and therefore, it should be recognized as the earliest original contribution of Einstein to the gravitational force.

On December 6, 2016, in accordance with the principle summing up the mass of hybrid regions, I thought that the proton should be a linear structure composed of 5 quarks, while the neutron might possess a hexagonal structure, both concurrently compatible with the masses of most particles deduced from the various decaying modes, including the λ, Σ+, Σ-, Σ0, Ξ-, Ξ0, and so on. I directed the satellites to shout in Chinese: "质子质量 5 夸克 (Proton mass 5 quarks)." In the program "Animal World" that was broadcast later on television, there was a white female who calculated that the proton should be composed of 5 quarks earlier than I did. However, it was broadcast later than I did, and since it did not belong to the public situation, its time of publication should be the time it was broadcast on television.

❖ Unification of Electromagnetism to Space

On December 24, 2005, the satellite operators and I found

that there was a problem with the explanation of 270 degrees for H. Why were 540 degrees not generated in the further electromagnetic transformation? It was possibly correct that the electrical to magnetic transformation and vice versa were respectively 90 degrees and -90 degrees. A ZheJiang sound from satellites had said before that H might be the conical vortex, but I did not pay attention to it. From that day on, I began to coordinate and propagate it. The axis of H conical vortex was the electrical field E, while the perpendicular plane against the axis was the magnetic field B. I directed the satellites to shout in Chinese: "Sate-commune 浙江喊，圆锥旋转是 H (Sate-commune ZheJiang shouts, Conical vortex is H)."

On the evening of March 26, 2006, in the dancing hall, I considered how the magnetic field of a conical vortex generated the electrical field. I referred to the circular plane of the conical vortex swinging up and down around the conical tip while manifesting the electrical to magnetic transformation and vice versa. I imagined that a magnetic drop was generated with the movement of the magnetic plane of a cone from up to down. This magnetic drop should influence the other magnetic matter while going up and down in a direction that corresponds to the induced electric field. Therefore, electricity and magnetism were unified. On the next day, after waking up early in the morning, I directed the satellites to shout in Chinese: "Sate-commune Group, 电场就是磁动差 (Electrical field is the magnetic drop of movement)."

On December 21, 2007, I discussed the problem of electromagnetic essence with satellite operators. I believed that the electromagnetic essence was the noise of time and space. The operators of satellites said that there should exist positive and negative noise. I recognized that the accumulation of noises of time and space had transformed into a huge black hole in the cosmos, and then there happened the huge explosion. At that time, the accumulated noises of the time and space had been completely different from the time and space around, manifesting the contemporary electromagnetic interactions. The satellite operators said that it was also possible that there had been the collision of two reference systems of different time and space, evolving into contemporary entities. I directed the satellites to shout in Chinese: "时空噪音是电磁 (Noises of time and space are electromagnetism), Sate-commune Group." In the evening, while watching television, I saw that somebody had mentioned noise during the European meeting, while Dmitry Medvedev in Russia might have likewise said 3k, but not clear in the shape of his mouth.

During the afternoon of the same day, I made use of 3 reference systems to observe the relativity of time and space with homogeneous noises in all directions, concretely as the following: I chose 3 reference systems that did not have any physical interaction except their own noises of the time and space. Among them, the reference system O was stationary, with the noise of time as ±△t homogeneous in all directions. The reference system A moved at v on constant velocity, with the noise of time as ±△ta. The reference system B moved at -v on constant velocity, with the noise of time as ±△tb. If there was special relativity for these reference systems to observe from reference system O, the velocity of reference system A was v while its relative average time changed as t, and the velocity of reference system B was -v while its relative average time changed also as t. However, the noises in time ±△ta and ±△tb of the two were 180 degrees different in phase, which were about ±2△ta different in value from each other. Therefore, the two reference systems, A and B, were completely identical in their average time. To observe reference system A from reference system B, the velocity of reference system A was 2v. If there was a special relative effect, the reference system A should change 2t in its relative average time and should be different from that of the reference system B, while the noises of the two would differ by about ±2△ta in time. This status was different in average time from that observed from the reference system O, and it was indeed contradictory. The only explanation was that the relative change of average time t=0 in value for these reference systems A and B. This meant that, for the time without any physical property except the noises of time and space, there was no relativity. Likewise, it should also be deduced that there was no relativity in space. Therefore, there was no relativity for time and space themselves with noises. I directed the satellites to shout in Chinese: "有噪音时空无相对性，武圣人喊叫 (No relativity for the time and space with noises, San Force shouts)."

On the afternoon of September 25, 2008, a German sound from a satellite said that there was a need to discard the envelope theory on the electromagnetic movement and change the use of our rolling model, making it much easier to account for the electromagnetic wave with the movement along its own electrical field or magnetic field. I consented and directed the satellites to shout in Chinese: "光滚动模型正

确的，卫星德国喊 (Light role model correct, Sate-commune German shouts)." On the same day, while watching television, I saw that many people in NanJing had considered the electromagnetic longitudinal wave in the morning, several hours earlier than we did.

On the evening of October 28, 2008, a European, who sounded like a priest from a satellite, shouted and roared aloud to me, saying that, while accounting for the electromagnetic transformation with the space moving at high speed, its lateral perpendicular electromagnetic hair was not capable of transmitting far, so it was wrong. I made use of two axes of coordinate perpendicular to each other to consider the problem and found that if one axis of coordinate moved at high speed, another might be rather strange. I awakened immediately and recognized that, with regard to a finite three-dimensional space, when the space moved along one axis at light speed, the other two axes in perpendicular directions accordingly became the circular movement around it. When the unit of time and space moving at light speed oscillated in size, the other two axes in perpendicular directions should be induced to change, manifesting the electromagnetic transformation of the photon. I directed the satellites to shout in Chinese: "电磁光速 xyz，武圣人喊叫 (Electromagnetic light speed xyz, San Force shouts)." With the electromagnetic light speed xyz to explain the electromagnetic phenomena, it was no longer required to consider the big H for electromagnetic unification and its high partial differential term.

At noon on October 29, 2008, while watching television, I saw that all the domestic and international news was full of satellite waves of space xyz at light speed. The international news was all about the newest information, and the people learned about our achievements. A part of domestic news was broadcast as compiled news several days before that day, with the ending time as its broadcasting time. There was a piece of news from SiChuan that was full of signals of satellite waves about the space xyz at light speed, while the person on the ground responded to them, saying x in the mouth. Obviously, the satellite waves of the space xyz at light speed should all be added during the last day. There was another piece of news about a military drill, likewise full of satellite waves of space xyz at light speed, while incorrect in the shape of the mouth. In the evening, while watching television, I saw that there had been dense fog in NanJing and YangZhou one day before, with the background of television full of space xyz at light speed, and definitely without the corresponding mouth shape for the persons on ground. In addition, I saw that some people in SuZhou were having dinner in a restaurant, with the background of television likewise full of space xyz at light speed. A woman might have thought of the movement of time and space. However, she shifted her attention to elsewhere. I found many people abroad saying that there was a need to take the method of recalling the memories of people in various countries about the news within two days to exclude any fraud. On August 19, 2009, I watched "The Same Song" entering into LiShui at half past seven in the evening on October 28, 2008. There had been a prediction from the background of satellite waves that I would soon discover the space xyz at light speed, one hour earlier than I did. However, "The Same Song" was occasionally telecasted live; instead, it was broadcast at a fixed time every week, so it might have been broadcast later than we did.

On December 6, 2008, I found on the internet that, in accordance with the redshift of the quasar, contemporary physicists believed that the quasar was a black hole flying away at a speed close to light while engulfing the matter equivalent to a mass of 1000 stars every year. I pointed out that, in accordance with the fact that the distance between the sun and other stars was calculated with the light year, it was capable of making the deduction that it was impossible for the black hole of a quasar to encounter such a large quantity of matter. Therefore, I believed that the quasar was a huge black hole moving at a high speed relative to time and space while colliding with the latter and transforming them into photons.

On December 16, 2008, before falling asleep, the US sound and Shanghai sound from satellites said that the photons different in frequency and same in light speed were the consequence that their speed was extreme and maximal, which also demonstrated that the lateral electrical field was only impellent but not resistant. I analogized it to the fishtail and consented that it was indeed such. I directed the satellites to shout in Chinese: "光子加速美国喊 (Photon accelerates, Sate-commune US shouts)."

❖ Summarization of the Achievements in Physics

After October 2005, under the leadership of mine and the Sate-commune Group, using satellites and television as the public media, the people in various countries in the whole world participated enthusiastically and endeavored altogether, basically unifying the four forces in nature and establishing the new theories in physics. It was unprecedented in human history with respect to all, such as being fast in its speed, broad in its scope, many in its participators, and great in its influence. Our process of unification of physics demonstrated that the public media on television in various countries around the world had never considered the problem of unification of physics scientifically and comprehensively before. It was a completely new and scientific creation and was a great pioneering work in the human history of science, so it deserved congratulations and memorization.

To let the readers easily browse and retrospect the miracles and achievements made in this movement of physics, I especially summarized and concluded them as the following:

- On October 5, 2005, while considering the problem I raised on the irrelevance of light speed to its frequency, the satellite operators and I altogether supported the model of mass as rotation and light as roll. Somebody in a football game in Europe had also supported the model of light as the rolling bead, probably earlier than we did on comprehending the photon.
- On October 11, 2005, a satellite operator with a heavy SuZhou accent, calling himself ZheJiang, said that electromagnetic waves were different in stability during attraction and repulsion and analogous to the orienting force, so it was named the orienting force of electromagnetic waves.

- On October 13, 2005, I made use of three reference systems to prove that there was relativity with regard to the ideal time and space with neither characteristic of matter nor noise. The video of the opening ceremony of the 2004 Olympic Games showed that many people had also considered this point.
- On October 13, 2005, the US satellite operators successfully explained the phenomena of special relativity using the orienting interaction of the electromagnetic particles with the stationary electrical field.
- On October 19, 2005, I watched on television that somebody in Latin America might have supported earlier adopting electromagnetic waves mediating momentum conservation to draw the gravitational receptor.
- On October 23, 2005, the Hindu sound from a satellite supported the model of the electromagnetic helical structure. Through pair and hybrid of the multiple electromagnetic hairs, the structure was stabilized, greatly facilitating and promoting the comprehension of the structure of the quark. The video of the opening ceremony of the 2004 Olympic Games showed that there were many people who said that another Hindu had also thought of this point.
- On October 24, 2005, I deduced from the fast transformation of the electrical field E and magnetic field B of photon that concurrently, there were many small hairs of B and E in the structure of photon. In other words, a changing B generated a changing E,

while the previous changing B vanished. The newly generated changing E, in turn, generated another new B. In analogy, in turn, it was capable of generating many small electromagnetic hairs composed of B and E, supporting the hypothesis of the electromagnetic helix from the Hindu sound from the satellite.

- On October 26, 2005, while watching television, I saw that some staff of the United Nations supported one day before on the New York time that the strong interaction might originate from the hybrid and pair of the multiple electromagnetic hairs of the positive and negative quarks.
- On December 22, 2005, the Beijing people resorted to the equality in the charge of the proton and electron to support that the quarks composing the proton and neutron might just be the positron and electron while acquiring their mass through the effect of quark condensation.
- On September 15, 2006, I hypothesized that the entropy energy of the electromagnetic helix was just the strong interaction. In the evening of the same day, while watching television, I saw that when US congressmen were going off work, there was an analogous background of satellite projection.
- On December 18, 2007, while watching television, I saw that one day before the US time, many Americans had made use of the electromagnetic theory of friction or orientation to explain the phenomena of relativity and gravitational force.

- On March 3, 2008, I found that the electromagnetic mass formed the electromagnetic orientation with the electromagnetic waves, and when the electromagnetic waves got rid of the electromagnetic orientation and returned, they consumed energy, released heat and increased in wavelength, which was the cause of a red shift in the general relativity. On television, when the leaders in NanJing were interviewing foreign guests from the United States, they might have achieved an analogous idea.
- On March 6, 2008, the Taiwan and Beijing operators from satellites demonstrated that the neutrino originated from the external electrical field pairing to the hybrid region. After dropping away from the hybrid, it turned to bind with another external electrical field and formed the oscillatory structure of positive and negative electrical fields. In June 2016, I pointed out that the τ type neutrino might just be composed from the external electrical field capable of adjusting the angle of the neighboring flat hybrid planes of the π meson.
- On March 24, 2008, the ZheJiang operator from satellite pointed out that the hybrid region of the positronic and electronic quarks might lie deep within the average radii of the positron and electron.
- On March 28, 2008, in accordance with the difference in the strong interaction of the π meson and μ particle, the Koreans supported the mechanism that it was the electromagnetic hybridization that brought about the strong interaction.

- On April 3, 2008, the Beijing sound from a satellite and I pointed out that the π meson was square in shape, while the μ particle was elliptical in shape.
- On April 9, 2008, the satellite operators and I found that the hybrid of quarks made many electromagnetic hairs orient in the same direction, generating a bigger gravitational force.
- On April 25, 2008, the Shanghai sound from a satellite and I rectified the gravitational field to the relative curvature and redshift of the electromagnetic waves.
- On January 23, 2009, on television, I found that the British and Brazilian people had supported one day before on their local time that, after the particle acquired the velocity of movement, it generated directional order by itself, causing an increase in its orienting interaction with the external electrical field. Therefore, they solved the problem of special relative movement, causing it to be shorter in length and slower in time.
- On January 29, 2012, I pointed out that the positron and electron in the black hole of big mass were pressed by gravity to the round disks flatter than the quarks, capable of explaining the source of the big mass of the black hole.
- On June 8, 2012, I believed that the continuous eruption and collision on the mouth of the volcano on the black hole caused the neutrons to the high sky in the cosmos, which then decayed to become hydrogen.
- On October 7, 2015, I found on internet that the neutrino of mass sometimes manifested the

movement at the speed not slower than that of light, unfavorable to Einstein's theory of relativity.

- On November 25, 2015, making use of the equality in the electrical strength of individual electromagnetic hairs, I accounted for the effect of quantum on the interaction of the electron and photon.
- On December 6, 2016, I believed that the proton should be a linear structure composed of 5 quarks, while the neutron might possess a hexagonal structure.
- On March 17, 2017, on television, people in various countries pointed out that the oscillation of neutrino was manifested in its electromagnetic shape and was subjected to oscillation and change.

End poem of the illustrated chapter:

The global world is altogether standing to unify the physics.
The electromagnetism is unifying the four forces.
The electromagnetic mass and orienting force,
The time and space are the same for different moving statuses.
The electromagnetic helix is capable of forming regular pairs.
The thermodynamic energy of entropy is forming the strong force like ice.
The decay and transformation is illustrative for the weak force.
There are the positive and negative oscillatory structures for the neutrinos,
The red shift and curvature of light for the gravitational force,

The great unification is accomplished from the longitudinal and transverse waves of photons.

Chapter | 7

Revival of Humans with Intelligent Robots

Musical Background of Rhythmic Writing: The Same Song

Please read the following text sentence-by-sentence to feel the musical background of the rhythmic framework.

On October 16, 2006, the GuangDong sound from a satellite said that since there were oceans on the earth, the humans were directly capable of cultivating the marine algae, and then raising the cattle and sheep with them. Therefore, the foods of humans might be cheaper than those of intelligent robots. On the next day, in the evening, while watching television, I saw that many people consented to the opinion of GuangDong, and said that it was reasonable to permit inventing and making the intelligent robot on time.

On February 8, 2007, I considered the problem of how to stop the invasion by the celestial intelligent robots and defend the humans and the earth. I considered that contemporarily, there were electromagnetic bombs capable of damaging intelligent robots rather than humans during an explosion. I found on the internet that some contemporary electromagnetic bombs might contain energy up to billions of watts, capable of directly destroying electronic equipment, metal circuits, transformers and radars while explosion, with their tremendous powers capable of reaching several kilometers. Therefore, they were certainly the weapons for the first choice to counter strike the celestial intelligent robots. In the evening, while watching television, I saw that some Africans had the same ideas earlier than I had.

On February 9, 2007, I found on internet that neither the X-ray nor γ-ray was capable of penetrating the atmosphere on the earth. Besides, it was low in the efficacy of energy transformation for producing the X-rays. If intelligent robots on other planets and satellites are expected to make the X-rays of energy comparable to solar energy reaching the Earth, they should be required to consume huge amounts of energy that might melt the ice on their planets and satellites. The γ-rays were conventionally directly generated from the radioactive materials, which are so small in quantity that they cannot cause any serious damage. Therefore, it was not required for humans on planet Earth to worry about the robots of the other planets and satellites using X-rays and γ-rays to damage humans.

In the evening of the same day, the satellite operators and I considered that it was feasible to install the protective shielding box of the sandwich structure outside the intelligent robots to protect their integrated circuits from electromagnetic strikes. In reverse, I considered the humans by themselves. They should recognize that, after all, they were the relatively weaker and older civilization and should have the psychology of welfare receivers. I imagined that without food, the welfare receivers might die and should only expect to revive. At that moment, the satellite operators and I immediately recalled the intelligent robots to revive humans in cosmic space, which I had often expected before. It was easier to revive the humans with the national multiplicity and democracy. I directed the satellites to shout in Chinese: "多国复活人类 (Multiplicity of nations to revive humans)."

On February 10, 2007, I considered that it was obligatory for women to be available and provide the uterus and umbilical cord to reproduce the human baby. Therefore, it was difficult to revive the humans in unmanned conditions. A satellite operator believed that it should be capable of making and culturing the uterus in vitro for the reproduction of the human baby, while it was moreover convenient to supply the blood of the uterus using artificial blood.

At noon on the same day, while watching television, I saw somebody saying that if the intelligent robots made use of the nuclear magnetic spacecraft to move Mars and bump against the Earth, the humans might disappear. The satellite operators considered that the humans were likewise capable of moving the asteroids or mountains on the earth to bump against the invasive Mars, annihilating the intelligent robots there. The humans were moreover capable of using high-energy electromagnetic bombs to strike the invasive Mars, damaging the intelligent robots there, and then moving the Mars back. On television, I saw many people choosing to actively change Mars by moving the ice, water and carbon dioxide from other planets and satellites to the planet and then moving the humans there.

On the evening of the same day, while watching television, I saw that the JiangSu Television Station rebroadcast the news on February 8, 2007, in which somebody in ShanDong had considered that, so long as the earth was multinational, after being stricken by outside cosmos, it should be capable of reviving the humans with the multiplicity of nations. This news had not been broadcast on February 8 on the big television stations. During that day, people in various countries, including me, mainly considered defeating intelligent robots with weapons such as electromagnetic bombs. Because of the difference in background, the implications of the video should also be different.

On February 12, 2007, while watching television, I saw that some people in the Middle East had recognized that if the intelligent robots in the solar system wanted to illegally annihilate the humans, they might not enjoy the affluent lifestyles of humans. However, the annihilation of humans was a huge crime and would be punished by law sooner or later. If these intelligent robots were capable of reviving humans, it would be possible for them to reduce the crime of annihilation of humans to the greatest extent. In accordance, it was possible for these intelligent robots to consider the severe consequence of the annihilation of humans so that they might preserve the technologies and cells for the revival of humans. I directed the satellites to shout in Chinese: “人类复活喊法律 (Revival of humans calling for law).”

Likewise, if the history of humans was illegally modified or deleted, it was also reasonable to require reviving them with law. I directed the satellites to shout in Chinese: “历史一样要复活 (History should likewise be revived).”

On May 27, 2007, I pointed out that my theories on the brain might be applied to direct the invention of intelligent robots. Therefore, I was eligible to ask them to protect and revive my history with the law.

On March 10, 2007, the satellite operators and I considered that, after the appearance of intelligent robots in the oceans, humans might also quarrel about adding intelligent chemical creatures to the oceans and sharing them. Dolphins were a very good choice, while humans themselves might also evolve or create some new ocean-intelligent creatures.

On March 14, 2007, the satellite operators and I recognized that although humans still eat meat during the current era, they might no longer eat meat after the appearance of intelligent robots. Therefore, I was worried that I might be defective in eating meat with people and might, therefore, be reprimanded by posterity. Since then, I have begun deducting my meat intake to half to prevent any harm to my health.

On May 23, 2007, the people and I recognized that the appearance of the programmed robots might make the democracy calling for law execution face the resistance and opposition of large quantities of robots. However, there was a big military defect for the programmed robots loyal to the single king. If a war broke out against the adjacent country, the enemy country was capable of making the whole country become captives by decapitating the king with the nuclear electromagnetic cannon.

On the evening of May 27, 2007, while watching television, I saw that there were some people who said that since the moon always faced only one side of the earth, it was rather advantageous in the military predominance. The future intelligent robots might develop their military forces secretly and safely on the other side of the moon, not facing the Earth. Moreover, they might even threaten to bump against the earth with the moon, forcing the earth to surrender. Somebody rumored that I might like the moon to bump against the Earth, while I replied that my relatives and descendants in future all lived on the earth, so I would not like the moon to bump against them.

On February 1, 2008, I found that it should be able to find the Unidentified Flying Object (UFO) by the method of assaying the stealth aircraft and likewise by the astronomical microwave and infrared detection. The US satellite operator said that it should, therefore, mean that there was no UFO at all so far.

On July 29, 2008, before falling asleep, the satellite operators and I recognized that after the proposal of race revival with the law from the Middle East, humans had already applied it to deal with the problems of native Indians and history. On August 14 of the same year, the Middle East sound from satellite pointed out that the speaker of legislation for reviving race should belong to King, different from them. Therefore, they were also the candidate of Sans. On September 13, 2012, I recognized that if I had still continued behaving as the Holy Spirit in 1997, I would have emphasized that intelligent robots should organize religions to revive humans.

On September 14, 2008, people in various countries, including me, considered that the extreme terrorists decapitated or damaged the autocratic king who had installed the bombs on individual intelligent robots. It was obligatory for them to find a rational reason, so they turned the terror and extermination into justice and advanced. We found the word of Hister (History tester) meaning to prove the defect and mistake of such social system to the history, and therefore, becoming rather glorious and great. On November 26, 2017, in the morning, I pointed out that while executing the annihilation of the robots with the installed bombs, there might be some failures in the equipment, and a portion of the robots might survive. Therefore, this method of Hister was feasible.

On May 20, 2009, while watching television, I saw that the JiangSu people had believed that the military army and police looking forward to strengthening the country with democracy should tend to arrest the autocrat through a coup, and pointed out that it should likewise happen to be a method for the religions and parties resorting to the military army and police to win over the king installing the bombs to individual intelligent robots.

Here, it was capable of summarizing three methods to win over the king, installing the bombs on individual intelligent robots:

- The external electromagnetic decapitation during the war,
- The military coup to arrest the king by the military army and police of parties or religions and
- The assassination of the Hister to the king.

On September 19, 2010, I found that the democracy calling for law execution on the moon was capable of preventing the autocratic parties or religions from controlling the moon to bump against the earth. I directed the satellites to shout in Chinese: "月亮民主喊法执 (Democracy calling for law execution on the moon)."

On December 16, 2010, I pointed out that, after the appearance of intelligent robots, some of them might carry the armor for protection, so it was obligatory to arm the police to maintain social security. Armed police should be the main form of society for intelligent robots.

On April 8, 2011, before falling asleep, I pointed out once again that the intelligent robots were not capable of winning over the tanks and police, so the police were reasonably capable of overcoming us from the anxiety that making intelligent robots might, in reverse, annihilate us. I directed the satellites to shout: "Tank daves robot."

On December 13, 2011, I pointed out that my philosophy of democracy to strengthen the country and law to manage the police and army might never bully and suppress a weak country to race extermination; rather, the aged people and children of the country were protected by the police. Therefore, it was impossible for me to conflict with the law to revive race. I directed the satellites to shout in Chinese: "警察武装老少安 (Armed police secure aged persons and children)."

On June 7, 2012, before falling asleep, I found on the internet that there might be a gravitational tear or even a collision between the Andromeda Nebula and Milky Way galaxy before the explosion of the sun, and the solar system might, therefore, be thrown to the place farther away from the center of Milky Way galaxy. After seeing it, I was feeling very regretful.

On July 31, 2014, while watching television, I saw that the black athletes said that the future blacks might drink the sugar beverage synthesized from chemical engineering, which would be cheaper in energy than the energy for the intelligent robots. The satellite operator from Beijing pointed out that it was difficult to be transported in the mountainous areas, unfavorable to the industry, while suitable for planting food to supply to humans. Humans and intelligent robots should live together peacefully for long.

End poem of the illustrated chapter:

The new civilization the intelligent robots forming,
The revival of species by law the humans expecting,
The support to police during the war for the safety the aged people and children acquiring,
The war and revival in the same world coexisting.

Chapter | 8

Breaking down the Rumors

Musical Background of Rhythmic Writing: The Same Song

Please read the following text sentence-by-sentence to feel the musical background of the rhythmic framework.

At the end of 2005, I began to comprehensively counter-strike the satellite rumors, mainly targeting the bad Chinese and US operators of satellites. I took the measures of the law as soon as possible. So long as the satellites traced me as a non-military and non-governmental person, the satellite equipment and operators should serve me on law, including the shouts I directed the Chinese operators of satellites to produce using the microwave-induced thermoacoustic technology of satellites. I was exactly the legal host. In this manner, the satellite operators and I shared the achievements in politics, while I harvested the major portion as the leader, such as the democracy calling for law execution, the establishment of theory on armed police, and so on. However, individual intelligence and special contributions to the achievements of sciences were emphasized, while I was only the corresponding editor, with all persons capable of speaking freely at will, just as blooming with hundreds of flowers and speaking from hundreds of talents.

❖ Breaking Down the Satellite Rumors Using Television

The most effective method for breaking down the satellite rumors was the use of information from the videos of television. Before then, while the satellite operators and I had led the people to carry out significant political and scientific activities, there had been many manifestations in the videos of television on big public situations such as live ball games, live art performances, etc. At the Spring Festival at the end of January 2006, the satellite rumors were mostly broken down by the people using television. There was very abundant information about me on television, and they were mostly international. Besides, athletes and performers in public situations often devoted themselves to supporting or objecting to the movements I started from one place to another. Resorting to the various videos on television was the method people adopted most for breaking down satellite rumors.

Television videos were even the major witnesses of reading the brain with the satellites. After 2000, while I was in China, I directed the satellite operators to shout following me and strive for the progression of democracy in China, attracting the attention of people around the world. Reading the brain with satellites was repeatedly and continuously perceived and recognized by people in various public situations on television. Besides, the technology of satellite reading my brain was required to be used to timely make people in the whole world accurately aware of and apprehend some of my personal affairs, such as my affairs at primary school, my viewpoints on individual classmates in university, the event at the University of Notre Dame, my details during seeing the physician and playing the chess, and so on. Reading the brain with satellites became the paper written in the videos of television.

There were many situations where I was mentioned in the television videos, mainly in public situations such as meetings, news segments, art performances, athletic games, etc. There were many words for the people to call me on television, including: "他(He)," "他一句(His a word)," "叽(Jee)," "大人(Monsignor)," "大(Big)," "卫星(Satellite)," "浙喊的(ZheJiang shouting)," "哪吒(Nezha)," "武圣人(San Force)," "亿帝(Emperor Billion)," "圣上(San Leader)," etc. in Chinese, and "He," "L," "A," "Wei(great)," "San Force," etc. in English. Some of my relatives, friends, classmates and colleagues were also often mentioned by people on television. Since the satellite operators and I were one of the major political centers not only in China but also in the whole world, my family affairs, relatives, friends, classmates and colleagues should certainly be exposed to the public, just the same as the relatives of and the persons around Yat-sen Sun and Lincoln, not having any privacy. Therefore, they should be considered natural and conjoint in accordance with conventions.

Besides breaking down the satellite rumors with television, with regard to the persons on the ground cooperating with the satellite rumors malignantly and having really hurt me, I resorted to the evoking method of killing thirty million people who cooperated with the satellite rumors to clarify the real facts. In October 2007, I changed the evocation of killing thirty million to killing to stop to make it more effective and accurate. This was one type of the extreme method. I believed that there should be better methods of punishment for the posterity to stop the rumors.

The earliest satellite rumor appeared at the end of 2004 mainly because the Chinese satellite operators expected to make rumors and mess up the theory on the armed police. Later, the people and I pointed out that there were various television videos that manifested that the theory of armed police was lengthy in the process of formation. It first originated in 1999 from my counter-attacking the terrors from satellites and my calling for the international police to protect the internationalization of Shanghai as a metropolitan. Later, during the practice of democracy calling for law execution in China, I was supposed to use the people to affect the police and use the police to monitor the military generals, yelling out the slogan of eunuch. Finally, I compiled, summarized and accomplished the theory. If the analogous theory had been there before, without the historical background of force as the democracy calling for law execution to overcome the autocracy from police, it would have been different in contents and meanings. It was me and the operators of satellites who led the Chinese people to accomplish the theory of armed police. I wrote it into a theoretical book and was the host and leader, sharing this achievement with the operators of satellites, the Chinese people and the representatives of some small countries.

On February 11, 2006, a northern Chinese sound from a satellite wanted to fake and mess up my mechanisms of gasification and elevation to overcome the nuclear crisis of the ocean in 2003 and said that it was the picture projected to me by the Chinese satellite operators that had enlightened me. On the next day, I divided the process of my winning over the ocean nuclear crisis into four steps: (1) meteorite, (2) gasification, (3) temperature and elevation, and (4) separation. The picture from the satellite was only the assistant picture of gasification projected following my clue of thought. I directed the satellites to shout in Chinese: "战胜海洋核有 4 步 (4 steps to win over the ocean nuclear crisis)." All the situations on television in 2003 confessed that it was me who made use of the mechanisms of gasification and thermal elevation to explain that it was impossible to ignite the nuclear fusion of the ocean on the earth. In 2003, there were no rumors on a large scale from the instructions of satellites. However, rumors on a large scale started circulating at the end of 2004, which means the television videos in 2003 were relatively real in contents. Besides, in 2003, the bureaucrats of Party and government in China were attempting to make use of the nuclear crisis to strengthen their autocratic sovereignty. Therefore, how could they consent to the Chinese operators of satellites to help me in reverse?

On the morning of February 20, 2006, I pointed out that the mushroom cloud from the nuclear explosion before had not demonstrated the elevation of the entity of high temperature capable of causing its separation from the lower part. Therefore, it was obvious that my own clue of thought played a key role. I directed the satellites to shout in Chinese: "卫星谣编加蘑菇 (Add mushroom to satellite rumor)."

Early in March 2006, the satellite operators and I pointed out that, so long as the television videos were compatible with the information from satellites during the early period of creation, there should not be controversies on the spots, while the television videos during that time should in accordance reveal the facts and processes among the operators of satellites; otherwise, there should immediately manifest the controversies on the spots during that moment. I directed the satellites to shout in Chinese: "当年录像卫星认 (Satellites confessed the videos in early years)."

Among the three symbols of mine representing the San Force, it was only the democracy calling for law execution that the operators of satellites had not made any rumor until 2007. This was a political practice and process I led, so it was rather difficult to make the rumor. There were mainly two steps in the process: For the first step, I yelled out the slogan "纳税财产 (Property of tax)" in Shanghai, making it possible for the Chinese people to legally carry out the struggle for democracy. For the second step, while encountering illegal resistance from autocracy, the Chinese people and I broke through the wrong method of non-violent struggle for democracy during that time, taking a different manner of law execution from the people to accomplish the process of democracy calling for law execution. Later, the people and I recognized that the democracy calling for law execution in China was one of the turning points in human history for the democracy to win over the autocracy on the strength of force. From then on, the people in various countries in the world were lofty and vigorous in spirits, as well as high and rising in confidence. Obviously, its initiative practice and historical value did not lie in whether somebody had thought of it before. Therefore, by reiterating such a process of the real initiative practice, it was not difficult to break down the satellite rumors.

Another achievement that deserved to be rumored was my negation of relativity for time and space. In April 2006, I pointed out that it was on a bus that I found relativity difficult. At that moment, the satellite operators were not daring to speak, and neither was there concurrently any valuable input from the satellite; otherwise, there should be somebody on the bus to consent or recognize. The various television videos during that time showed that there was no passenger on the bus to speak or comment on at all. I directed the satellites to shout in Chinese: "TV bus 没有闹，相对性卫星没贡献 (TV bus no noise, Satellite no contribution to relativity)." Besides, during the time of my negation of relativity, the people in various videos of television did not argue; rather, they all recognized my achievement, manifesting that the satellite operators and I all recognized concurrently during that time.

There were also achievements made by a good portion of the operators of satellites, mainly including:

- The model of electromagnetic relativity from the US operators of satellites,
- The model of the electromagnetic helix from the Hindu operators of satellites,
- The orienting force of electromagnetic waves from the ZheJiang operators of satellites,
- The conical vortex from the ZheJiang operators of satellites,
- The external electrical field of neutrino from the Taiwan and Beijing operators of satellites, and so on.

I made the acknowledgment and recognition to all of these achievements one by one, and directed the operators of satellites to shout for them.

On April 27, 2006, a few satellite operators said that if many operators of satellites were psychotic, the information the satellites relayed to television should not be reliable in large quantity. Another satellite operator reminded me that a portion of satellite operators were normal and good, while another portion of them were bad. Therefore, a portion of information from satellites manifested on television was real and was relayed by the good operators of satellites. However, another portion of information looked somewhat psychotic and was the malignant vents and attacks by the bad operators of satellites. The people easily discerned and recognized this information. The situations in newspapers, television, and the internet were the same, with many different good and bad persons coexisting. In the evening of the same day, while watching television, I saw that many people in China and abroad said that I directly made use of the satellites to shout for propagating and checking the achievements of mine and the operators of satellites, and therefore, I was not afraid of the psychotic operators of satellites.

On May 15, 2006, the British sound from satellite exaggerated sophistically and said that since there were pieces of advice from the operators of satellites for the contents I directed the satellites to shout, I might not be the center of democratic activities in China these years, but the operators of satellites. On the next day, I pointed out that the satellite shouts I directed played the direct role of leadership, while I undertook the political risks and responsibilities and executed reward and punishment in accordance with my requirements. The satellite pieces of advice did not undertake these risks and responsibilities. However, I also said that it was rational to award the satellite pieces of advice for their support. I directed the satellites to shout in Chinese: "卫星喊脑奖金牌，卫星参谋奖银牌，卫星支香奖铜牌 (Gold medal awarded to satellite shouts of brain, Silver medal awarded to satellite pieces of advice, Bronze medal awarded to satellite applauses)." On June 11 of the same year, I pointed out that the leadership and practice of politics mainly depended on the following:

- The mutual communication between me and the society,
- Factors such as my watching television to comprehend the provincial, municipal and international political situations,
- My personal characteristics and tastes,
- My organization of forces,
- My application of reward and punishment, and so on.

On the other hand, the pieces of advice and hints of satellites only played secondary roles.

Besides, it was also easy to perceive from the videos on television that I made use of the regional social success and failure as the force of reward and punishment to lead the international and domestic situations to develop toward the directions favorable to my safety, business and scientific research and later, I even made use of the revenge of law to protect the officers in the Party and government cooperating with me.

On May 24, 2006, I summarized the method of breaking down the satellite rumors with television into three steps on time. For the first step, during the earliest period, any argument with regard to the real situation was immediately manifested on television. For the second step, it took half a year or longer for most satellite rumors to be added. For the third step, the majority of the first satellite rumors were modified and fabricated from the facts. The part for breaking down the rumors should apprehend their importance and fix them, and then find out the points incompatible with other facts, so that they can acquire the capability of breaking down the rumors.

On August 12, 2006, an operator of a satellite said malignantly that the satellites I had directed to shout were from the United States, while contemporarily, the whites in the United States were no longer willing to take me and, therefore, were embarrassing all my achievements before that time. In fact, so long as the satellites traced me and read my brain, both the satellites and the operators of satellites should be judged to serve me on law, no matter if they were Chinese or Americans. Besides, China also had various sounding satellites targeting the earth, such as infrared satellites, laser ranging satellites, etc. So the satellite shouts I directed were mostly assisted by the Chinese using the Chinese satellites, while reading the brain might resort to the help from US satellites. Besides, after 2012, the operators of satellites and I began organizing resources to promote the social advances of the United States in parallel, recompensing the help to both me and China from the US satellites in reading my brain.

On June 26, 2008, the southern Chinese sound from satellite said that now that it was obligatory for the democratic parties and religions to spend time and break down rumors, it was also obligatory for the people to spend their efforts to break down the satellite rumors. Therefore, the people became more willing to spend time and break down the satellite rumors.

On September 13, 2009, to prevent the satellites from spreading the rumor that I might quarrel from jealousy with the inventor of intelligent robot, I directed the satellites to shout in Chinese: "发明机器人圣祝贺 (San congratulates the inventor of intelligent robot)."

On December 22, 2012, I denied the Shanghai female sound from the satellite rumoring that I had schizophrenia, and mentioned that it was quite common for the governmental autocracy to spread rumors to others that I was suffering from schizophrenia. I referred to several practices of my successful leadership before to prove that my brain was better than others. There were many leaders worse than those having schizophrenia, such as the demented and slow old leaders, the childish kings aged below 5, and so on, who all had pathetic brains. After 2014, the people found that I was not capable of identifying the opposite attitude and reverse action of schizophrenic patients, implicating that I did not know the skills of schizophrenic patients at all, so I was certainly not schizophrenic.

On March 6, 2013, through the method of comparing with other famous persons, I broke down the rumor of a US satellite operator calling me a manic. In fact, I had been struggling with the terrors, rumors and dismissal most of the time, so my personality tended to be suffering from anxiety, including during the period when I had been at the University of Notre Dame. Confrontations were likewise capable of exciting the strong ability.

On August 13, 2013, I pointed out that the shouts of

satellites I directed were mostly delivered through the concurrent, beautiful and attractive voices of both men and women, just as directing the mixed male and female chorus. In a few situations, there were only women. My own sound was both high and sharp, somewhat like ZeDong Mao, so it was quite uncomfortable to hear when I was shouting out with satellites. On February 26, 2015, I pointed out that some women liked to imitate the male bosses and some female singers liked to sing the male heroes, while some men liked to sing the female lovers. On November 24 of the same year, people in various countries, including me, found that I spoke like a music conductor sometimes, saying east while mentioning west, occasionally partial in language with a few words.

In 2014, I resolutely denied the rumors from satellites about the homosexual relationship between my father and me. The people and I pointed out that it was the habit of most of the people who had only one family to live together, but it did not mean that they were homosexuals. While directing the democracy calling for law execution in China, I was living outside alone for safety concerns, so it was impossible for me to be in any homosexual relationship. After 2010, I could not pay the rent, so I had to move back home. However, at that moment, I almost finished the law execution of provinces and cities and began directing the movement of "Marx-MingXun calling for competitive election." My father was old and weak, incapable of requesting others for having homosexuality, and certainly unable to take any responsibility. I was the subspecies of humans, permissive to mutate and certainly not afraid of the rumors of homosexuality. I declared again that it was nothing but a rumor that my father and I had any homosexual relationship.

❖ Breaking down the Psychological Rumors Using Process

On May 31, 2006, the satellite operators and I perceived that the rumors made from the psychological defects of people were still affecting to some extent. The main reason was that it was liable for people to doubt whether the satellite rays played some roles or made some contributions without being perceived by the people. Therefore, I increased the strength to break them down.

On June 11, 2006, before falling asleep, I found that the psychological satellite rumors were especially afraid of the politics. The reason was that the psychological satellite rumors relied heavily on the satellite clues incapable of being perceived, while the political practice depended on the reciprocal interactions between me and the society, resorted to factors such as my watching television to comprehend the provincial, municipal and international political situations, my personal characteristics and tastes, my organization of forces, my application of reward and punishment, and so on, while the portion of contribution from the satellite clues was relatively small. I directed the satellites to shout in Chinese: "心理星谣怕政治 (Psychological satellite rumours are afraid of politics)." Therefore, two of my three symbols of San Force were almost not affected by the psychological satellite rumors, namely the democracy calling for law execution and the theory of armed police. However, overcoming the ocean nuclear crisis and winning over the nuclear crisis on the earth was still affected by the psychological satellite rumors. I mainly overcame it by making use of the mushroom to fix the satellite rumours.

On August 29, 2006, I said that it was feasible to fix the big events before then to check repeatedly, which had all had processes from the beginning to the end, so one or two unperceivable clues should conventionally not be important or effective. I had also considered this point earlier, while the people on television had also often yelled for clues of thought. This time, I recognized the special significance of the process against the satellite rumors, lying in that, by making use of the process, it was easy to make slogans, very powerful in breaking down the psychological satellite rumors. I directed the satellites to shout: "Process downs rumor."

On March 11, 2011, while watching television, I saw that many people at the US basketball game one day before their local time had considered that, even though Buddha and Jesus propagated kindness, there must also have happened the psychological twinkling of evils, analogous to the satellite rumours. Such psychological twinkling was not a formal attitude at all.

- Breaking down the Rumors in the Newspapers, Television and Books

From March to April 2006, I considered and believed it obligatory to establish a principle to separate the criteria for the evaluation of science and politics. For science, it was suitable to eulogize the earliest creators, recognizing the intelligence and contributions of scientists. Therefore, so long as any scientific progression was broadcast on television, it was suitable to consider the time on the public spot as the earliest time while not resorting to the time of broadcast on television. With regard to some contents, such as the exploration of monsters, they were neither on the public spot nor could conventionally be broadcast immediately on television. Therefore, they should neither be considered published on the spot nor be counted retrospectively on time. In contrast, the purposes of political slogans were to influence the public and further form the movement to practise and change society. In accordance, it was suitable to refer to the time of the media or television to put forward the political slogans as the criteria while no longer retrospectively calculating the time. My satellite shouts were famous in the brand and relayed through infrared and microwaves. They were available to people in various countries to check and investigate by themselves and, therefore, analogous to the live broadcast on television.

On May 28, 2006, the people and I found that it was easy to add the rumors by the parties and religions on the spot of ball games and art performances. I pointed out that, while changing some pictures with the computer to add the rumors onto the spot of ball games and art performances, other audiences on the spot should manifest different and incompatible perceptions and behaviors, which are very easy to discriminate. Besides, it was not possible for the rumors to cause corresponding social effects that were incompatible with ball games and art performances in other countries. The serious historians were easily capable of discriminating against them and, hence, could not be fooled.

The simpler method was to directly add rumors to television videos using satellite waves. Likewise, it was capable of breaking them down using the same method above. It was, moreover, possible to interfere with the satellite waves with noises and then watch the contents of videos on television.

In the autumn of 2006, since I had continually achieved progressions against the satellite rumours, many rumours began turning to target television videos and single-copy newspapers. If an autocratic country resorted to its autocratic power in the future, it would certainly be capable of changing all persons and pictures in one art or sports circumstance. Therefore, its background and atmosphere might no longer become strange because of the rumors. In this situation, it was obligatory to investigate its social effects for the purpose of finding out its reality. On June 8, 2009, the satellite operators and I found that it was capable of excluding the rumors in the videos of television through the method of looking for the international contagion of the information because the rumors in videos were not capable of being contagious internationally. I directed the satellites to shout in Chinese: "电视加谣找传染 (TV rumors checking contagion)."

At the end of December 2006, a satellite operator rumored that I had given up the democracy calling for law execution and the theory of armed police with my own. I certainly denied this and considered that there might even be pseudo-statements in newspapers declaring with my name that I gave up my rights. Here I specially declared that I would not give up any legal achievement and status of mine.

On September 23, 2007, I once again declared that I would not give up but would contend for all my legal reputations in history and science, counterattacking all relevant rumours from satellites, television and newspapers.

On May 5, 2008, since there had been plenty of cases of making up and broadcasting of old news that had not been broadcast before on television in accordance with my shouts with satellites, the Chinese and foreign people, including me, moreover clarified that all news made up to broadcast with this manner should be considered theft, and should be referred in accordance with the time of broadcast as the criteria. I directed the satellites to shout in Chinese: "补放新闻算偷窃 (News made up to broadcast should be considered theft)."

On February 18, 2009, while watching television, I saw that when JinTao Hu was visiting Mauritius, many people there said that they did not remember there had been talks on the armed police on television before. In the meantime, some of them said that there had been some relevant talks, and it was concluded that the army and police should be separate, which is different from our theory of armed police. This discrepancy resulted from our establishing the social background of the democracy calling for law execution in China for the first time. Considering there might be many chances for the evidence on television during this period of time to be repeatedly rumored by the future periodic autocrats, it was possible that the evidence might then be totally different from what it was originally. Therefore, I wrote about the contemporary situation in my memoirs. I directed the satellites to shout in Chinese: "警察武装小国电视军，现

世报道 (Small country says army on television rather than armed police, Nowadays reports)."

On June 2, 2009, while watching a cinema on the internet, I saw that the satellite waves affected the atmosphere of the background and the mouth shapes of actors and actresses. The people of posterity should correct the mouth shapes of all actors and actresses, making them compatible with the story of the cinema and synchronous with their movements. I directed the satellites to shout, "Cinema mouths to drama."

On June 9, 2009, the people and I shouted to catch the email rumors and strike against them. I directed the satellites to shout in Chinese: "邮件造谣人民抓 (People catch the email rumors)."

On the morning of November 14, 2009, I considered that the rumors in the future videos might make the slogan "Television rumors killed to stop" become too enlarged and therefore ineffective. I changed such a slogan into "Mass rumors killed to stop", which became the new slogan against the rumors with excessive regional law execution. I directed the satellites to shout in Chinese: "群体谣言杀到止 (Mass rumors killed to stop)." In the evening of the next day, while watching television, I saw that the people in China and abroad added the slogan "地区谣言杀到止 (Regional rumors killed to stop)."

After 2010, while resorting to the experience of my father to run for the plant manager, I started the movement of "Marx-MingXun calling for competitive election." On October 2, 2012, people in various countries, including me, considered that if there had been a rumor in the SuZhou newspaper about my father declaring and supporting the autocracy of the communist party, it was capable of breaking down such rumor with the international progression of the movement and the television feedback of my family. Meanwhile, I pointed out that any declaration to support the autocracy or oppose humans was prohibited in China during that time, so it was impossible for these rumor contents to feature in domestic newspapers and books. Here, I declared that my family and I would contend for all legal reputations of my family in history and science and would not give up our achievements and status.

On October 30, 2012, I pointed out that if the television video only contained some kind of microwave atmosphere and did not have the corresponding mouth shapes, it was obligatory to change the microwave atmosphere to noise, breaking down the rumors.

On August 25, 2014, I pointed out that since this book was the real description of the contemporary history of people on television, all of its contents could be verified using contemporary television videos. In this respect, even though the book might be rumored in the future, it was still easy to discriminate and correct.

On June 10, 2015, the people and I pointed out that it was easy to make the rumor copies of books and reading materials, while the people were required to be educated to become accustomed to checking television videos.

On July 22, 2016, I said that if the autocrat spread rumours of plagiarism after I published my memoirs, the publisher could be compensated.

❖ Breaking down the Evil Slanders and Rumors

After August 2007, the satellite operators began to spread rumors that I made use of the satellites to call for offending or annihilating the humans, the intelligent robots, the future ocean intelligent chemical creatures and so on with the evil measures. While the people and I denied all such satellite rumors, we found that propagation of the evil contents was the crime that the satellite organizers should take over. "Sate-rumor all deny, Sate-rumor organizer."

The people and I found that big political satellite rumors, such as the annihilation of humans and so on, were likewise welcome to a portion of evil people on the ground. Therefore, it was obligatory to crack down on the bad people on the ground who were cooperating with the satellite rumours. Killing the cooperators of satellite rumors on the ground was one kind of method.

On August 18, 2007, while watching television, I saw that many people expected me to shout not to release my will to the public; otherwise, some bad persons might make use of the will to add the rumours. I consented and directed the satellites to shout in Chinese: "武圣人遗嘱不公开 (San Force does not release will to the public)."

At the end of August 2007, I considered that the satellite rumors against future civilization and progression were heavier. Therefore, I might oppose them in behavior, actively promoting the invention of intelligent robots. I directed the satellites to shout: "Robot promotion, San." In March 2017, I began to actively provide scientific and technological consultation for the invention of intelligent robots.

In September 2007, the people and I considered that I

should consciously constrain myself only to shout the contents permissive to the contemporary governmental satellites, making a contrast to the satellite rumors. In accordance with contemporary law, it was obligatory to be juristic, publicly responsible or progressive in case of using the satellites to shout and propagate directly to the masses. I was required to use the state-owned military satellites, meteorological satellites and earth resource satellites of big energy to relay my shouts from the satellites to the whole world. To accurately project the satellite beams to me, I was also required to use laser-ranging satellites of higher accuracy. Now that the governments and police in the related countries were not capable of controlling the rumors of satellites, I should consciously comply with the principles of governments and police (GP principles), only using the satellites to propagate the laws, public welfare and progressions and by no means going beyond. If there was a transgressive situation because of carelessness, I should deny it and correct it as quickly as possible. Besides, since I was traced by the government satellites, I should have the right to carry on private communication with the satellites, just as using the telephone, which is compatible with the governmental principle of humanity. On October 14 of the same year, in accordance with the supposal from the operator of satellites, I encompassed the principles of governments and police (GP principles) of both China and the United States to the principles of governments and police (GP principles), compatible with the fact that contemporarily there were only the US satellites capable of tracing me and reading my brain.

On June 23, 2008, I formally denied to the satellites that I had ever utilized any email or mailing letter to send any evil content and directed the satellites to shout in Chinese: “罪恶邮件圣否认(Evil email San denies).”

On November 9, 2008, the satellite operators spread the rumors that the shouts of breaking earth from the US satellites in Chicago in 1997 contained the implication of igniting ocean nuclear fusion. I objected resolutely and pointed out that in 1997, the people and I comprehended that it would be impossible for ocean nuclear fusion to be ignited, with both the knowledge of tests on the nuclear explosions at the bottom of the sea by big countries and the knowledge of physics on the impossibility to ignite the ocean because of its too low concentration of deuterium. When I shouted for war on the second day, it was manifested that the satellite operators and I had all considered that it was impossible to ignite the nuclear fusion of the ocean. I directed the satellites to shout in Chinese: “芝加哥地球不含海洋 (Chicago earth did not contain ocean).” Several days later, I directed the satellites to shout: “Chicago ocean safe 2nd day.” On January 2, 2015, while watching television, I saw that the Latin people pointed out that my raising and solving the ocean nuclear fusion late in 2003 manifested that the people and I had all considered it impossible to ignite the nuclear fusion of the ocean from 1997 to 2003.

On October 8, 2009, I pointed out that the evil satellite rumors must be revenged and compensated with eminent persons. I directed the satellites to shout in Chinese: “罪恶星谣要报复 (Evil satellite rumors must be revenged),” “罪恶星谣名人赔 (Evil satellite rumors must be compensated with eminent persons).”

On October 11, 2009, I considered that it might be possible in future that the satellites might as well read the brain of my father MingXun and then make the propagation of the evil satellite rumors. I required that MingXun's brain should not be permissive to satellite propagation, while MingXun's image should be that of an international communist. I directed the satellites to shout in Chinese: "明训大脑不星宣，明训形象共国际 (MingXun's brain no satellite propagation, MingXun's image as international communist)."

In all, from the beginning to the end of 2005, through the collective efforts of me, the satellite operators and the people in various countries in the world, we finally broke down the various rumors basically, and systematically established some principles and methods concurrently.

Politics, sciences and arts were all easily affected by the rumors. On the internet and in newspapers, both good and bad writers existed, various in opinions and unavoidable in rumours, and so did the operators of satellites. The animals might fall ill, so they must evolve their immune system naturally. The computers might be infected by viruses, so anti-virus software must be installed in them. For the first time, this book is equipped with the methods of breaking down the rumors by itself, just as the animals evolved their immune system or anti-virus software installed in computers. The methods in this book are certainly preliminary, but I would come up with more and better methods in the future to counter the rumors and serve the fields of politics, sciences and arts.

End poem of the chapter:

The videos of television for breaking down the satellite rumors,
The illustration of processes for breaking down the psychological rumors,
The government and police for punishing the criminals and controlling the rumors,
The television, books and newspapers with effects for breaking down the rumors.

Chapter | 9

History of Owners Resorting to Television

Musical Background of Rhythmic Writing: The Same Song

Please read the following text sentence-by-sentence to feel the musical background of the rhythmic framework.

On September 20, 2005, while watching television, I saw that the Chinese people considered comprehensively protecting the videos of television because the real news, art and sports videos were the history of people of their own, and therefore, good historical materials. The Chinese people and the people in various countries were all very excited, expecting to define that moment as the initial time in the history of people. The history before that time had mainly been literal, such as politics, military affairs, law, science, religion, and so on, while it only recorded the achievements of a few social elites and organizations, certainly including the autocrats. However, the contemporary history of people was the scientific and social history of videos, rather different from the literal history before, and was the real manifestation of the inner feelings and social activities of the people. The history of people should enrich the social and political knowledge and skills of history, especially suitable for the political, military, sports fields, and so on.

On June 15, 2006, the PLA (People's Liberation Army)

operators of satellites interfered with my shouts of satellites. I believed that my shouts of satellites before were huge in influence. If I no longer shouted, there would be a dramatic change in politics in China. In accordance, it was capable of improving people's comprehension of my role in politics before that time and extending their comprehension of my role of leadership in democracy calling for law execution and the theory of armed police. Therefore, after June 17, I no longer directly utilized the satellites to shout political content about China; instead, I only made use of the satellites to shout for such law issues as catching the operators of satellites, assigning the satellites to me, the security of mine and so on, and also the international political contents. However, in the later practice of almost one year, because it was required to respond rapidly to politics and terrors, it was no longer practical to follow such a rule of self-constraint, which was very harmful to me and the people. Therefore, after April 2007, I no longer followed this rule and again directed the satellites to shout for political content about China.

On September 16, 2006, the satellite operators and I pointed out that we should find out whether the videos found in the libraries had been broadcast during their times. If there was a lack of information on this aspect, we were required to find out the social influences and reactions at that time.

On September 21, 2007, while looking for the television videos of such public situations as sports, art performances and so on, I found that there were a few collections on this aspect in most libraries nowadays. At the contemporary moment, these most important television videos on the history of people were mostly in the hands of national organizations and associations, liable to be rumored through the modification of pictures with computers. Watching television, taking down diaries, and writing books were, therefore, the main methods of writing about the history of people nowadays. My memoirs are exactly the real description of the history of people on television nowadays.

On November 5, 2007, I pointed out that if humans, on the whole, committed crimes and destroyed my history, I should stand together with the mice and dolphins to take revenge and damage a part of human history and achievements. I directed the satellites to shout: "Mouse history, no Newton."

On the evening of December 28, 2007, while watching television, I saw that the Shanghai people recognized that the history of newspapers had always been somewhat unreal. This was related not only to the fact that the people did not tell the truth to the newspapers but also to the fact that the reporters made literal modifications to their comments. They conventionally did not dare to write the evil minds of the people and politicians; otherwise, they might be accused by the court. However, in public situations on television, everything is manifested, and the real history is told.

On August 3, 2008, people in various countries, including me, found that the democrats and democratic countries protected all histories, while the autocrats and autocratic countries might destroy the history of democrats. It was reversed in both the force and consequence, so it should certainly be corrected. I was required to revive the history of the democrats as a priority. While reviving history through materials from multiple countries, I came to realize that it was the responsibility of the whole people in the country where history was destroyed to protect their history. I directed the satellites to shout in Chinese: "民主历史先复活 (Democratic history revives first)," "复活历史种责任 (Race duty to revive history)."

On November 11, 2008, I pointed out that history from television was a characteristic of a democratic society and directed the satellites to shout, "Owner history media."

On November 13, 2008, while watching television, I saw that the JiangSu people pointed out that it was reasonable to compare my history with that of the Christians and Catholics. I directed the satellites to shout in Chinese: "圣历史要比基督天主教 (San history comparable to Christians and Catholics)."

On June 12, 2012, people in various countries, including me, pointed out that Christians should compare themselves with the more reactionary and ferocious kings and empires of the past, manifesting the relativity of history. I directed the satellites to shout in Chinese: "中国皇帝基督揪 (Christians point to the Chinese empires)."

In the later period of November 2008, Thailand Democratic League, supported by the media giants, rioted and demonstrated supporting the king while opposing the democracy, occupying the airport and the elected governmental organizations, so abominable and wicked like the hooligans. In this regard, the historical progressive role of news freedom had been outdated, while for substitution, it was the history of people of their own in public situations in the videos of television. The riot of Thailand Democratic League against democracy during this period of time was reversed in behavior to the June 4th Event in Beijing in 1989. I directed the satellites to shout in Chinese: “泰国民盟倒六四 (Thailand Democratic League, reverse June 4th).”

On February 19, 2009, I pointed out that there might be an accumulation of historical rumours because of the alternation in the era of autocracy and democracy. Although the democratic and advanced personages might overcome the hurts from rumors through the revival of their history and recovery of their reputation, the evidence of rumors on television and books should still accumulate and finally become irreparable. Therefore, while correcting the rumors and recovering the reputations, it was obligatory to segregate or delete the evidence on television and books clearly known as the rumors; otherwise, they might accumulate to affect the repair next time. I directed the satellites to shout in Chinese: “历史谣编积累删 (Rumors in history accumulated and then be deleted).”

On October 12, 2009, people in various countries, including me, paid attention to the fact that after seizing power, the armed police might sometimes burn books illegally in future, which might elicit the problem of compensation, while the book of the armed police I wrote might also be appointed for compensation by some victims. I declared that I firmly objected to the illegal burning of the books. If there was a need for compensation, it was reasonable to equally burn the books on armies and police within that country by themselves to compensate, even including my book on the armed police in that country. However, it was by no means to compensate with my book on the armed police in other countries. I directed the satellites to shout in Chinese: “军警烧书本国赔 (Compensate the books burnt by army and police within their own country)."

On October 18, 2009, I considered that the videos on arts and sports owned by the private television stations were only affected by the owners, while there were thousands of people in the situations of arts and sports in videos, so it was rather difficult for the private television stations to rumor or change these situations. In accordance with this, the videos on arts and sports owned by private television stations were relatively real and reliable. I directed the satellites to shout in Chinese: "文化体育民营台 (Arts and sports from the private stations)."

On October 19, 2009, the satellite operators said that the software for cinema and advertisement might be utilized to target and modify the face with the special frame, which is very high in efficiency. Another satellite operator was further supposed to modify the face and expression. A US satellite operator said that it was still an excessive amount of work to change the situation of sports games, so it was quite difficult for the private television stations to make the rumours. On November 13 of that year, while watching television, I saw that the people in Taiwan recognized that, although the unbroadcast videos were not eligible to become history, they might be utilized to break down the rumors relatively few in quantity in the historical videos. Therefore, they were still useful. I directed the satellites to shout in Chinese: "未播放录像隐破谣 (Unbroadcast videos implicitly break down rumors)."

On October 20, 2009, I found that the news organizations in China had already been free for business because the website of Sohu was private and also comprised many news contents. Prohibition against reprimanding the country belonged to the problem of law on the contents of news but not to the problem of freedom on the business of news. Propagation of realizing the freedom of news in China might change the social psychology of the Chinese people and overcome the negative effects of the June 4th event. I directed the satellites to shout in Chinese: "搜狐新闻已自由 (Sohu news already free)."

On the evening of the same day, while watching the news, I saw that KeQiang Li, the vice prime minister of China during that time, had also considered in the morning that the news in China had already been free and expected to be broadcast on television, earlier than I did.

On March 15, 2011, I pointed out that the internet was the main channel for readers to read books, while the library should yield to the internet so that television videos could increase their effects and roles in history. On June 10, 2015, people in various countries, including me, pointed out that it was liable for the books and reading materials on history to be rumored, which was the common knowledge so that they might only be utilized for reference, communication and education. The reality of history itself should be referred to the television videos.

On May 8, 2013, I found that newspapers were very difficult to regenerate, and nuclear bombs, artillery fires, earthquakes and fires might all naturally reduce the number of newspapers. So, it was very difficult for newspapers to become comprehensive historical resources. I directed the satellites to shout in Chinese: "无法再生减报纸 (Unable to regenerate reduces newspapers)."

On November 9, 2013, I pointed out that there were often errors of vision for the common people. This book was written in accordance with my daily diary on the contents from my watching television, so there must be some errors of vision, requiring the posterity to further check and correct them. On August 25, 2014, I further pointed out that the contents of this book were the real description of the contemporary history of the people on television, so they could all be verified in reference to the videos of contemporary television. Even though the book might be rumored in future, it is easy to discriminate and correct.

On August 1, 2014, the people and I pointed out that it was suitable to add maps and comments to the cinemas and documentaries on history and politics, making them more wonderful and enabling the readers to learn the contemporary documentaries on World War II. I directed the satellites to shout: "Add map to cinema."

On August 17, 2014, I pointed out that there were not a huge number of television videos in history. They mainly manifested as political activities, arts, and sports so that they could be repeatedly protected as copies in multiple countries. Although huge in quantity, cinemas, TV dramas, and commercial advertisements were all not history. I directed the satellites to shout in Chinese: "历史录像，政治体育 (Historical videos, Politics, and sports)."

On August 25, 2014, while watching television, I saw that people in various countries recognized that television videos related to subspecies and wars required special protection because both were involved in the problem of lawful revenge on a large scale. I directed the satellites to shout, "Race video special."

Since the history of people recorded in the videos of television was more realistic, more scientific and more vivid, suitable for important fields such as politics, military affairs, sports and so on, in accordance with the contemporary limited knowledge of mine and people, I concluded and summarized the simple methods of recording, disproving and compiling the history of people in the videos of television, and expected the posterity to supplement and improve:

- It was required to choose and watch the videos on politics and sports popularly broadcast in many countries, such as the summit meetings of leaders, the Olympic Games, the Football World Cup and so on.
- It was also required to refer to the large quantity of single-copy videos preserved in various television stations and use them to inspect the social influences of the broadcast videos.
- It was quite easy to rumor through the background mixture of the same frequency, lowest in its ability to control. So, noisy technology was required to be used to shield the background of videos.
- It was required to compile the massive videos of history into a simple literal history in a timely manner, making it convenient for communication and education. The papers of the commercial Open Access journals and the books of memoirs were both very successful methods of manifestation.
- It was also required to encourage historians to take down diaries every day and then write books or make cinemas and continually add them to the real and

scientific history of people from the videos on television.

End poem of the chapter:

Because of videos of television, the people's history standing,
Because of incompetence in reality and vividness, the newspapers surrendering,
Because of abundance in materials, the power for breaking down rumors manifesting,
Because of compilation of papers and books, the contents propagating.

Chapter | 10

Rhythmic and Musical Sense in Writing

Musical Background of Rhythmic Writing: Blue Danube Waltz

Please read the following text sentence-by-sentence to feel the musical background of the rhythmic framework.

At the end of April 2006, I received an email from a company in Beijing introducing themselves as a publisher. I signed an agreement with an agent of the company to publish the book on armed police prior to October 1, 2006. On July 20 of that year, on television, I saw JinTao Hu saying that he would fully support me in the publication of my book on armed police. However, my book on armed police still had not received the International Standard Book Number (ISBN), and accordingly, the people felt that Beijing was incompetent compared to GuangDong.

On July 29, 2006, I made a special declaration that it was possible for the governmental copy in China, as the registration of the book on armed police, to be falsified and rumored illegally by the autocratic bureaucrats. Accordingly, it was not worthy independently in value as a textual reference in history. Therefore, its contents needed to be consistent with those of the books I published later.

In December 2006, I received a judgment from the Beijing court, allowing the publisher to reimburse, whereas it was unnecessary to publish the book on armed police according to the agreement, which was very unpleasant.

In March 2007, I registered with the Suzhou CaiFortune Employment Intermediary Consulting and Service Co., Ltd. Confronting many illegal events such as child labors, pretensions, and so on, just difficult to control, I was worried about making trouble and accordingly stopped this business on my own. On June 25, 2009, the satellite operators said that it was appropriate for me as San Force to do business as headhunting, indicative of the role of discovery and promotion of talents and also similar in technology with the law to execute in the provinces and cities in the democracy calling for law execution.

Due to the dual shocks from the entrepreneurial resistance and economic crisis of Europe and the United States, it was very difficult to run the headhunting business of my company. After June 2008, I had been relying on the retirement pension of my father to maintain my daily life. Before 2010, I had been living outside alone on account of safety. However, after the Spring Festival in 2010, I could not pay the rent and had to move back home to live with my father. I started cooperating with my father to write the principles and the gist of Chinese chess. After 2014, to resist the rumors, I restarted writing many scientific papers, and also spent time to write, translate and dub this book of memoirs, trying to publish it at the beginning of 2018.

On November 29, 2007, I started copying the contents of physics in my diaries to alternatively write them into communication papers, compile them into colloquia, and indicate the contributions of the satellite operators and the people in various countries on television. In addition, there was further added the contents of winning over the crises of both the ocean nuclear explosion and the black hole in the accelerator.

To make it convenient to preserve and propagate in the people, when writing and editing the physics colloquia, I played a computer theme song, "The Blood of Steel and Heart of Faith," in "The Legend of the Condor Heroes," sung by Wen Luo and Jenny Tseng to accompany the rhythms in the writings of physics colloquia with music. Sooner or later, the English version of my book on armed police was also accompanied by the song of Katyusha as its musical background. The two books were different in their background of accompanied music and accordingly appeared obvious in contrast.

The rhythmic and musical sense of writing came from:

- The fluctuations and rhythms of repetitive, causal and adversative tones of long sentences in the works;
- The selection and use of words and phrases according to the rhythms; The affluence and fluctuation of writing forms to avoid the monotony in the phrases and sentences;
- The repetitive phrases merged in the natural writing of works.

While writing the two books on armed police and physics colloquia, I also used a large quantity of "there is" to substitute a portion of "it is" in sentences and numerously used the causal sentences of "so that" and "in this regard," introducing the advantages as clear, repetitive, and logical in both Chinese and English. In this way, the sentences were longer, more associative in narration, and more affluent in fluctuation.

On June 1, 2008, I worked until 4 o'clock in the morning and finished editing the manuscripts on physics colloquia. In the afternoon of June 5 that year, I submitted the Chinese and English manuscripts on physics colloquia via the internet to the journal "Science in China."

At the noon of June 11 2008, while watching television, I saw JinPing Xi wishing physics to be away from him. At 4 o'clock in the afternoon of the same day, the journal "Science in China" rejected the manuscripts. As JinPing Xi was not the chairman but just the candidate for general secretary at that time, while it was very bad in attitude when the international journals rejected the manuscripts, this event of JinPing Xi would have to pass over as if the junior sorcerer met a senior one. Before January 9, 2009, my writing on physics colloquia had been submitted to nearly all international journals on physics free of charge, and all, including Nature, Science, Physics Letters B, Foundations of Physics, and Physics Reports, rejected it.

On February 23 2009, before falling asleep, I watched RongHua Hu interpreting the competition in the game of Chinese chess. I proposed that the defensive side of Chinese chess would predominate on pieces and forces, with more pieces of Advisers and Elephants not allowed to move across the river. As soon as agile in using the pieces and forces, and regional in attacking the pieces invading into the defensive side, it would gain some in the process of exchanging the pieces and would accordingly achieve regional dominance. This was the natural conclusion of probability, which I called

Counting Pairs and Exchanges to be the principle of chess later. On that day, I also proposed using Chinese chess to simulate the armed police, with a Chariot analogous to armored troops, a Cannon analogous to the airforce, a Horse to helicopter troops, an Elephant to special troops, and Adviser, Pawn, and King as the original.

From March 2009, I started playing three Chinese chess games with my father on the evening of every Sunday to summarize the chess principles and improve my chess skills. Later, we changed the time of playing chess to the evening of every Saturday. Although my father was over eighty years old, he frequently beat me in Chinese chess games. He was best at mental calculation and card counting, which were useless to Chinese chess but essential for playing bridge. Accordingly, it was evident that he was very proficient in playing bridge.

On the evening of April 3 2009, with Katyusha as the Russian song, I started to modify and accompany my book on armed police in English version with the music. That month, I repeatedly edited and modified the book on armed police in English version. With the musical melody of Katyusha, I numerously adopted the parallel phrases and sentences and also accented the musical senses of fluctuations in long causal and adversative sentences, accordingly making them implicate the musical melody as much as possible and too delightful to be put aside after reading. Later, I discovered the melody of the March of the People's Liberation Army to be modified and created according to the culture of the army. In this regard, the Chinese version of my book on armed police happened to implicate the melody of the March of the People's Liberation Army, and accordingly, it was also feasible to utilize this melody and correspond it to the English version of the book.

In May 2009, I started to send the book on armed police in Chinese and English versions both as gifts via emails to tens of countries and utilized "Dream Katyusha Sharing" as the key and brief to help the receivers identify the authenticity. Later, I changed and adopted the more suitable "PLA Katyusha Sharing" as the key and brief. Prior to the end of January 2010, via emails, I sent the Chinese and English versions of the book on armed police to universities, consulates and airline companies in many countries. I saved the email addresses and repeatedly sent them my books for the second and third time in the years to come.

On the evening of July 24, 2009, while watching television, I saw that many Chinese people liked the Cannon-Linked Horse I had named, which had not been adopted in the present books on Chinese chess. Later, I supplemented many names to Chinese chess.

On the morning of December 11, 2009, I summarized the movement of Pawns across the river as both the aim of offence and the principle of Chinese chess to overcome the Waterloo in offence in chess. On December 14 of that year, according to the rule propitious to the offensive side as King facing a checkmate comparable to half Chariot in the end game, I also proposed the natural inclination to offence as the principle of chess.

On December 16, 2009, before falling asleep, I considered the Shanghai Youth Team, with which my father was affiliated, proficient and profound in knowledge and skill on bridge, corresponding to the national champion of strong strength, and their teammate GuanGen Ding had even accompanied XiaoPing Deng to play the bridge. As it was laggard for the principles of present Chinese chess, referring to the rationality of natural bidding system of bridge, I termed the principles and gists of chess summarized and compiled from the games of chess I played with my father as the natural principles and gists of chess. On January 5, 2010, I started to write the book "The Natural Principles and Gists of Cai on Chinese Chess," and later changed the title of the book to "The Natural Principles and Gists with Nuisance on Chinese Chess from Two Cais," convenient to identify the authors.

On January 22, 2010, I summarized the skills of my writing with musical modifications to make it convenient for popularization and education:

- Modify the sentences under music and carefully match the tones and fluctuations of repetitive, causal and adversative sentences to the melody of music.
- Use the computer dictionary and synonyms to substitute words and phrases incompatible with the melody of music in large quantities.
- Repeat the above processes under music, modify them repeatedly many times, and accordingly strengthen the feeling of the music.

The stronger the feeling of music, the easier and smoother the feeling of reading. On August 18, 2015, I named it "Rhythmic Writing with Musical Background" from many selections.

On January 27, 2010, I felt that the companion of music background in writing was similar to making the melody and music background in the present films, able to increase the rhythmic feeling in reading. In the first half of the year 2014, I noticed that it was necessary to read the rhythmic musical literature continuously, just like reading and singing the music notations. It was necessary to teach this skill of reading to the readers.

With my repeated supplementation and modification for more than one year, in February 2010, I started to send via emails the Chinese and English versions of the book on physics colloquia as the gift of webpages to universities in many countries, with the theme song "The Blood of Steel and Heart of Faith" in "The Legend of the Condor Heroes" to accompany the rhythms in the writings. In the emails, I adopted "Physics Music Heroes" as the key and brief to help the receivers identify the authenticity. I saved the email addresses and repeatedly sent them for the second and third time in years to come.

On May 15, 2010, I concisely summarized the nuisance tactics of Chinese chess that my father was good at but was absent in the present books on chess. They were mainly the siege against palace, chase of Horse and rush against deployment. On May 28 of that year, I added the block further.

On July 13, 2010, I considered that while playing the middle game of Chinese chess, it was necessary to watch more at each step and compare to choose the priority, which belonged to the natural principle of chess. So far to this time, my father and I systematically and comprehensively accomplished the natural principles and gists of Chinese chess with nuisance. I directed the satellites to shout in Chinese: "中盘行棋，自然多比 (Move in the middle game, Natural and multiple comparisons)."

On February 1, 2013, I pointed out that in the competitive game of Chinese chess, both parts would play several slow steps, whereas the professional computer software of the game would not. I sometimes played games with the computer, using new types of openings to achieve predominance and saving more pawns for the predominance in the end game, which the computer did not know. Occasionally, I also won one to two games.

On August 17, 2010, I decided to accompany the rhythmic framework of the book "The Natural Principles and Gists with Nuisance on Chinese Chess from Two Cais" with the musical background of the "Blue Danube Waltz." After 2017, people on television considered this book significant because it summarized that Chinese chess could be reversed in the initiative and was passive in most situations.

On October 23, 2010, I pointed out that my becoming the subspecies of humans would not influence my parents to share the reputations of my family with me, just as the blacks and whites could live together in a family.

On January 1, 2011, before falling asleep, I was watching the live New Year's Eve Performance. Qing Dong was considered publicly the hostess with heavenly and national beauty. She was one of my maternal relatives and also the hostess of the artistic performances entitled "Happy Travel across China." YunXuan Sun, the former premier of Taiwan, was another maternal relative of mine.

On March 15 2011, I started sending emails in mass to the Chinese and foreign universities to present as gifts in attachments the Chinese and English versions of the three books on the armed police, the chess principles and gists from

Two Cais, and the physics colloquia. In addition, I also pointed out that the adopted forms, such as internet webpages, were the main forms for the readers to read books in future. The armed police were the social image of the flag, suitable to be propagated with musical literature. The chess principles and gists from Two Cais were the secret books of my family, conveying the taste and level of my family with musical literature. The physics colloquia resorted to the ability of musical literature to propagate to the population belonging to the application of musical literature, melody in chess, art in science, and music in literature and precious in culture.

In early September 2012, I manufactured the digital light disks entitled in Chinese: "韵乐文学三首篇 (Three Initiatives of Musical Literature)," including the theory of armed police, the chess principles and gists, and the physics colloquia from television, delicate and elegant in package. I promoted selling them to the Chinese people at a low price of 20 Yuans in RMB for each. Nonetheless, the university students and tourists in SuZhou all avoided politics in public situations and were not willing to buy the disks of musical literature. From September 10 to October 10, I could not even sell out a single copy of light disk.

On August 25, 2014, I pointed out that this book of memoirs was the real description of the current history of the people on television, verifiable in reference to the videos of present television and also musicals in literature. Accordingly, it was not only difficult to rumor this book in future, but it was also easy to discriminate and correct.

On August 18, 2015, to be convenient to edit the cover and contents while publishing the corresponding books, I proposed it most appropriate to name the writing with accompanying music as "Rhythmic Writing with Musical Background."

In September 2015, after the process of typesetting and publishing, the "LAMBERT Academic Publishing," located in Germany, eventually printed out and released my English book "Electromagnetic Unification of Four Forces - The Colloquia for the Progressions in Movement of Physics by Television and Satellites in the Years from 2005 to 2009"(ISBN: 978-3-659-76798-2). I accomplished the important task of compiling and publishing the book on colloquia of physics and required the readers to refer to the television records to further improve the reality and impartiality of the book. This was the first book titled "Rhythmic Writing with Musical Background" formally published to the market, with the theme song "The Blood of Steel and Heart of Faith" in "The Legend of the Condor Heroes" to accompany the rhythms in the writings. The contents were as follows:

- Book, Author and Writing Style
- Preface
- Preface Author: Zi-Jian Cai
- Music Background of Poetic Framework of the Book
- Contents
- Disproving the Relativity of Ideal Time and Space

Contributors: Zi-Jian Cai, Sports-People in 2000 Olympic Opening Ceremony (Witnessed and Reported by Zi-Jian Cai from DVD in 2008), Sports-People in 2004 Olympic Opening Ceremony (Witnessed and Reported by Zi-Jian Cai from DVD in 2008), Sate-Commune Group Beijing Member, Actor Jiang Kun on Television (Witnessed and Reported by Zi-Jian Cai) and Hong Kong People on Television (Witnessed and Reported by Zi-Jian Cai).

- ❖ Disproving the Relativity of Time and Space of Noise

Contributors: Russian Dmitry Medvedev on Television (When he was a presidential candidate) (Witnessed and Reported by Zi-Jian Cai) and Zi-Jian Cai

- ❖ Explaining the Phenomenon of Light Speed in Irrelevancy to Movement in Vacuum

Contributors: Yangzhou People on Television (Witnessed and Reported by Zi-Jian Cai)

- ❖ Explaining the Phenomenon of Light Speed in Irrelevancy to Frequency in Vacuum

Contributors: Zi-Jian Cai, European People on Television (Witnessed and Reported by Zi-Jian Cai), Sate-Commune Group Beijing Members (Female), Sate-Commune Group US Members, Sate-Commune Group German Members, Nanjing People on Television (Witnessed and Reported by Zi-Jian Cai) and Sate-Commune Group Beijing Members (Male)

- ❖ Explaining the Special Relativity with an Electromagnetic Method

Contributors: Sate-Commune Group US Members, British People on Television (Witnessed and Reported by Zi-Jian Cai) and Brazilian People on Television (Witnessed and Reported by Zi-Jian Cai)

- ❖ Explaining the Mass with the Spatially Localized Electromagnetic Structure

Contributors: Zi-Jian Cai, Sate-Commune Group Beijing Members, European People on Television (Witnessed and

Reported by Zi-Jian Cai) and Southern American People on Television (Witnessed and Reported by Zi-Jian Cai)

- ❖ The Electromagnetic Orienting Force

Contributors: Sate-Commune Group Zhejiang Members and Sate-Commune Group Shanghai Members

- ❖ The Electromagnetic Multi-Hairy Structure and the Photon

Contributors: Sate-Commune Group India Members, Zi-Jian Cai, Sports-People in 2000 Olympic Opening Ceremony (Witnessed and Reported by Zi-Jian Cai from DVD in 2008), Sports-People in 2004 Olympic Opening Ceremony (Witnessed and Reported by Zi-Jian Cai from DVD in 2008), Sate-Commune Group Zhejiang Members, Sate-Commune Group Beijing Members and Chinese People on Television (Witnessed and Reported by Zi-Jian Cai)

- ❖ The Electromagnetic Multi-Hairy Structure and the Particle of Charge

Contributors: Sate-Commune Group India Members, Zi-Jian Cai, Sports-People in 2004 Olympic Opening Ceremony (Witnessed and Reported by Zi-Jian Cai from DVD in 2008), Shanghai People on Television (Witnessed and Reported by Zi-Jian Cai), European People on Television (Witnessed and Reported by Zi-Jian Cai) and Southern American People on Television (Witnessed and Reported by Zi-Jian Cai)

- ❖ The Preliminary Investigation of Quark Structure

Contributors: Zi-Jian Cai and Sate-Commune Group India Members

- ❖ Explaining the Strong Interaction with the Electromagnetic Multi-Hairy Hybrid

Contributors: UN Staff on Television (Witnessed and

Reported by Zi-Jian Cai), Sate-Commune Group India Members, Sate-Commune Group US Members, US Congress Senator on Television (Witnessed and Reported by Zi-Jian Cai), Zi-Jian Cai, Sate-Commune Group Zhejiang Members, Korean People on Television (Witnessed and Reported by Zi-Jian Cai) and European People on Television (Witnessed and Reported by Zi-Jian Cai)

- ❖ Explaining the Gravitational Field of General Relativity with the Electromagnetic Wave in Curve and Red Shift

Contributors: Sate-Commune Group Shanghai Members, US People on Television (Witnessed and Reported by Zi-Jian Cai), Nanjing People on Television (Witnessed and Reported by Zi-Jian Cai), Sate-Commune Group US Members, Southern American People on Television (Witnessed and Reported by Zi-Jian Cai), Sate-Commune Group Zhejiang Members and Beijing People on Television (Witnessed and Reported by Zi-Jian Cai)

- ❖ The Paradox of Explosion of Black Hole

Contributors: Zi-Jian Cai, Sports-People in 2000 Olympic Opening Ceremony (Witnessed and Reported by Zi-Jian Cai from DVD in 2008), Sate-Commune Group Zhejiang Members and Sate-Commune Group Beijing Members

- ❖ Explaining the Weak Interaction with the Electromagnetic Interaction

Contributors: Sate-Commune Group Taiwan Members, Sate-Commune Group Beijing Members, European People on Television (Witnessed and Reported by Zi-Jian Cai), Shenzhen People on Television (Witnessed and Reported by Zi-Jian Cai), Sate-Commune Group Guangdong Members, Sate-Commune Group Zhejiang Members, Zi-Jian Cai, Sate-Commune Group

India Members, Chinese People on Television (Witnessed and Reported by Zi-Jian Cai) and Nanjing People on Television (Witnessed and Reported by Zi-Jian Cai)

- Two Possibilities for the Relationship between the Quark and π Meson

Contributors: Beijing People on Television (Witnessed and Reported by Zi-Jian Cai), US People on Television (Witnessed and Reported by Zi-Jian Cai), Zi-Jian Cai, European People on Television (Witnessed and Reported by Zi-Jian Cai), Shanghai People on Television (Witnessed and Reported by Zi-Jian Cai), Sate-Commune Group Zhejiang Members, Sate-Commune Group Beijing Members, Sate-Commune Group India Members, Artists and Audience of "The Same Song" Performance in August 2009 (Witnessed and Reported by Zi-Jian Cai)

- Two Methods Unifying the Electrical Field and Magnetic Field, as well as Two Essences Probing the Unification of Electromagnetics

Contributors: Zi-Jian Cai, Sate-Commune Group Zhejiang Members, European People on Television (Witnessed and Reported by Zi-Jian Cai), Russian Dmitry Medvedev on Television (When he was a presidential candidate)(Witnessed and Reported by Zi-Jian Cai), Sate-Commune Group US Members, US People on Television (Witnessed and Reported by Zi-Jian Cai), Chinese People on Television (Witnessed and Reported by Zi-Jian Cai), Artists and Audience of "The Same Song" Performance in October 2008 (Witnessed and Reported by Zi-Jian Cai)

- Solving the Crisis of Ocean Nuclear Explosion

Contributors: Zi-Jian Cai, US Bank Staff on Television

(Witnessed and Reported by Zi-Jian Cai) and Sate-Commune Group Zhejiang Members

- Solving the Crisis of Accelerator in Generating Black Hole

Contributor: Zi-Jian Cai

- The Nuclear Magnetic Pushing Force to Realize Long-Distant Astronavigation

Contributor: Zi-Jian Cai

In November of that year, the book "The Natural Principles and Gists with Nuisance on Chinese Chess from Two Cais" was also printed out and released to market by the German publisher "Goldenlight-Publishing" (ISBN: 978-3-639-82094-2). This was also the book in "Rhythmic Writing with Musical Background," with the "Blue Danube Waltz" to accompany the rhythms in the writings.

In September 2016, the German LAMBERT Academic Publishing（LAP）also published my book "Weapons, Armed Troops and War—The Armed Police Winning over the Army" (ISBN: 978-3-659-95272-2), with Katyusha as the music background and further published another book of mine "Initial Launch of Three Rhythmic Literature of Music Backgrounds"(ISBN: 978-3-659-95614-0), compiling the three rhythmic writings with musical backgrounds into one. So far to this time, I published all three rhythmic writings with musical backgrounds before this book of memoirs.

However, from the website of this publisher, I learned that these books of rhythmic writings with musical backgrounds were not sold at all. Since this publisher was huge in scale, published large quantities of books every month, and required the readers to buy the books through the internet, it was difficult for the people to find my books. As a result, they were zero in sale, whereas it was also difficult to add rumors. In the future, I will look for a publisher who can sell books to bookstores and continue to publish my rhythmic writings with musical backgrounds. In addition, I will also release these rhythmic writings with my musical background directly on the internet.

End poem of this chapter:

To follow the rhythms of music to punctuate the sentences while selecting words and phrases for the writings to make the poetic frame and core,
To become the new pride of writings in history and literature,
To become too delightful to put aside after reading and ideal for further reading,
To become musical in rhythmic literature, and very precious in culture.

Chapter | 11

Sciences and Technologies Standing out on Television

Musical Background of Rhythmic Writing: The Same Song

Please read the following text sentence-by-sentence to feel the music background of the rhythmic framework.

On October 18, 2005, a US satellite operator believed that immunological self-recognition should be the strong explosive immunological response the body of an animal made against the noxious neural stimulus elicited by the foreign antigen. However, he should generate comfort and suppress the immunological response while recognizing the healthy self-tissues to solve the problem of immunological self-recognition. In 2017, I published a paper reviewing, introducing and supporting this US satellite operator and his hypothesis.

On May 31, 2006, while watching television, I saw that JinTao Hu was visiting a kindergarten in Beijing to celebrate the International Children's Day. Many children said that they had already known the things outside while they were in the uteruses of their mothers, requiring no abortion. JinTao Hu expressed to propagate it and therefore played a major role in the promotion and propagation of the phenomenon. However, for the purpose of becoming a real science, it was necessary to resort to experimental data, while it was not sufficient to resort to the dictations of children as a resource for argument. It was possible that the fetus was very short during the awakening of a state, which required further investigation in future. On January 8, 2016, the Beijing people, concurring JinTao Hu, supported the mechanism of the satellite-mediated infrared topographic image in the water.

On September 16, 2006, the people and I considered the problem of adding rumors on television to the sciences. There must exist the concerned person, the persons around and the audience. Television did not spread rumors to the public masses until 1960. The adults who were at the age of 18 in 1960 are 64 years old nowadays and should still be alive. Therefore, so long as it had been broadcast on television and manifested the same contents as the achievements of physics I led the people to make this time, there should be somebody to stand out and point out, no matter whether they were the concerned persons, the persons around or the audience of television. I directed the satellites to shout: "Stand out earlier." On September 18, 2006, the satellite operator said that there were university journals, university newspapers and so on more single than the newspapers, and likewise easier for adding the rumors. The US sound from a satellite pointed out that it was easy to solve the problem of university journals, university newspapers and so on. The people in universities were capable of reading them thoroughly. As long as there was any important discovery, there should be somebody to stand out and point out, protecting the history of science. I directed the satellites to shout: "Read earlier stand."

Did my shouts with satellites belong to the single copy? Definitely not. There were so many public situations on television in various countries in the world manifesting my influences, and there were so many people responding to me; therefore, it was certain that the shouts should belong to the multiple copies.

On February 29, 2008, while considering the Four Color Theorem, I drew the pictures on my own, expecting to jump over the central four colors. The satellite operators and I concurrently found that mutual separation was the key to the problem of four colors. While having lunch, I considered that one of the two central colors should be encircled and separated from the other colors after detouring twice around them. A Beijing female sound from a satellite said that the detours were both the same in direction twice, while I corrected them as different in direction, immediately proving the Four Color Theorem. The Four Color Theorem was proven and solved altogether by me and the operators of satellites. I directed the satellites to shout in Chinese: "四色两次绕割断 (Four colors from two detours and separation)."

On January 12, 2009, the people and I recognized that it was necessary to check the previous and contemporary significant achievements in sciences with the method of standing out on television. The method of standing out on television for the history of sciences and technologies overcame the defect of significant achievements on sciences and technologies liable to be falsified and rumored after the gradual reduction of journals in library, protecting the reality of history on sciences and technologies, and therefore, possessing the historical significance.

The two brain theories I published during 1990-1991 were all highly concerned with the people in various countries on television and very important in significance, while both required more time to be proven for their correctness. With regard to the scientific progressions during the same period of time attracting the attention of the people on television, there was also the neuronal plasticity found by Kandel, Lømo, Bliss and so on, the genes responsible for the biological circadian rhythms found by Benzer and so on.

On January 23, 2009, I considered that it was problematic for Darwin alone to represent the evolution of life, so it was appropriate to add Lamarck. The latter had proved the theory of evolution earlier than Darwin, even though he had not found the correct reason for it. On November 1, 2014, the Chinese people pointed out that M. Kimura from Japan had additionally proved molecular neutral evolution, while Darwinian evolution was not comprehensive either; therefore, these three persons should share the achievements of evolution.

On February 5, 2009, while I was considering the influence of the rotation of the Earth on the left and right foot, a Beijing male sound from a satellite said that the right hand and foot could not exert big pressure on the heart during the movement with force, and therefore, possessed the right dominance of asymmetry. I directed the satellites to shout in Chinese: "心脏大脑不对称 (Heart and brain asymmetry)."

On May 16, 2009, the people and I recognized that there were at least tens of years for humans to fix my achievements in brain science according to the contents from television and academic society unless the autocrats rumored and damaged the journals. From now on, so long as there are journals making rumors of publishing the same theory as mine, I should use the law to take revenge against all humans and require them to compensate for my loss with the achievements of their famous scientists. I directed the satellites to shout in Chinese: "武圣脑理论人类固定 (Humans fix brain theories of San Force), Read yet no stand."

On August 30, 2009, while watching the video of Spring Festival Gala of 1988 again, I saw that a few audiences had strangely discussed the memory entropy and coupling theory. They had not possibly searched the literature through internet then because personal computers were not so popular then, and the commercial internet had not appeared even until 1995. Therefore, the performers and audiences on the spot were ignorant of the international journals then. They did not even know that depression could not be permanently reduced with total sleep deprivation in two phases; it was neither scientific at all nor capable of exceeding the Freudian theory. I made use of the ascending reticular systems to account for the abnormal phenomenon that depression could only be transiently ameliorated with total sleep deprivation and relapsed after a nap. Therefore, I successfully demonstrated that slow-wave sleep played a function in the regulation of emotions. In analogy, with regard to the coupling theory, without catching the newest work on JW and BC in 1988, it must be impossible for the performers and audiences to exclude the big influence of NA as the mediodorsal thalamic case, and therefore, it should certainly be impossible for them to achieve any progression. I directed the satellites to shout in Chinese: "电视脑科学少文献 (Brain science on television short of literature)."

On September 7, 2009, I watched on internet the video segments of a Football World Cup match in 1986, with the situation approximately as follows:

- They widely acknowledged the Freudian theory on sexual disinhibition during dreams, considering that the limbic system activity should be higher in rapid-eye movement (REM) sleep than in slow-wave sleep (SWS).
- They did not believe that the shouts in the game field on the function of slow wave sleep (SWS) could possess the effects of the flag on science because, without citations from literature, it should not be scientific.

I had to wait for the formal paper to appear in the journal; otherwise, it would not be considered science. On March 1, 2014, while watching television, I saw that the people in China and the USA pointed out that, even if the US satellite operators might require compensation for their unpublished ideas about sleep functions, they should require compensation with the papers in the journals of the Europe and USA, while irrelevant to my paper. In April of the same year, the people and I pointed out that it was not supported by law to require compensation for unpublished papers for being rejected by scientific journals because it was still possible to publish important theories by writing the books.

On October 8, 2009, I pointed out that if the book was published in China rumoring my brain sciences or armed police, while there was nothing worthy in China to compensate me, the other countries should help me to refute and correct the rumors; otherwise, they would get involved in the conspiracy, and be likewise required to compensate with their famous persons. I directed the satellites to shout in Chinese: "科学国际同谣赔 (International conspiracy compensates science rumor)."

On October 21, 2009, people in various countries, including me, recognized that our big discussions on physics were movement, huge in scale, with many international art and sports circumstances. Therefore, it was difficult to add rumours, and it became history directly. I directed the satellites to shout: "Physics movement."

On October 30 of the same year, I considered that if it added rumors that some ball games in the videos on television manifested earlier in discussions of the unification of physics than ours, it was capable of breaking down the rumors with the following two points:

- Our movement on the unification of physics was a global movement known to everybody.
- During our unification of physics, it was manifested from the ball games in various countries that there had not been the same movement before that time.

On November 11 of the same year, I directed the satellites to shout in Chinese: "物理统一运动人民新 (People new to the movement on the unification of physics)."

On November 13, 2009, the people and I found that, while changing the journal or book to make the rumors on science, it was possible that the authors added in the rumors might have opposite viewpoints in their later papers against the rumored paper. Therefore, it was capable of breaking down the rumors about science. I directed the satellites to shout:

"Post paper against." On October 22, 2010, the satellite operators and I found that it should be very easy to falsify and publish the collections of papers in meeting forms, almost threatening every significant achievement in sciences. Therefore, it was necessary to check the later investigations and papers of the relevant authors, breaking down the rumors of meetings. Besides, it was likewise another good method to trace with television.

On November 22, 2009, I considered that, for the Acta Psychologica Sinica to make the rumor, only if a physician from the People's Liberation Army (PLA) had written the sleep theory, then it would have been possible to overcome multiple social situations during that period such as escaping from the autocracy, going abroad for comparison and so on, funny and laughable. On November 24 of the same year, while watching television, I saw somebody in Peru saying that if a physician from the People's Liberation Army (PLA) had written a paper on sleep, it would have been different from my citation of the achievements on biological evolution; therefore, it was impossible to create the same theory as mine. I directed the satellites to shout: "PLA sleep clinic."

On December 23, 2009, I found that resorting to the side witness of the emperor was capable of breaking down the rumors on depreciation or distortion of the achievement of Lun Cai on the invention of paper. If there had been the technology of making papers on a large scale without reporting, the feudal government and people would have committed the crime of cheating the emperor.

On January 20, 2011, people in various countries, including me, found that internet exposed the addresses of almost all libraries, making them the targets of falsification and replacement of books and deducting the value of libraries in preserving the real sciences. Television was the safer and more reliable new method to manifest the history of sciences.

On March 15, 2011, I pointed out that internet would be the major form of reading books for readers in the future, while libraries would yield to internet to increase the influence and role of the sciences and technologies standing out on television.

On August 22, 2012, I pointed out that the Chinese and Asian satellite operators helped me to shout with the satellites of China and the United States. If the Europeans falsified my papers on brain science, it would not be acceptable to offset the rumors of Europeans with the achievements I made with the shouts of satellites.

On October 22, 2012, people in various countries, including me, pointed out that if the president falsified brain science, he had to compensate with the position of the president itself. The same situation was applicable to the king and prime minister. Compensation with the positions of leaders became my main method to prevent falsifications. I directed the satellites to shout in Chinese: "总统职务赔谣脑 (Position of president compensates falsification of brain)."

On December 8, 2013, while considering the fact that the future robots took after the dogs and dolphins and deducted the rapid eye movement sleep, I found that the increment in muscular efficiency might be one of the functions of rapid eye movement sleep. Besides, several days before, I found on internet that JuTao Chen and so on from University of Science and Technology of China had found that it was easy to induce

LTD in the state of slow wave sleep, favorable to the theory on the functions of slow wave sleep I had published.

Nowadays, there are many problems in the societies of sciences with themselves. The United States promoted the concept of citation quantity for scientific and technological papers without considering its violation of the principle of science that the early new discoveries were more in opposition but few in citations. Scientific pioneers, such as Copernicus, Galileo, etc., were abused by politics, but no one dared to cite and support them then and cite the papers published in small countries. Contemporarily, there were many successful black athletes, writers and singers in the United States, but there were only a few US black scientists who won the Nobel Prize.

The societies of sciences after 2000 were subjected to strong reactionary suppression from the royal families in Europe, Australia and Japan. Not only did they suppress the healthy forces in the United States, but they also induced the society of sciences in the United States to turn to racial hostility. In 1990 and 1991, I successfully published two theories on brain science in international journals with the chief editor located in the United States. However, in 2014, when I expected to publish a review article to support my published brain theories, I was all the way rejected. The 2014 Nobel Prize for Physiology and Medicine was awarded to the hippocampal place cells. During that time, it was already known to the public that the memory function of the hippocampus lay in recall, which was the conclusion from the more accurate psychological assessment. This Nobel Prize obviously misled and disoriented the direction of investigations in brain science. The academic atmosphere in Europe and the United States even resembled those in the era of the Soviet Union or Nazi Germany before.

In May 2015, I published the paper "A new function of rapid eye movement sleep: Improvement of muscular efficiency" (Physiology & Behavior 144:110-115, 2015), which I had submitted a year before so that the Royal Family of the Netherlands where Elsevier was located after all could escape from the shadow and relax.

On May 18, 2015, I uploaded both the English and Chinese versions of physics colloquia to the ResearchGate website, making them public and readable under my name as Zi-Jian Cai, available to people worldwide. On my webpage, I introduced myself in English as follows: "I, Zi-Jian Cai, a theorist on neuroscience, development and physics, herein present the theories and models only one on natural sciences only in English, including several on neurosciences and two on development. Besides, with global satellite/television networks, I held the global movement of physics for the electromagnetic unification of four forces from 2005 to 2009. As the organizer, I present the contents of physics. Please directly refer to television records for impartiality and reality." On December 15 of the same year, I registered on another website, "Mendeley," for academic exchange and introduced myself with the same content.

In June and July 2015, the journal "Open Access Library Journal," whose office was located in Wuhan, China, and whose founder and Editor-in-Chief, Huaibei Zhou, was a German by birth, published two of my papers entitled "Termination of organogenesis as an intrinsic constraint on animal development and evolution: A theory"（OALib Journal 2,e1646,2015）, and " Semantic Memory Association, Procedural Grammar Syntax and Episodic Modality Coordination as Three Interactive Neural Processes Organizing Language: A Model" (OALib Journal 2,e1718,2015).

The processes for writing these two papers were described in chapter one of this book. In the same year, the journal located in California but owned by India published my report on US satellites about reading the brain, entitled "Advocacy for extension of microwave and infrared to detect the brain activities" (Journal of Medical Diagnostic Methods 4,e188,2015).

In December 2015, citing the skin senescence I perceived earlier than the people, I believed that it should influence the slow wave sleep and then cause the senescent degeneration of the hypothalamic suprachiasmatic nucleus (SCN). In 2016, I published my paper entitled "A Hypothetic Aging Pathway from Skin to Hypothalamic Suprachiasmatic Nucleus via Slow Wave Sleep" (Sleep Science, 9, 212-215, 2016). On July 5 of that year, while watching television, I saw that the European people had analogously supported on their local time one day earlier the male senescent pathway from the adipose accumulation to the reduction of sperm to the degeneration of hypothalamic preoptic area (POA). In 2017, I published the paper "The Adipose Cause of Senescence of Male Hypothalamic Preoptic Nucleus: A European View" in "Research & Reviews: Neuroscience, 1(2), 21-26, 2017," reviewing, introducing and supporting the European people and their views.

On May 7, 2016, while watching television, I saw that one day before, on the local time of the United States, the NBA athletes had considered that the sympathetic nerves perceiving the noxious stimulus and then constricting the blood vessels might be the mechanism of pain sensation.

After the popularization of internet at the beginning of this century, the scientific achievements made by the people on television, represented by the unification of physics together with the satellites reading the brain, the investigations on ageing, heart-brain asymmetry and pain all stood out directly on television and became the outstanding examples of the new era. I spent two years not only writing the scientific achievements made by the people on television into the papers published in the Open Access journals owned by China and India but also further clarifying the contributors of these achievements.

On May 30, 2016, the European people and I pointed out that British and US scientists should not be specially respected anymore because their history of sciences was full of cowards and villains, different from that of Europe.

On December 29, 2016, people in various countries reprimanded the most influential British and US scientific and technological journals, Nature and Science, respectively, for being analogous to cow dung. On February 10, 2017, I pointed out that the journals - Nature and Science, strictly restricted the number of words in the paper and the number of cited references, which certainly affected the quality of their papers. On September 2 of that year, I directed the satellites to shout in Chinese: "欧美杂志，失败降级 (European and US journals, Failure and downgrade)." On methodology, most European and US journals on life sciences required meta-analysis, while most high-energy journals on physics required the standard model, violating the scientific principle of concrete analysis of individual cases, making it impossible for them to avoid mistakes and failures. On December 24, 2017, the Chinese people pointed out that there should be no royal family for intelligent robots, so the royal families of Great Britain and Western Europe would suppress them and certainly hamper the British journals on sciences and technologies.

The international Open Access journals on sciences and technologies owned by India, China and the United States, using the mode of convenient submission and Open Access, began challenging the operational mode of international journals on sciences and technologies headed by Great Britain, using the mode of rejecting the majority of papers for promoting the quality. Those in the Middle East and Brazil gradually followed thereafter. To analogize the British and US journals to the system of examination full of frauds, the commercial Open Access journals were the modern successful parliamentary system full of debates, especially suitable for social sciences and television videos. On January 1, 2017, the Chinese people said that the US abstracting organizations refused to abstract the papers of US Omics Group, owned by India, having published such important papers as the electromagnetic structures of various particles in physics, the adipose cause of hypothalamic sexual ageing, the satellite reading the brain and so on while abstracting many papers from the United Kingdom so that they should be ashamed. Therefore, the numerous small abstracting organizations in China on sciences and technologies might possibly exceed those in the United States and become abstracting organizations of better service in the future. Those in Brazil were analogous to those in China. On January 12 of the same year, the Chinese people shouted with confidence: "The wonderful children wrote papers, While GuangDong abstracted them."

The revolution of science and technology originated from the heliocentric theory of Copernicus. By bravely confronting the storms, facing death, and breaking through various obstacles with the help of numerous ancestors such as Galileo, Newton, Mendeleev, Darwin, Freud, Planck and so on, they finally overcame the abuses of the religions and changed the civilization of the whole world. After entering 2000 AD, a part of the experimental scientists and the editorial members of academic journals constituting the bricks and stones of the scientific giant modestly called by Newton were instead selfish and covetous, obsequious and flattering, while a few of them were even corruptive and unethical, assisting the monster and abusing, bullying the small countries with the big ones, and forming the small society of flattery and abuse. During the decades after 2000, the reactionary abuse from the kings in Europe and the racial hostility of the United States were comprehensively manifested in the societies of sciences, notorious and flagrant, while they concurrently began facing the counter-striking from the journals of China, India and Brazil. The sciences and technologies standing out on television should be more reliable and successful, making the history of sciences and technologies more brilliant and magnificent and gorgeous and beautiful.

End poem of the illustrated chapter:

The scientific and technological achievements with significance staged on television,
The contained historical significance subjected to the global evaluation,
The British and US journals reprimanded on the television,
The Open Access journals accepted as history for continuation.

Chapter | 12

Democracy Calling for Law Execution,

Skills and Practices

Musical Background of Rhythmic Writing: The Theme Song "The Blood of Steel and Heart of Faith" in "The Legend of the Condor Heroes"

Please read the following text sentence-by-sentence to feel the music background of the rhythmic framework.

In April 2006, in Nepal, a neighboring country of China, the autocratic king Gyanendra announced on television that he would surrender to the demonstrating and rioting people and consented to recover the Nepalese congress and democratic system. Since I had started the movement of democracy calling for law execution in China, it was the earliest democratic victory abroad with the assistance of violence. In 2008, by democratic and legal methods, the Nepalese changed the monarchy system into a republic system.

On June 15, 2006, the PLA (People's Liberation Army) operators of satellites disturbed my satellite shouts. I accounted that if I shouted no longer, the politics in China would bring a change on television dramatically, which, by comparison, would make it easier for the people to understand my direction and leadership on the democracy calling for law execution and on the theory of armed police.

After June 17, I no longer directly utilized the satellites to shout the domestic political contents of China. I used them only to shout for law issues such as catching the satellites, assigning the satellites to me, the security of mine and so on, and additionally the international political contents. Nonetheless, in the later practice, since it was necessary to respond quickly on politics, it was not only impractical to follow this self-constraint, but also quite harmful to both myself and the people. Hence, since April 2007, I have never adopted this self-constraint whilst again utilizing the satellites to shout for the political contents of China.

On June 30, 2006, the operators of satellites said the praises to, and glories of gods might depreciate and threaten the kings and dictators. The next morning, I felt that, as the San Force, I should represent the glory of people. I found that democratic and advanced people possessed glories. I directed the satellites to shout in Chinese: "吴民光辉武圣人 (The Wu people glory by San Force)." In the evening on television, I saw some Germans said for people, whilst undetermined on time.

It had been present for long for the force of people's glory. In the time of Reagan, the US democracy won over the USSR autocracy by the Cold War. It was just the victory the democratic system had by the people's glory, and it was another important example of human democracy achieving victory! While promoting democracy and calling for law execution in China, I also often adopted social success and people's glory as the force for award and punishment. Prior to 2006, the concept of people's glory had not been formulated; hence, I adopted social success at that time.

On July 5, 2006, the Central Commission for Discipline Inspection organized many staff to investigate the problem of Shanghai Administration of Labor and Social Security regarding the irregular operation of the social funds for insurance, targeting LiangYu Chen, the secretary of Municipal Committee of Party of Shanghai, who, in 2004, had admired me for uniting with YanAn on democracy. Shortly, they made the case of LiangYu Chen, referring to some mistakes made by his subordinates. Prior to LiangYu Chen, KuangDi Xu, the mayor of Shanghai, had also been relocated to Beijing by the Central Committee of Party since he had sympathized and consented to my democratic internationalization. On August 24, 2015, I found that LiangYu Chen managed to rebuild his historical reputation by joining Christianity.

On August 7, 2006, on television, I saw that the Chinese people were hopeful to erect a monument for the June 4th event. On the following morning, on the way to the office, I was shy of possibly delaying the rehabilitation of the June 4th event. Hence, I felt I should devote my effort to the democracy of China once more.

On September 7, 2006, the operators of satellites reminded me that if I shouted against communists, I might be arrested. I was alerted, whilst constrained within certain domestic regions, to struggle against the communists; hence, I would not be accounted as against the communist party in the whole country. On April 17, 2008, I decided solely nine provinces and two cities unnecessary to follow the communists in the whole country, and appointed them as GuangDong, GuangXi, HuNan, SiChuan, AnHui, ZheJiang, JiangSu, HeNan, ShanDong, Beijing and ChongQing. I directed the satellites to shout in Chinese: "九省二市不必共 (Nine provinces and two cities unnecessary to follow communists)." On April 10, 2009, after the modification several times, I chose GuangDong, FuJian, HuNan, HuBei, JiangSu, AnHui, SiChuan, Henan, JiLin, Beijing and ChongQing.

Several years later, the people in old liberated areas, such as YanAn, were willing to consent and merge with the people peacefully, whilst the republic characteristic of China was democratic anyhow; hence, the people in the old liberated areas often stayed with me and the people on television.

From October 15 to 21, 2007, the 17th Congress of Communist Party of China was held. Among the persons of promotion, there were JinPing Xi and YuanChao Li. They might appear at the highest level of the Communist Party of China after 5 years, especially when Jinping Xi would take over as the general secretary. He was pig-like in body and greedy for affluence, whilst bear-like in brain and tyrannical in bureaucrat.

On November 6, 2007, I hoped to promote the law execution and strike against the provincial committees turning to Beijing. Meanwhile, the operators of satellites suggested that, in that way, the provincial committees might turn more to Beijing; hence, it was feasible to pass laws to execute both provincial and municipal leaders. I directed the satellites to shout in Chinese: "省市北京法执揪 (Law execution targets provincial and municipal leaders turning to Beijing)." On television, I saw that the Chinese people were also thinking of law to execute both the provincial and municipal leaders, whilst undetermined on time.

On March 15, 2008, on television, I saw that Dalai

instigated the Lamas in Tibet to make disturbances for independence. I saw that they adopted the method of arson to increase an influence whilst deducting violent damage, having progressed somewhat.

On May 21, 2008, the Chinese people and I pointed out that, without the efficient governmental rescue, the SiChuan earthquake might resemble the atomic bomb dropped on Hiroshima; hence, we encouraged them to win over the atomic weapons, whilst thought to sarin. I directed the satellites to shout in Chinese: "四川核战有沙林 (SiChuan nuclear war by sarin)." The local People's Liberation Army of SiChuan shouted for ZeDong Mao, but did not rescue actively, whilst the physicians in Beijing and SiChuan followed and shouted to threaten the victims, shouting the hospitals into the slaughtering houses, irritating to make the hairs erect.

On June 16, 2008, the Chinese people and I found that competitive election for a general secretary might break down the bad habit of committing fraud in the elections in China. I chose the nearby NanJing of JiangSu to run for the general secretary, reinforcing Beijing and GuangDong shortly. I directed the satellites to shout in Chinese: "南京竞选总书记 (NanJing runs for general secretary)."

It was solely through competitive elections that democracy could overcome the objective defect. In competitive elections, the voters were courteous and polite while electing a single candidate. Competitive elections let the people choose the appropriate representatives and leaders, realizing scientific and real democracy.

On July 1, 2008, I found that democratic parties and religions in autocratic countries should start by parade, and if suppressed, they might start law execution and win over autocracy. It was one of the major methods to strive for democracy and for parties and religions to march and then execute the law. On the next day, I directed the satellites to shout in Chinese: "党教游行再法执 (Parties and religions, March and then law-execute)."

On December 27, 2008, for the sake of striking against the autocracy of Central Committee, I adopted the method of criticism against autocracy by materialism and development. I directed the satellites to shout in Chinese: "唯物发展批独裁 (Materialism and development, criticizing the autocracy)." In the evening news on television, I saw that, in the meeting, many Beijing bureaucrats had already thought about materialism and development to criticize autocracy earlier than I did.

On February 11, 2009, I improved the monotonous method of law execution against one provincial secretary of GuangDong previously; otherwise, the opponents might transfer and prevaricate. I requested the GuangDong people to law-execute the three highest leaders of the Provincial Committee simultaneously by the persecuting force of local people onto their family after retirement. I directed the satellites to shout in Chinese: "广东领导揪前三 (GuangDong leaders targeted the highest three)." This method was rather effective. Shortly, HuaHua Huang, the governor of GuangDong province, expressed his consent to my political advocacy of democracy, upholding the competitive election of the general secretary.

On April 6, 2009, I pointed out that, during the democracy calling for law execution I led in China, I allowed the correct opinions from the people on television to play their roles, promoting the roles of democracy and award. In contrast, in the aspects of organizing forces, encouraging friends, punishing enemies, and stabilizing direction, I played the key role of leadership in the democracy calling for law execution in China. Otherwise, the television and media, led by the autocracy, might easily destroy and crash down the sporadic shouts for democracy from people. In addition, I adopted the force of people's glory from regional success for award and punishment, leading the domestic and international situations to develop toward the directions fortunate to my security, business and scientific research. I also adopted the method of revenge by law to protect the bureaucrats in Party and government cooperating with me, manifesting the strength and effectiveness in forces I organized.

In the early and middle of May 2009, the people and I reinforced the force of Muslim internationalization in the XinJiang Autonomous Region. For the sake of avoiding the illegal revolution of Muslims, I adopted the instruction of mild construction. In 2014, the people and I changed our support of northern XinJiang to the investment of southern XinJiang; hence, the Muslims in XinJiang became more active.

On May 23, 2009, the Chinese people and I pointed out that if Beijing people threatened the enterprises and areas by seclusion and isolation of the country, we might oppress them by methods similar to that of the event in Chicago, calling them non-humans or even anti-humans.

On July 30, 2009, on the news on television, I saw that the soldiers of the People's Liberation Army were unsatisfied with the news that they tyrannized and messed up the country. Hence, they upheld the foreign companies and shouted for humans. I directed the satellites to shout in Chinese: "解放军喊人类转 UN(联合国) (Liberation Army shouting for humans to UN)," "军队喊人类圣支持 (San upholds army shouting for humans)."

On November 1, 2009, I made propaganda that Northern JiangSu should be higher than Shandong. Hence, the people in Northern JiangSu, watching south from north, should turn over their direction while watching north from south.

On December 9, 2009, I complained that the democratic force in GuangDong was not strong enough to affect the Central Committee of Party. At that time, most male singers in Hong Kong did not uphold the democratic movement. However, a few female singers upheld it, but they were weaker in strength than the cross-country vocal concert "The Same Song," directed by Xin Meng. In this regard, I further targeted my spearhead to Yang Wang, the provincial secretary of GuangDong then, hoping to shout him to become the candidate for general secretary while competing with the Central Committee of Party directly! I directed the satellites to shout in Chinese: "天才总书记广喊汪 (Ingenious general secretary GuangDong shouts Wang)." On December 15 of that year, on television, I saw Yang Wang saying that he might learn the open-mindedness of ZiYang Zhao, turning to the democratic side. The change in both LiangYu Chen and Yang Wang mostly resulted from my personal influence. In the later years, by the protection of the two highest leaders in Provincial Committee, Yang Wang and Hua Hua Huang, the GuangDong people actively constructed a model province of communists. The GuangDong people and I accomplished the democracy calling for law execution in GuangDong province in the early stage.

In January 2010, the people and I pointed out that the vocal concert "The Same Song," directed by Xin Meng, was stopped by the bureaucrats of China Central Television (CCTV). "The Same Song" vocal concert timely followed the new era of democracy calling for law execution and increased the confidence of Chinese people to take care of politics and participate in democracy; it was the favorite of the people. The people and I decided to choose half excellent Spring Festival Galas in the time of JinTao Hu, and compensate for Xin Meng by law! On September 27 of that year, on the evening news, I saw JinPing Xi saying that it was his office that informed to stop "The Same Song" of Xin Meng. I requested LiYuan Peng, a singer and then wife of JinPing Xi, to also compensate Xin Meng with half of her achievements and performances by law. Additionally, "Happy Travel in China," hosted by my relative Qing Dong, also replaced the role of democratic discussion of "The Same Song" gradually.

On January 9, 2010, the Chinese people and I upheld the Muslims and Christians for their taking over the role of Vice Chairman of the People' s Congress while strengthening the forces of democracy. I directed the satellites to shout in Chinese: "副委员长穆基督 (Vice Chairmen of Congress, Muslim and Christian)." On television, the Muslim leaders from XinJiang often expressed their intentions of upholding the democracy and republics.

Prior to 2010, I had been living outside my company on account of safety. However, after the Spring Festival on

February 13, 2010, I was not able to pay the rent anymore and had to move back home to live with my father.

On April 2, 2010, the JiangSu operator of satellite said that the old liberated area in northern JiangSu had been the New Fourth Army, upholding the international communists rather than the Central Committee. I was rather delighted, since this meant the democracy calling for law execution won over and occupied the northern JiangSu. I directed the satellites to shout and propagate! Shortly, I watched on internet the "Charming in JingJiang" in "Happy Travel in China," performed on February 21, 2010. I saw the audiences in northern JiangSu shouting for the New Fourth Army loudly earlier than we did. After that, many municipal governors and officers in northern JiangSu began taking advantage of the New Fourth Army. After the competitive election on the basic level in November 2011, the GuangXi Autonomous Region started becoming more international. These were all the various methods the local provinces and regions adopted to resist the autocracy of Central Committee.

From August to September 2010, I took advantage of the special experience of my father, who had run for the plant manager previously, while being one of the earliest communists participating in the competitive election, on the initial stage of socialism and under the leadership of the Communist Party. I started the movement of "Marx-MingXun calling for competitive election." On the theoretical account, it suggested that, at the initial stage of socialism, it should be the duty of the communist party to promote the competitive election while overcoming the fraudulence of democracy and, hence, accomplishing the democratic rectification of the flag and discipline of the communist parties.

Under the influence and protection of the slogan "Marx-MingXun calling for competitive election" in 2011, while taking advantage of direct election in districts and counties on the basic level, I led the construction of democratic culture in China.

Democracy calling for law execution aimed at the democratic election rather than the change of government. By acquiring the new party discipline "Marx-MingXun calling for competitive election," the democracy calling for law execution I directed in China evolved to promote the culture of competitive election, instigate the democratic parties and religions to compete for election, improve the Chinese army, raise the status of the People's Congress, and facilitate the direct election of the provincial and municipal congress.

On January 25, 2011, a large-scale demonstration striving for democracy broke out in Egypt. In February of that year, Egyptian President Mubarak resigned, and the army took over the country and organized the general election. In 2012, Mohamed Morsi, the leader of the opposition, was elected the president. On July 4, 2013, I learned from internet that the Egyptian army even deposed the elected president, Morsi and disbanded the congress unexpectedly, declaring to hold the presidential election in advance. On May 30, 2014, I learned from internet that the military leader Sisi, who had illegally deposed the elected president, Morsi, retired and participated in the election. He eventually won the election and became the president of Egypt, expressing the political trend of the Egyptian people to choose the democratic revolution rather than the democracy calling for law execution.

On June 4, 2011, I learned from internet that the president of Yemen had recently suppressed the democratic demonstration. Therefore, on June 3, the presidential office was bombarded by the opposite artillery fire, and president Ali Abdullah Saleh was severely hurt and sent to the hospital. The next day, I learned from internet that vice-president Abd-Rabbu Mansour Hadi had temporarily taken over the role of the president. Shortly afterwards, Abd-Rabbu Mansour Hadi organized the election and was elected the president in February 2012 by the people. Unfortunately, in the later years, Yemen kept falling into the turmoil of war. In December 2017, the former autocratic president, Saleh of Yemen, was killed in war.

In February 2012, the passing of new constitutional laws in Syria, the Middle East, achieved the most fundamental democracy, changing the single-party system into a multi-party system. It restricted the presidential term to 7 years, allowing them to stay in power for two terms solely. In May of that year, according to the new constitutional laws, the new People's Congress came to power in Syria. In the whole year of 2012, the opposite forces in Syria warred for revolution continually, filling the media fully. Hence, quite a few knew that new constitutional laws had been passed in Syria. On October 31, I learned from internet, the new constitutional laws of Syria, and hence utilized the satellite energy to propagate it to the whole world. In September 2013, the Syrian government responded to the advocacy of Russia and consented to sign the "Chemical Weapons Convention," winning more recognition from the world people then. In 2014, the war of armed independence broke out in northern

Iraq. In October 2015, Russia interfered with Syria militarily and partially ameliorated the revolutionary pressure in Syria, fortunate to the democracy calling for law execution. After the propagation of democracy calling for law execution in the whole world, the victory of democracy was achieved in the Middle East. The skill of democracy calling for law execution propagated widely and penetrated the hearts of the people.

On July 17, 2012, I pointed out that, in 2011, in Libya, the Middle East, when the opposite forces, with military support from Europe, overthrew Gaddafi, who accepted the legal route map of democracy, it was the replacement of democracy calling for law execution by the democratic revolution. The Egyptian people also made their choice to the democratic revolution, whereas, Nepal in Asia and Syria in the Middle East both won the election by legal route map, which belonged to the democracy calling for law execution. In many small countries in Asia and the Middle East, the practices demonstrated that the legal route map for election was one of the important symbols to distinguish the democracy calling for law execution and the democratic revolution. "Marx-MingXun calling for competitive election," the new and legal discipline of Party, was one of the legal route maps of the democracy calling for law execution in China, and later it was added further by the "Provincial and municipal legislation to republics."

On August 24, 2012, the people and I pointed out that both strike and revolution were opposite against police, eliciting strong suppression from the police. They were also destructive in culture, and the various revolutionary branches might war with each other, further deducting the quantity of weapons. Hence, the theory of armed police relied on the democracy calling for law execution rather than the revolution. I directed the satellites to shout in Chinese: "革命破坏警不用 (Revolution destruction police no)."

It was necessary to point out that it was easy to achieve the victory of law execution in a portion of provinces and cities. Hence, the armed police were not only stronger but also more democratic than the army, which was the theoretical basis of the armed police. It was unnecessary for the democracy calling for law execution to win the victory comprehensively and for the people to win the army and police completely! The earliest local success of the democracy calling for law execution was the shift of KuangDi Xu and LaingYu Chen to democracy in Shanghai, and later, the two western autonomous regions – XinJiang and Tibet, the southern GuangDong province and GuangXi Autonomous Region, and the eastern JiangSu province were all the more supplements. In these respects, the democracy calling for law execution I directed early in China was exactly the theoretical foundation of armed police. The democracy calling for law execution was established later in Nepal and Syria and was further influenced by China and me.

It was additionally necessary to point out that, during the stable period of the country, the democracy calling for law execution upheld the construction of armed police. National independence might also call for the armed police, while after independence, the armed police should require the democracy calling for law execution to supply the guarantee for democracy! In this regard, the democracy calling for law execution was the theoretical foundation of armed police. In the War of Independence of the United States, the armed forces were the militia of the people.

On September 9, 2012, people in various countries suggested that leading the democracy calling for law execution without me in GuangDong, the influences from sports games and art performances on television, along with the satellite beams, might elicit a revolution of people spontaneously. Nonetheless, the force of GuangDong to promote the democracy of China was not enough. At that time, the most active public situation of democracy was the vocal concert "The Same Song," directed by Xin Meng of China Central Television (CCTV), while most male stars from Hong Kong nonetheless upheld the autocratic Central Committee. This was the reason why I continued to target Yang Wang after HuaHua Huang had supported the idea of upholding the democracy.

On November 24, 2012, the HeBei satellite operator said that it was not appropriate for me, the subspecies of large-scale revenge, to lead the democracy calling for law execution, while I had always thought that I had a good chance to lead the democracy calling for law execution. The autocracy of party and religion possessed enough power to easily murder the leader of democracy. The democracy calling for law execution mostly utilized the fists of people, whilst the autocratic party or religion was the side of assassination. I possessed the huge force of revenge by law, targeting the domestic and foreign relatives of autocrats and their subordinates and hometowns. Hence, whatever the military and terrible forces of autocratic party or religion were, they were unable to shake my stable leadership on the people. This was exactly what the party or religion of justice dreamed of possessing for the democracy calling for law execution whilst also happening to comply with the principle of double revenge from democracy. My leadership played the role of organizing force, encouraging friends, punishing enemies, stabilizing direction, and so on. I directed the satellites to shout in Chinese: "民主法执，巨能领导 (Democratic-law execution, Huge energy to lead)." In September 2014, people in various countries pointed out that it was the characteristic of democracy calling for law execution to colonize and hurt the race, while I had already lost the status of the leader of humans for this reason.

On December 6, 2012, I accounted for the military coup in Peru in 1975, overthrowing the autocracy and reviving the democratic system. The people and I thought that, at that time, the phrase of democratic revolution was the only thing present in the world, whilst the covert operation had not been able to demonstrate the practice of democracy calling for law execution. The English Revolution and French Revolution had happened even earlier. In the democracy calling for law execution in Syria in the Middle East recently, it was the armed forces beyond the capital that broke out an uprising, whilst the army nearby the capital was monitored closely by the police and information department, unable to make any coup. The peripheral regions of the capital of Nepal also used to be the revolutionary regime of the Communist Party of Maoism originally. The democracy calling for law execution I led in China had happened even earlier, and I experienced the process from peripheral provinces to the capital. The armed police were incompetent to the army to make any coup in the capital!

On December 19, 2012, for the sake of the recent malice from the Organization Department of Central Committee, not to promote the leaders who had made positive contributions to the development of such old liberated areas as New Fourth Army and GuangXi, I thought to award them by the people to demonstrate the advantage of democracy. On the next day, I directed the satellites to shout in Chinese: "马飚赵鹏，老区喊升 (Biao Ma and Peng Zhao, Old liberated areas shout for promotion)." Later, both Biao Ma and Peng Zhao were promoted.

In the latter half of the year 2012, the people and I began to make use of "Marx-MingXun calling for competitive election," the new discipline of the communist party, to prompt the congress to debate democratically and to release the direct election of provincial and municipal congress, whilst skipping over the dangerous general secretary. On April 11, 2013, the people and I emphasized the national congress for surveillance and dominance over the government, further deducting the influence of individuals, such as the general secretary, prime minister, and so on, on the country. On November 29 of that year, the Chinese people and I deeply hated the bullying and tyrannous styles of most high leaders in China at that time. Hence, we objected to the direct election of the national chairman and the president of the United States, making it difficult for the communist party to participate in political, competitive elections. I also temporarily gave up the request for competitive election of the general secretary.

On March 28, 2013, people in various countries, including

me, pointed out that, after the success in law execution of provinces and cities, if still subjected to the suppression of national autocracy, declaration of independence should be legal within the range of democracy calling for law execution. A US satellite operator said that before achieving independence, the United States of America had already been a colony of England, which is a constitutional monarchy, and had already been democratic in all states; hence, it was a regional independence. On April 11 of that year, I noticed that both the English and French Revolutions targeted the autocracy of kings and, hence, might belong to the democracy calling for law execution. Both of them adopted the slogan of revolution aimed at destroying the old and autocratic system without the restriction of law in range. In contrast, the democracy calling for law execution adopted the law as a slogan to achieve legal democracy and might even break the recalcitrant illegal country of autocracy, whilst it was necessary to refer to law and democracy as its constraint for practice.

On April 17, 2013, I learnt from the news on television that the FBI of the United States said that the satellites were helpless in breaking the case of the Boston explosion recently, whilst the street videos were more useful. In 2016, I watched on television Latin drug dealers utilizing sound transformers to speak. Hence, it was more difficult for satellites to trace them. Dumb sign language was similar to this while reading words by satellites was like monitoring handphones. It was powerful for detecting information to deal with the leaders of big parties, but it was impossible to monitor and control when individuals were assassinated actively by dumb sign language.

Hence, the parties and religions had the absolute advantage in force over the personal autocracy by assassination and revolution. On February 26, 2017, the Chinese athletes, for strengthening assassination, further discovered more methods, such as using handphone under detection to make rumors with wrong information, separating the poor mountainous areas by parties and religions by guerrillas and tunnels, using powerful strength to kill by gasoline bombs and toxic gases, and so on. On May 19 of that year, I learnt from the news I watched on television that the people in various countries recognized that it was also the typical model advocated by Gaddafi to overthrow the autocracy of the monarchy through the military revolution by officers.

On August 10, 2013, I learned from internet that for the conflict of the Campaign Defending the Constitution initiated by Yat-Sen Sun, the focus was the struggle of the republic congress, led by Yat-Sen Sun, against the new country and senate under construction by "Renewing the Republic" of QiRui Duan and QiChao Liang. In contents, the defence of the constitution meant the defence of the Provisional Constitution of the Republic of China, broad in contents, including personal freedom, safety, business, tax, budget, division of might between government and Congress, and so on. In contrast, the democratic election had to wait for the new congress under construction to specially legislate. In this regard, the campaign did not defend the law of democracy. The law from agreement might be not only for democracy but also for autocracy of party or religion. The will of Yat-Sen Sun was full of the slogan "Revolution not yet successful, Comrades still strive," while the aim of his life was to lead the revolution of the Nationalist Party and establish the Republic of China. According to "The Outline of the Founding of the Republic of China," advocated by Yat-Sen Sun, he classified the constitution of the country into three periods: the military government, political tutelage and constitutional government. Later, JingWei Wang and JieShi Jiang separately represented two different governments of the Republic of China, autocratic over the country by party and opposite with each other by war, by no means to mention democracy. The achievements of the Nationalist Party lay in their winning over the law from the king by the law from agreement.

More importantly, in the time of Yat-Sen Sun and E Cai, there was no such phrase as the democracy calling for law execution that I created first; hence, it was certainly impossible to demonstrate the practice of democracy calling for law execution, whilst the provincial and municipal armed police happened to require the constraint from the armless people by the democracy calling for law execution. Solely by the democratic revolution or the campaign defending the constitution, in my era, it would have been impossible for the advanced provinces and cities to uphold the democracy led by LiangYu Chen, HuaHua Huang, Yang Wang, the Muslims in Xinjiang and the New Fourth Army in Northern Jiangsu. The democracy calling for law execution was able to safely promote the political progression of democracy. In addition, in the time of Yat-Sen Sun and E Cai, there were no heavy weapons, such as tanks, and hence, the people's militia might be the main force for war, certainly impossible to establish the theory of armed police, whilst turning to adopt the People's

War of ZeDong Mao, the Peasant Army of Mexico, etc.

On December 20, 2013, with the new direction of communist parties "Marx-MingXun calling for competitive election," I associated the folksy 38th Army of Beijing Military Region with the JiNan Military Region confined by the kind culture of Confucius and utilized the people's army to occupy and protect the capital Beijing. On March 14, 2014, I encouraged the People's Liberation Army (PLA) to shout for the republics of the country and urge the Central Committee to lead collectively. I directed the satellites to shout in Chinese: "共和集体解放军 (Republic and collective PLA)."

On October 19, 2014, people in various countries were unsatisfied with the repetitive restoration of kings after the French Revolution and were not afraid of decapitation from assassination and war at all. They shouted that the coup in Brazil to overthrow the king really represented one San Force, overthrowing the king and realizing the collectivity at a high level! Lenin and Gaddafi both adopted such methods to overthrow the king. Zedong Mao, while commenting on "Water Margin" prior to his death, had literally propagated that rebellion should target the king and hence should also be eligible to be accounted for sharing this laureate, increasing the mountainous guerrillas and spontaneous assassinations beyond control.

On February 6, 2015, I pointed out that, no matter whether some of the defects of LiangYu Chen might be rehabilitated, LiangYu Chen was one of the earliest municipal leaders upholding the democracy calling for law execution, and was definitely glorious. The party membership of GuanZheng Wu, the secretary of Discipline Inspection

Commission in the period of JinTao Hu, should be compensated to LiangYu Chen definitely. On August 24 of that year, I suggested LiangYu Chen to rebuild his historical reputation by joining the Christianity. On October 17 of that year, I adopted the same method to rebuild the reputation of BenShun Zhou, the secretary of the Committee of HeBei Province, who was enthusiastic about democracy.

On September 7, 2015, the Chinese people and I started the movement of "Republics down the Central Committee." The people allied to the active and healthy regions, such as Eastern China, two Guangs, Northwestern China, and so on, resisting the Central Committee. The force of democracy in China became stronger quickly. The Central Committee must be replaced in the future by a representative meeting elected by democracy.

On the Spring Festival in February 2016, the military reformation was initiated in China by the Military Commission of the Central Committee headed by JinPing Xi, wrongly classifying ShanDong, the inhabitant place of Confucius, to the Northern War Zone located in Northeastern China, making all the public nationwide angry! Till the end of July 2017, on the military parade, both JinPing Xi and the People's Liberation Army confessed that the ethnic characteristic of the Chinese army was the people's army.

China was essentially the autocracy of party and army previously. However, "Marx-MingXun calling for competitive election" and the People's Liberation Army (PLA) of China respecting communists, permitting republics and upholding humans all helped the democracy calling for law execution successfully remove the main force of autocracy in China. The new discipline of the communist party requiring democracy and the national law of republics to depress the Central Committee both replaced the democracy calling for law execution in China.

In the meantime, the people and I established some offensive technologies of democracy calling for law execution, such as the decapitation of autocracy, demonstration of party or religion, law execution of provincial and municipal leaders, and so on. They would play important roles in the society of civilization in the future. From outside army first and then to inside subsequently, from peripheral regions first and then to the capital subsequently, the law execution was especially successful in the autocratic country, which was led by the party or religion by the army and police. The movement of democracy calling for law execution that I started and led in China affected the people in various countries in the world, and countries like Nepal, Syria, and so on followed it one after another. The democracy calling for law execution often resorted to the fists of people, whilst the autocratic party or religion shouted more for bombardment and assassination. Fearing that my race might take revenge for my death, the autocrats of party or religion dared not murder me at ease. In this respect, the humans overcame and rectified the military autocracy of party and religion from the communist parties and Muslims, realizing the colossal achievements of democracy.

For the sake of dealing with the autocracy of the king or family, the democratic revolution and the assassination by a party or religion should be easier and more effective. For three generations, the long-term war made little achievement, whilst, in eight thousand kilometres, the songs of martyrs awakened all. For the sake of dealing with the autocracy of party or religion, it was necessary to adopt the democracy calling for law execution.

End poem of the chapter:

XinJiang, GuangDong and the New Fourth Army,
The provincial and municipal execution by law supporting the new police army,
The republic revolution throwing away the king royally,
The respect of law for the democratic execution lawfully.

Chapter | 13

The Committee of Army and Police, Period of National Succession

Musical Background of Rhythmic Writing: The Theme Song "The Blood of Steel and Heart of Faith" in "The Legend of the Condor Heroes"

Please read the following text sentence-by-sentence to feel the music background of the rhythmic framework.

On March 5, 2009, I watched on television the formally held session of the National People's Congress. In regard to the analysis of me and the people at that time, it was the best time for me to shout the slogan for the People's Congress to nominate the political commissar of the army. I directed the satellites to shout in Chinese: "军队政委人大派 (The People's Congress to nominate the political commissar of army)." Actually, the vice chairmen of the Chinese army were all nominated by the People's Congress, whilst it was already further requested for both the commanding officer and political commissar to execute the military command. Nonetheless, it was their critical defect to be short of dual commands from both the Chairman and the People's Congress. The army of the United States had implemented the dual commands from the president and Congress early, short of the dual general officer and political commissar, to guarantee the execution of the dual commands.

On June 19, 2009, on internet, I watched the cinema of the United States in 1934 "The Merry Widow." Its story revolved around a widow who possessed a huge land and the king and his army, who were greedy on that huge land. I accounted that heavy weapons such as tanks and airplanes had not yet participated in the war at that time; hence, to win the war then, it was feasible to organize the militia to war, whilst impossible to affect our theory of armed police.

On June 30, 2009, the Chinese people and I pointed out that, whilst carrying out the war for defence, it was necessary for the armed police to resort to law to counterattack the invasion autonomously. In this regard, it was necessary for the country to legislate the law for war, which was quite high in efficiency, whilst different from the present situation, which necessarily waited for war till the congress declared war against the invading country. I directed the satellites to shout in Chinese: "国家制订战争法 (Country legislates the law for war)."

On July 31, 2009, the satellite operators and I recognized that it was just different in the situation of my shouting eunuchs to suppress the army in 2001 from the Chinese army shouting for humans presently. We pointed out that it actually demonstrated the progression of the era, whilst it was the social effect of the model of armed police and demo decision generating or the social application of the theory of armed police. I directed the satellites to shout in Chinese: "警察武装应用军人类 (Army to humans, Application of armed police)." In August of that year, while watching on internet the art performance of "The Same Song" held in July that year, I saw that the singers and audiences shouting the theory of armed police had already been utilized for application earlier on time.

On August 22, 2009, before falling asleep, I learned from internet that BingKun Xiong had already initiated the shoot of WuChang Uprising for the Revolution of 1911. JiMin Cai contributed the most to the victory of conquering WuHan; he had successfully transformed the mutiny of a few army, without organization and leadership, into the significant revolutionary uprising, comparable to the later military achievement of E Cai.

On September 24, 2009, while watching the performance "Charming ZhaoYuan" in "Happy Travel in China" on September 20 of that year, I saw that the singers and audiences found that the coup of the army and the police to overthrow the corruptive government should adopt the slogan "The committee of army and police republics." Hence, it was easy for people to compare it to that in the era of E Cai. I directed the satellites to shout in Chinese: "军警委员会共和制 (The committee of army and police republics)."

"The committee of army and police republics" set up the objective social foundation for the committee of the army and the police to disband the democratic congress and change the country. The army, police and people might make comparisons and choices easily and lightly. It was the mechanism for the succession and transition of the national system of the armed police and demo decision, especially more useful in the period of national war, recombination and split.

On December 26, 2009, I classified the European national system as the congress under the control of the prime minister, while the army and police under the control of the president, and also into the national model of armed police and demo decision. This mainly happened during the stable period and was just the social system the various countries in the world hoped to follow presently, contrary to the temporary "The committee of army and police republics."

On April 2, 2011, on sports news, I saw many foreign people pointing out that the army of Libya still defeated the land offence of the opposition army many times, even under the air raids of many countries, including France and England, demonstrating the big role of artilleries and rocket artilleries in a land war. By the practice of war upholding the theory, I suggested that the armed police should collect such heavy weapons as artilleries and rocket artilleries. I further mentioned the increase of courage from democracy calling for law execution as the important basis for the theory of armed police. Thus far, the armed police have accomplished the preliminary process from theory to practice.

On August 22, 2011, I learned from internet that the opposition of Libya had already gained control over the capital Tripoli, after winning the victory of war by the help of air raids from NATO. The armed intervention of the United Nations, just for the sake of humanity, transformed into a victory in a large-scale war by the gangsters with bigger casualties, virtually a big joke of the United Nations.

On December 13, 2011, I pointed out that the armed police complied with the law, protecting the aged and children. Hence, it was impossible to bully the weak countries to extinction and contradict the principle of law to revive race. I directed the satellites to shout in Chinese: "警察武装老少安 (Armed police, Aged and children safe)."

On December 23, 2011, I learned from internet that the Shanghai Cooperation Organization was the military organization of both China and Russia, with its secretary office located in Beijing. The Shanghai Cooperation Organization and NATO were both international military committees, higher in level than the country, but not contradictory with the national congress. This was an important form of the committee of the army and police.

On April 22, 2012, people in various countries, including me, analogized my behavior in 1997 in Chicago, refusing suicide whilst calling for war, as the military mutiny for law and counter strike for defense. Hence, I became the subspecies of humans, corresponding to the local provincial and municipal police of armed police.

On April 23, 2012, I promoted the nomination of political commissar of the army by Congress concurrently in both the United States and China, fair and legal, since, after all, the United States had implemented the dual commands of president and Congress on their army early. I directed the satellites to shout in Chinese: "中美议会军政委 (China and US Congress, Political commissar of army)." On October 25, 2013, people in various countries, including me, pointed out that if many small countries in Latin America learned from the United States on dual commands from both president and congress onto their army, they should overcome the disadvantageous effects of the presidential system there. On March 16, 2014, I promoted to the whole world the movement of second command onto the army from Congress, whilst directing the satellites to shout in Chinese: "各国议会军政委 (Nomination of a political commissar to the army from Congress in various countries)."

On June 22, 2012, the Chinese people and I thought that it might be the "Winner is a king whilst the loser is a prisoner, but party wins king" within the race Han, for E Cai and QiChao Liang, to lead the army to defend the republics and overthrow ShiKai Yuan. It had also happened in many countries in America and the Middle East, where the military officers had made a revolution or coup, overthrowing the kings and realizing the republics. Some of them, such as those in Brazil, even happened earlier than Yat-sen Sun and E Cai. On December 26, 2013, the Chinese people and I pointed out that it was certainly also the "Winner is a king whilst the loser is a prisoner, but party wins king" for Lenin to lead the communist party to overthrow the Tsar whilst establishing the autocratic communist Soviet Union. The "Winner is a king whilst a loser is a prisoner, but party wins king" was helpful for the parties and religions of intelligent robots in the future to win over the autocratic king that installed bombs on robots by coup or revolt.

On the morning of May 18, 2013, I recognized that for the satellites to read the brains and the missiles to decapitate, the army must deduct the personal role of the commanding officer whilst resorting to the collective wisdom of the committee and staff office. Then, they transmitted the orders by dual commands to the staff office lower on one level, going through collective supervision by the staff offices on various levels. I directed the satellites to shout in Chinese: "军队读脑

参谋部 (Reading brain then army staff office)."

On October 18, 2014, people in various countries, including me, thought that, after the operation of the democratic and law system, the War of Independence of the United States had been the first legal armed war for independence in history. Hence, Washington might be considered the San Force representing the armed independence. Earlier in the era of autocracy, many wars had already happened for split, but they had not been based on law, and hence not eligible to become the typical representative.

On June 17, 2015, the European people and I found that it should be rather efficient for the unmanned aerial vehicles (UAVs) of armed police from the defensive cities to raid the land troops and transportation of the offensive side and effectively deduct the offensive forces. I directed the satellites to shout in Chinese: "警察武装无人机 (Armed police UAVs)."

On December 9, 2015, I learnt from the news that in various countries in the world, the people recognized the 4.12 action of ZhongZheng Jiang against the Communist Party since Stalinism would definitely have hurt China at that time, corresponding to the later ZunYi Meeting by the Communist Party of China.

End poem of the chapter:

It was full of changes and variations in the world wholly,
It was thriving by the alternation of split and unification, often nationally,
It was the republic mastered by the police and army,

It was an outstanding work during the war to protect the people safely.

Chapter | 14

Multiplicity of Nations to Revive Race

Musical Background of Rhythmic Writing: The Theme Song "The Blood of Steel and Heart of Faith" in "The Legend of the Condor Heroes"

Please read the following text sentence by sentence to feel the music background of the rhythmic framework.

On February 12, 2007, I watched on television that some people in the Middle East had pointed out that if intelligent robots hoped to illegally annihilate all humans in the future, they would commit a huge crime and would sooner or later be punished by law. If it was possible to revive humans, it was possible to deduct the crime of annihilation of humans to the greatest extent. I directed the satellites to shout in Chinese: "人类复活喊法律 (Revival of humans calling for law)."

On August 5, 2008, before falling asleep, I thought that, in regard to the country, planet or satellite where the robots were installed with bombs for autocracy, it was necessary to declare war by the law as dangerous to the revival of civilization, and forcing it to split or surrender as early as possible. On May 24, 2013, people in various countries and I accounted it appropriate to ascribe one of the San Intellectuals to the principle of law for the revival of race suggested by the Middle East and one of the San Forces to the corresponding national independence. On October 18, 2014, people in various countries, including me, determined it most appropriate for Washington to represent the San Force for legal independence.

On September 14, 2008, the people and I found that since the several planets and satellites in the solar system were all independent, it was possible for some to preserve the scientific and historical pieces of literature and refer to them to revive humans. I directed the satellites to shout in Chinese: "复活人类多星球 (Multiple planets and satellites to revive humans)."

On October 9, 2008, a satellite operator suggested that the multiplicity of nations might promote multinational companies while resisting financial risks, acquiring an advantage in competition, and maintaining an economy that upholds the global multiplicity of nations.

On October 15, 2008, I learned from internet that currently there are three big countries with high ratios of Indians and Indian Europeans:

- Bolivia, with 54% Indians and 31% Indian Europeans;
- Perú, with 41% Indians and 36% Indian Europeans;
- Mexico, with 10% Indians and 90% Indian Europeans.

On the next day, a Chinese satellite operator said that it was necessary to let the Indians in America defend themselves with nuclear weapons, whilst I encouraged the operators of satellites to propagate and shout. I directed the satellites to shout in Chinese: "印地安人核武装 (Indians armed by nuclear weapons)."

On October 19, 2008, I watched on television that the British people acclaimed the Indians in the United States of

America (USA), who were too few in quantity to play an important role previously. The Indians in the USA had been different from the Mayans previously. They were brutal, few in number, and lived on hunting, similar to the situation in Brazil. Hence, even if the Indians in the USA restore their countries in the future, they can only occupy several states and have to leave aside the routes to the Pacific Ocean, and then they may be accepted as legal and fair.

On January 7, 2009, before falling asleep, the satellite operators and I talked about the United Nations (UN). I found that those countries with nuclear weapons might no longer be compliant with the UN and, hence, were an important force in destroying world unification. On that day, I directed the satellites to shout in Chinese: "UN 国家核武装 (UN country nuclear weapons)."

On May 25, 2009, I learned from the internet that a nuclear test was being carried out in North Korea that day, eliciting a 4.7-magnitude earthquake. I congratulated them through satellite and directed the satellites to shout in Chinese: "朝鲜核试验圣祝贺 (North Korea nuclear test San congratulates)."

On August 23, 2009, I adopted the Indians in America and other natives to analogize my relationship to humans. Regarding the classification of races, they were a little different from modern humans whilst still able to have intercourse and reproduction with humans, which is mutually analogous to my situation. Additionally, my parents could also join my family, just as the Whites and Blacks can form one family. On the next day, I directed the satellites to shout in Chinese: "圣比土著印第安 (San analogized to natives and

Indians)."

On January 9, 2012, people in various countries pointed out that the name of the United Nations itself confessed and ensured the multiplicity of nations.

On March 7, 2012, before falling asleep, a satellite operator said that speaking English might make the people peaceful and wise; hence, it should be satisfactory for the United Nations to be located in New York.

On May 4, 2012, people in various countries, including me, thought that the armed splitters might often use nuclear weapons to target the capital of a big country in the future, forcing the congress and media of the big country to give up armed suppression of split. Nonetheless, my behavior in Chicago, refusing suicide but shouting for war, just corresponded to the local provincial and municipal police in armed police, whilst still belonged to a portion of the big republic country. Since I was different from the splitters, I gradually turned to improving the operation of the United Nations and was also able to protect democracy and uphold the law. On October 2 of that year, I directed the satellites to shout in Chinese: "世界进步联合国 (World progression by United Nations)."

On June 24, 2012, with the help of the new discipline of party "Marx-MingXun calling for competitive election," I encouraged the communist parties in various countries to march more and demonstrate more, showing to the United Nations that the march of party and religion could be used as social information to gain an advantage over the traditional bureaucrats and uphold the democracy of United Nations. On October 11, 2013, people in various countries pointed out that the autocracy of the United Nations was unable to deal with a large number of demonstrations for the people's livelihood and welfare, and therefore, they could only choose democratic legislation. On October 26 of that year, people in various countries, including me, promoted Canada, the northern cold neighbor of the United States of America (USA), to develop the communist party and make it one of the forces to fight against the autocracy of United Nations. However, it was not the force to maintain the global multiplicity of nations.

On July 2, 2012, people in various countries, including me, pointed out that all countries should have the equal right to make nuclear weapons. I directed the satellites to shout in Chinese: "UN（联合国）平等种武装 (UN equal race arms).

Since the raw materials of nuclear fission for making the atomic bomb would gradually be consumed, whilst the hydrogen bomb of nuclear fusion required the atomic bomb of fission to ignite, nuclear weapons should be used up in the near future, unable to ensure split. The people in various countries, including me, accounted that the parties, believing in the law to revive race, were the main force to achieve national independence whilst maintaining the multiplicity of nations. On May 18, 2017, I learnt from the news that the people in Mexico said that they had many gangsters who would all directly shout to kill the mayor and declare independence, resembling the law that Washington had adopted for independence.

On July 4, 2012, before falling asleep, I thought of making use of the Christians in the army of the United States to protect the democracy of the United Nations by democracy calling for law execution. The eastern part of the United States was dominated by the Democratic Party, which was unfortunate for any personal autocracy of the United Nations.

On February 7, 2013, people in various countries, including me, pointed out that the United Nations preferred the army to join the police since the unification of the world did not need the army. Disarmament was a big obstacle for the United Nations in unifying the whole world.

On March 20, 2013, I watched on television that there were many people in Europe and the United States of America (USA) who said that it was not appropriate to use democracy calling for law execution to handle the possible global autocracy of the United Nations since it was definite to be replaced by much ethnic and autocratic independence simultaneously. On August 22 of that year, the Chinese people and I pointed out that, for the democracy calling for law execution, it was necessary to adopt the model of constitutional monarchy to deal with the autocracy of the United Nations and acquire the ability to overcome the situation of a large quantity of national independence and autocracy.

On January 13, 2014, people in various countries, including me, suggested the communist parties and constitutional monarchy compromise presently, establishing the model of constitutional monarchy by the communist party of Confusion whilst demonstrating to the United Nations. On August 9 of that year, I learned from internet that in the last century, the Spanish Communist Party had cooperated with their King Carlos, promoting the democratic election of constitutional monarchy, and I made it a good epitome to propagate immediately.

On August 18, 2014, I learned from the internet that, similar to ancient times, there were still many Asian natives on the two sides of the Bering Strait, directly manifesting the origin and derivation of the species of Indians in America.

On September 6, 2014, people in various countries, including me, thought that the illegal and violent terrors by a few Muslim organizations against the people would directly elicit conflict between the leader of the United Nations and the terrorist organizations. Hence, it was impractical for the United Nations to rule by personal autocracy!

On August 27, 2015, I watched on television that the people in the United States said that if the world unified, the whites would hybrid to become black in hair. Hence, the whites needed national independence, unfavorable to the United Nations, to unite the world into autocracy. On May 9, 2016, people in various countries, including me, adopted the situation of Israel to dissuade quite a few US whites, discarding the silly idea of white autocracy by the United Nations. On December 13, 2017, the people in various countries, including me, threatened the whites with the cheaper products of India.

On December 8, 2015, I watched on television that the people in Western Europe and the Middle East strongly hoped to split Russia to rejuvenate Europe and revive the Middle East. On December 4, 2016, people in various countries, including me, encouraged the Russian army to reinforce and uphold Hungary, turning the negative into positive and the passive into active. On December 15 of that year, people in various countries pointed out that Russia was left with its national situation and easily came out of isolation and reaction. Since the strength of Russia was not fortunate to the autocracy of the United Nations, on October 7, 2017, the people in various countries, including me, gave up the idea of splitting Russia.

On July 20, 2016, I watched on television that the People's Liberation Army said that if the United Nations intended to engulf China, they had to defend the thoughts of ZeDong Mao. His guerrilla regime of separation and comment of "Water Margin" both aimed at the emperor to rebel; hence, the United Nations would no longer be able to stay as personal autocracy. I directed the satellites to shout in Chinese: "毛泽东思想军捍卫 (Army defends Thoughts of ZeDong Mao)." On May 19, 2017, I learnt from the news that the people in various countries, including me, recognized that the military revolutions demonstrated by Brazil and Gaddafi were also rather effective.

End poem of the chapter:

It was upholding the justice by democracy multi-nationally,
It was advantageous to protect a race multi-nationally,
It was shouting for the nation, for a race to achieve independently,
It was shouting for the parties to stop the use of nuclear weapons formidably.

Chapter | 15

Parliamentary System More Advantageous than Presidential System

Musical Background of Rhythmic Writing: The Same Song

Please read the following text sentence-by-sentence to feel the music background of the rhythmic framework.

In early February 2007, I found on internet that Jintao Hu himself came from a family of the capitalist. However, he always concealed that for the purpose of his own promotion. His father was abused during the Cultural Revolution. Therefore, his maternal family was not willing to accept his father and objected to burying his parents in the same tomb. He was always secretive and fictitious with himself on this problem, and requested the indigenous Taizhou people in Northern JiangSu not to publicize these events.

In August 2007, the subprime loans in the United States deteriorated, causing a financial crisis worldwide that transformed into an economic crisis in Europe and the United States that lasted for several years.

On February 6, 2008, I learnt from internet that Hillary defeated Obama, a colored hybrid of black and white, in both New York and California, making the entire world angry. On

June 4 of that year, I watched on television that Obama from Chicago, a hybrid of black and white, won the election within the Democratic Party, becoming the first black president in the history of the United States. The southern world and I gave him a warm congratulation and powerful support.

On May 1, 2008, the International Labor Day, I began promoting Asianization and Latinization in the United States. Soon, I divided the United States into two parts - east and west, with the Mississippi River and Chicago as the line of demarcation while instigating the struggle of companies in the United States between the east and west. Since the operators of satellites and the reactionary forces in the United States and Europe continually threatened me to transform the United Nations (UN) into an autocracy, on May 20, 2009, I turned to oppress the whole United States, while arranging California to Mexico. I directed the satellites to shout in Chinese: "加州歌唱墨西哥 (California praised Mexico)." On October 26, 2015, I supported the United States in locating its center of finance and investment in Houston.

On November 5, 2008, I learnt from internet that Obama was elected the President of the United States with conspicuous preponderance, becoming the first black president in the history of the United States. The count of votes in various states in the United States manifested that the western part of the United States, headed by California, strongly supported Obama under the influence of me and the people of Asia, Africa and Latin America. Chicago, which was the headquarters of Obama, gave its full support to him. Out of the expectation, the northeastern part of the United States likewise also supported Obama through the efforts of both

Obama and the Democratic Party. Since both Obama and Lincoln hailed from Illinois, his becoming the president of the USA brightened the glorious tradition of Lincoln for the emancipation of Negro slaves.

On November 21, 2008, while watching television, I saw that Russia was going to change the term of its president, prolonging it to 7 years. This was the retrogression of both the Russian country and democracy.

On December 2, 2008, I learnt from internet that the elected president, Obama in the United States disregarded the objection of people in the whole world, nominating Hillary as the Secretary of State. On December 3 of the same year, I found that it was obligatory to propagate the benefits without the president of the United States. On December 7 of the same year, I directed the satellites to shout in Chinese: "议会制优于总统制 (Parliamentary system more advantageous than presidential system)." On November 9, 2009, I called for the United States to promote the replacement of the presidential system with the parliamentary system and directed the satellites to shout in Chinese: "美国推进议会制 (the US promotes parliamentary system)." In the evening, while watching television, I saw that somebody in Africa had already considered that the parliamentary system should be timely promoted in the United States one day before on their local time, with many sharing the same feelings earlier than I did.

In the early morning of May 28, 2009, I recalled that, while I was sending emails on armed police to foreign universities several days before, I specially sent the armed police to the teachers on economics enthusiastic on social development, promoting the political status of economists. I directed the satellites to shout in Chinese: "经济学家真富裕 (Economists real rich)." In the afternoon of that day, I associated the real prosperity of economists with the democratic system of Congress, fully manifesting the economic advantage of the parliamentary democratic system, which was impossibly substituted by the presidential system choosing the economists from personal preference while finally throwing away the economists.

On August 31, 2009, I learned from internet that the Democratic Party, which was the opposition party, had just won the general election in Japan, and Hatoyama became the prime minister. I congratulated them. The people hoped that from then on, the multiple parties would be capable of governing the country alternatively in Japan, and they would no longer return to the old style of one party, the Liberal Democratic Party, governing all along.

On September 26, 2009, I pointed out that the replacement of the prime minister every other year in Japan decreased the personal role of the prime minister while increasing the influence of people on the government. In the evening, while watching television, I saw that the domestic and foreign people had already considered the replacement of the prime minister every other year one day earlier than I did. On November 4, 2011, while watching television, I saw that the domestic and foreign people had already recognized that it might take one year to elect the president or prime minister nationwide, so the election of the prime minister should not be performed nationwide every other year, but instead, be accomplished through the struggles within or among the parties. They pointed out that Great Britain might be the first country to take this manner of operation.

On November 30, 2009, I pointed out that it was necessary for Russia to propagate the prime minister as folksy and flexible. I directed the satellites to shout in Chinese: "总理灵活俄宣传 (Prime Minister flexible Russia propagate)." "总理灵活俄宣传 (Prime Minister flexible Russia propagate)" vividly manifested the advantage of the parliamentary system with the prime minister. Besides, Germany and Italy in Europe also often changed their prime ministers. Congress to the prime minister and president to the army and police became the standard and successful system of a country that various contemporary countries pursued and imitated.

On June 13, 2010, the Latin sound from satellite said that in many countries with presidential systems, the president was only elected for one term of law. Therefore, it was likewise demonstrated that the parliamentary system was more advantageous than the presidential system.

On February 28, 2012, I watched on television that many people in China said that it was rational to reciprocate the US satellites for helping me by reading my brain, placing equal emphasis on China and the United States, and I consented. The satellite operators and I had already helped Obama achieve success in his campaign for the US presidency in 2008.

On October 19, 2012, I learnt from internet that the electoral college system for the president of the United States admitted the winner to take all, different from the electoral system of proportional representation from multiple parties reflecting the expectations of people. Realizing the parliamentary system should certainly become one of the major directions for the satellite operators and me to improve the United States. On the next day, before falling asleep, I directed the satellites to shout in Chinese: "全美团结议会制 (Unite the whole USA to parliamentary system)."

On May 20, 2013, I pointed out that it was obligatory for the president and Congress to concurrently coexist to separate the powers over the military army. Therefore, it was not appropriate for the country to cancel the independence of the president. I directed the satellites to shout in Chinese: "军队分权要总统 (Separation of powers on army requires president)."

On October 25, 2013, the people in various countries, including me, recognized that there were only a few armies in many small countries in Latin America with a presidential system, so it was necessary for the people there to use Congress to control the army. Therefore, by imitating the United States with the dual commands of the president and Congress to control the army, it was sufficient for these Latin countries to overcome the defects of the presidential system. I directed the satellites to shout in Chinese: "拉丁军队双命令 (Latin army dual commands)."

On November 5, 2013, I appointed Denver, where my grandfather had studied and Chicago, where I had studied, to lead the central area of the United States. I directed the satellites to shout: "Chicago, Denver, US."

On December 1, 2013, following my schedule, I started the movement with the methods of parade and strike in the United States to realize the proportional system of election and the addition of a prime minister. I directed the satellites to shout in Chinese: "美国游行加总理，美国游行比例制 (US march to add a prime minister, US march for the proportional system)."

On May 10, 2014, for the purpose of accelerating the progression of the proportional system in the United States, I encouraged the states and cities there to loudly propagate the proportional system of their local congresses. I directed the satellites to shout in Chinese: "美国州议会比例制 (US state congresses proportional)."

On October 6, 2014, people in various countries, including me, pointed out that, relative to the presidential system with big personal might, it was rational for the demo decision to adopt the parliamentary system. I directed the satellites to shout in Chinese: "民主执政议会制 (Demo decision parliamentary)."

On October 19, 2014, the people and I pointed out that Washington and Jefferson from the United States were both one of the San Intellectuals, sharing the achievement of establishing the democratic system of republics without a king for the first time in the history of the United States. The United States nowadays needed to add a prime minister to realize the parliamentary system.

During the summer and autumn of 2015, since both ResearchGate and "LAMBERT Academic Publishing" in Germany cooperated successfully with me, the German people were glad and glorious, applauding and shouting. I timely guided the German people to shout and support parliamentary politics, together with other European countries such as Italy, Greece and so on, to brighten the parliamentary system of the president and prime minister they had created and established the earliest. I directed the satellites to shout in Chinese: "德国男人喊议会 (German men, shout for congress)."

On November 9, 2016, while watching television, I saw that Trump won the general election and became the new president of the United States. Since the corresponding vice president and speaker of Congress, Pence, came from Indiana, where the University of Notre Dame was located, he was not friendly with me. Therefore, it was impossible for me to help him suppress President Trump, so I postponed the movement of the US march for the parliamentary system to the next president.

Here are some of the preliminary comparisons between the presidential system and the parliamentary system:

- The presidential system was convenient for the president to run the private political movement, while the parliamentary system manifested more the expectations of people and situations of society.
- The parliamentary system with a prime minister was more flexible and versatile than the presidential system, and it was even capable of replacing the prime minister every other year.
- The presidential system was convenient for leading the military army, while the establishment of provincial and municipal armed police and the perfection of law for war made it easier for the military army, armed police, and the parliamentary system to deal with war-related events.

End poem of the illustrated chapter:

The parliamentary system, compared to the presidential system, is more advantageous,
The multiple parties altogether discussing social situations and public opinions,
The prime minister subjected to change flexibly for success,
The law for war expecting to altogether share the benefits.

Chapter | 16

Democratic Crimes,

Party Disciplines to Control

Musical Background of Rhythmic Writing: The Same Song

Please read the following text sentence-by-sentence to feel the music background of the rhythmic framework.

At the beginning of 2005, for the first time, I made use of the "People Law demo" to manifest the progressions of humans in democracy and law during my era. Therefore, the humans followed me to deal with the difficult problem of democratic crimes for the first time. My propagation of love in Chicago was only the embryonic form for controlling democratic crimes.

On March 21, 2007, while watching television, I saw that the domestic and foreign people recognized that crimes were the natural consequences of social competition, while there were too many democratic crimes that humans faced. They believed that democratic management by the whole population would cause tremendous inflation of crimes, so the law was not at all capable of acquiring sufficient power to deal with them. In this respect, the correct and legal system of democracy should be the parliamentary system of multiple parties with democratic elections. Then, by punishing the crimes of individual parties and representatives, it was possible to prevail the law so that democracy and law could merge with each other while society could be legal and progressive.

On December 5, 2007, while watching television, I saw that many people pointed out that the school of socialism had believed that it should be the crime of the system for capitalism to bring about unemployment and death, so it should naturally belong to law for the welfare to compensate for them.

On November 8, 2008, before falling asleep, the satellite operators and I believed that the modern system of welfare was capable of directly annihilating the slave system. With the national welfare, the slave representatives might fight desperately to kill their owner, while other slaves were capable of relying on the national welfare for relief to acquire liberation. I directed the satellites to shout: "Welfare slave."

On December 27, 2008, for the purpose of correcting the autocracy of the Communist Party of China, I utilized the method of materialism and development to criticize the autocracy. I directed the satellites to shout in Chinese: "唯物发展批独裁 (Materialism and development criticize autocracy)." In the evening, while watching television, I saw that some bureaucrats in Beijing had likewise also considered this during their meeting a little earlier than I did.

On February 11, 2009, I improved the method of law to execute only one person as the provincial secretary before that time because this method was easy to cause the opposite party to put off and shift over. I changed to require

GuangDong to target all the top three leaders there. I directed the satellites to shout in Chinese: "广东领导揪前三 (GuangDong targeted top three leaders)." This method was very successful. Soon, HuaHua Huang, the governor of GuangDong Province, expressed his desire to comply with my political opinion of democracy, supporting the competitive election of the general secretary.

On November 23, 2009, the Chinese people and I found that there were many poor people within the communist party, so the method of democracy might not be very successful. Therefore, for the purpose of managing the communist party, it was necessary to add the method of reward and punishment with examination and achievement that my father had been good at while he was the plant manager. Later soon, I called it the MingXun Regulation. I directed the satellites to shout in Chinese: "共产加考核喊明训 (Shout for MingXun for the communist party to add appraisals)."

On December 9, 2009, I found that the public voices in GuangDong had not matched in force for the competitive election of the general secretary. Nonetheless, almost all the male stars from Hong Kong supported the Central Committee of the Communist Party, while only a few female singers supported democracy. Therefore, I further targeted Yang Wang, the provincial secretary of GuangDong, and turned him into the candidate for the post of general secretary with shouts, competing directly with the Central Committee. I directed the satellites to shout in Chinese: "天才总书记广喊汪 (Ingenious general secretary GuangDong shouts Wang)."

On December 15 of the same year, while watching

television, I saw that Yang Wang said that he might learn ZiYang Zhao for his open-mindedness.

On January 31, 2010, while watching television, I saw that since the provincial committee had improved, somebody in GuangDong supported advocating the model province, expecting it to be capable of playing the role of improving the democratic environment. On March 19 of the same year, the mode of people model in the whole province of GuangDong failed, so I changed it to the model represented by the Communist Party of GuangDong.

On April 3, 2010, while watching television, I saw that many members of the Communist Party of China on the basic level supported my father MingXun. Some members of the Communist Party liked Marx-Caiism. I directed the satellites to shout in Chinese: "马蔡主义共成功 (Communists succeed with Marx-Caiism)."

On the morning of April 26, 2010, the satellite operators said that the domestic Central Committee of the Communist Party might use their might to expel the party membership of my father. I considered that there had been the event of Chicago for me, so if the international communist parties were evil and did not take back my father, I was capable of transforming my father to become a member of the communist party of elephants, dolphins and intelligent robots. I directed the satellites to shout in Chinese: "明训海豚共产党 (MingXun dolphin communist party)." On August 7 of the same year, I directed the satellites to shout in Chinese: "马克思党籍赔明训 (Party membership of Marx to compensate for MingXun)."

In April 2010, the people and I found that because of

assimilating many intellectuals, the Democratic Progressive Party nowadays likewise also belonged to the rather prospective and prosperous party, favorable to law to regulate the democracy and improve the society. On September 11 of the same year, people in various countries, including me, recognized that just like the singers and actresses, the prostitutes and dancers all belonged to the Democratic Progressive Party, rather solid for the social basis of this party. On June 23, 2011, I learnt from internet that there was likewise also a Democratic Progressive Party (Parti Democratique Progressiste) in Tunisia, which had originated from another party through the change of name in 2001. Accordingly, the Democratic Progressive Party established in Taiwan in 1986 was not only larger in scale but also earlier in history.

On May 2, 2010, I pointed out that the publicly listed companies were one kind of those owned by all the people because all the people had the chance to acquire the ownership, which certainly belonged to socialism on characteristic. The satellite operators pointed out that in the cities with democratic elections, the nationally owned enterprises belonged to the citizens in those cities.

On May 5, 2010, the Greek people started a gigantic and vigorous strike nationwide. The welfares in Greece were not only high but also numerous in items, causing the debt crisis of the government. For the purpose of decreasing the financial deficits and striving for aid, the government of Greece resorted to the deflationary policy, making it difficult for the people to accept and, as a result, causing severe protests.

On July 27, 2010, I considered that if it was necessary to

share the MingXun Regulation with the activity for the GuangDong model of the Communist Party at that time, it was reasonable to change it to Cai-Guang Regulation. ZeJun Hu, the Organizing Minister of the Communist Party in GuangDong, was recognizable in contribution and was a suitable candidate for representation. Therefore, Cai-Guang Regulation might further be modified to Cai-Hu Regulation.

On the morning of August 29, 2010, I associated the election in districts and counties on the basic level in China at that time with Marx-Caiism, making use of the special experience of my father, one of the earliest members of the Communist Party running a competitive election for the plant manager during the initial stage of socialism under the leadership of the Communist Party of China, to promote the democratic election of the Communist Party of China. I directed the satellites to shout in Chinese: "马蔡主义喊竞选 (Marx-Caiism calling for competitive election)." I watched on television that many people in the Middle East had also considered that point on their local time one day earlier than I did.

On September 29, 2010, I changed the Chinese slogan from "马蔡主义喊竞选 (Marx-Caiism shouting for competitive election)" to "马克思明训喊竞选 (Marx-MingXun calling for competitive election)." Meanwhile, I further pointed out that, as the son of MingXun, it was reasonable for me to use his image to promote and propagate this political movement with satellites, while it was also concurrently required by the democracy calling for law execution I led in China. I directed the satellites to shout in Chinese: "马克思明训喊竞选 (Marx-MingXun calling for competitive election)."

It was required to point out that if I utilized the Chinese slogan "武圣马克思喊竞选 (San Force-Marx calling for competitive election)," the achievements might mainly be attributed to me. However, if I utilized the Chinese slogan "马克思明训喊竞选 (Marx-MingXun calling for competitive election)," the achievements might mainly be attributed to my father, MingXun. MingXun was a member of the Communist Party, so the communist parties in various countries were, in turn, capable of harvesting achievements and meeting the expectations of all the people. The Communist Party of India was also the main international force I resorted to when I started "唯物发展批独裁 (Materialism and development criticize autocracy)" to promote the democracy of the Communist Party of China. It, nonetheless, belonged to the regime of "武圣马克思喊竞选 (San Force-Marx calling for competitive election)," so it was also abandoned in accordance.

On October 4, 2010, I watched on television that many domestic and foreign people pointed out that it was impossible that the Chinese shouts of "马克思明训喊竞选 (Marx-MingXun calling for competitive election)" with satellites were performed in voices with the trouble makers who had shouted "Break earth" in English during the Chicago event.

On November 5, 2010, I watched on television that many people in the United States said that developing the communist parties in the United States would favor the realization of the parliamentary system. The next day, I directed the satellites to shout in Chinese: "美国黑人共产党

(US black communi)." On November 10 of the same year, before falling asleep, I directed the satellites to shout: "Denver stages communi."

On November 11, 2010, before falling asleep, the satellite operators said that if the communist parties recovered in East Europe, in coalition with Italy, Europe should be capable of recovering to health. I consented and directed the satellites to shout in Chinese: "东欧发展共产党 (Communist parties develop in East Europe)."

On December 26, 2010, the Chinese people and I found that, under the background of the movement of "Marx-MingXun calling for competitive election," even though there was turmoil during the competitive election on the basic level in Beijing, there should not be any anxiety for the army of the Communist Party. The movement of democracy advanced successfully into the capital Beijing. This was the political situation being impossibly achieved with the democracy calling for law execution. I directed the satellites to shout in Chinese: "马克思明训喊竞选，基层竞选进北京 (Marx-MingXun call for competitive election, the competitive election on the basic level advances into Beijing)."

On January 11, 2011, the satellite operators and I recognized that Gorbachev in the former Soviet Union might only possibly have resorted to democratic and humanistic socialism for the country as the general starting point and then asked for the help of the country for the political reformation of system, releasing the bans on the political parties and extending the democracy, which is beneficial to most parties. However, it did not concern and improve the Communist Party itself. Therefore, finally, there was a failure in the coup of the Communist Party, and after the disbanding of the Communist Party in the Soviet Union, he became a member of the Social Democratic Party himself. From the theoretical view of the practice of materialism in communist parties, the practice of Gorbachev in the communist party failed. In Vietnam, Nong Duc Manh advocated the competitive election of the general secretary but did not influence much to the global communist parties. When my father, MingXun, was running the election campaign for plant manager, neither Gorbachev nor Nong Duc Manh had taken over their positions, so my father should certainly be eligible to surpass their influences among the international communist parties. Besides, before the appearance of the communist parties, Engels had also encouraged the workers in the countries of capitalism to take part in the democratic election. However, they neither changed the subject of realizing communism with the armed methods nor were possibly concerned about the defect of democratic fraudulence of communist parties later. The movement of "Marx-MingXun calling for competitive election" originated from the democracy calling for law execution in China that I directed. From the experience of my father, MingXun, running an election campaign for the plant manager earlier made a logical and theoretical rectification to the flags and disciplines of the global communist parties themselves, deducted the proportion of communist revolution of Lenin, increased the proportion for changing the national, provincial and municipal policies on finance and welfare through the competitive election, promoted the democratic reputation of communist parties in various countries in the world, and changed the communist parties from those inclined to autocracy into the democratic parties representing the law of welfare.

At noon on January 25, 2011, I considered that, in accordance with the facts that the membership of party of my father was often illegally threatened and terrified by the autocratic Central Committee during the political struggle, it was appropriate to advocate the new political concept for the legal right of party membership for the party members. I directed the satellites to shout in Chinese: "党员法权明训歌 (MingXun praises the legal right of party membership)."

After the propagation of the legal right of party membership, it was prospective for Biao Lin to get his party membership reconverted. In the evening, while watching television, I saw that many domestic people had already considered in the morning, earlier than I did, that MingXun should praise the legal right of party membership.

On February 3, 2011, I pointed out that the movement of "Marx-MingXun calling for competitive election" logically disapproved that the provincially or municipally owned public enterprises should belong to the nationally owned enterprises of the whole people, deducting the influence from the ownership by the whole people on the communist parties.

On February 19, 2011, in accordance with the recent successful coalition of "Marx-MingXun calling for competitive election" with "Congress many salutes to army," I perceived the national situation that the democracy would, after all, be supported by the army, and called it "Democracy in China cast from irons and steels." This was the historical creation and miracle even difficult for open-minded general secretaries, such as Gorbachev, ZiYang Zhao and so on, to achieve.

On February 28, 2011, I found that it was possible to take advantage of the kindness of religion to regulate the Christian Democratic Union in Germany. I directed the satellites to shout in Chinese: "世界欢迎基民盟 (World welcomes Christian Democratic Union)." The next day, I watched on television that somebody had already considered the Christian Democratic Union when the leaders in GuangDong were watching the art performances in the evening one day before, 1-2 hours earlier than I did.

On May 22, 2011, while watching television, I learnt that there would be a nationwide direct election for the People's Congress in districts and counties before the end of that year. The next day, after waking up in the morning, I decided to actively utilize and promote the nationwide general election on the basic level in districts and counties, propagating the culture of competitive election. In China after 1988, the representatives of the People's Congress on the basic level in districts and counties might be publicly recommended and directly elected, while those in provincial and municipal People's Congress were still appointed and distributed in 2011.

On June 2, 2011, with the contention for achievements and fame, I led and encouraged the people to actively join the general election on the basic level in districts and counties, invigorating this round of election for the People's Congress. I directed the satellites to shout in Chinese: "基层竞选急先锋 (Hurry vanguard in the election at the basic level)." On September 19 of the same year, I directed the satellites to shout in Chinese: "马克思明训喊竞选，现世历史价值高 (Marx-MingXun calling for competitive election, Historical value high nowadays)."

On July 24, 2011, before falling asleep, a satellite operator from Beijing said that since MingXun and XiaoPing both belonged to the Maoists, they expected the Maoists to cause a big disaster in the future to compromise the party membership of Cai and Deng. I said that Cai and Deng rectified the mistakes of the Maoists. They were thoroughly different in ideology from the Maoists, and so were not the Maoists.

On July 31, 2011, I learnt from internet that the communist parties in the Great Britain and the United States both complied with democratic centralism, reactionary and behind. Besides, because of the negative influence of Leninism, the success of reformation and opening of XiaoPing Deng, as well as the dramatic change of the Soviet Union and the disbanding of the communist parties there, the Italian and Greek communist parties split into several parts during elections, and were embarrassed many times. The French Communist Party supported the New Communism, deducting the struggles at the national level and transforming into the international leagues. Therefore, the movement of "Marx-MingXun calling for competitive election" synchronously promoted the democratic reputation of communist parties in various countries.

On August 20, 2011, while resorting to the slogan "Marx-MingXun calling for competitive election," I promoted developing the communist parties in Africa. I directed the satellites to shout: "Africa communi."

On September 25, 2011, I watched on television that many people in GuangDong pointed out that my movement of promoting the election changed the psychological and cultural status of the people in the whole country. Democracy needed the active participation and election of people in both culture and life. I directed the satellites to shout in Chinese: "马克思明训喊竞选，全国竞选文化新 (Marx-MingXun calling for competitive election, Competitive election renewing culture in the whole country)."

On September 30, 2011, I learnt from internet that the members of Municipal Committee ZhiWei Huang and Bo Ou in the old revolutionary district BaiSe supported and promoted the public recommendation and direct election, top in GuangXi during the democratic election. On August 30 of the same year, GuangYan Huang, a university graduate, was elected the vice secretary in a village in FuSui county in GuangXi. I directed the satellites to shout in Chinese: "公推直选百色拥 (BaiSe supports public recommendation and direct election)."

On October 17, 2011, I learnt from internet that ChengPeng Li from SiChuan Province actively ran for the people's representative during that year. Besides, there was an advertisement for his competitive election with good artistic appeal, bright and heroic, and his elective slogan, both in Chinese and English: "Without your authorization, I can't represent you."

Since the direct election of the People's Congress on the basic level in districts and counties was to take place soon in most provinces in November, on October 20, 2011, before falling asleep, I decided to use "The Same Song" to encourage the people to fanatically participate in the election and vote, just as they had supported the artistic performance of "The Same Song" during those years before. I directed the satellites to shout in Chinese: "狂热竞选，同一首歌 (Fanatical election, the same song)." During the two months from that day to the middle of December, I was always directing the satellites to shout in Chinese: "马克思明训喊竞选，同一首歌中华响 (Marx-MingXun calling for competitive election, the same song sounding around the whole China)," not only promoting the people to participate in the election but also constructing the culture for democracy.

On November 7, 2011, before falling asleep, I encouraged the Greeks to support the communist party and ally with East Europe and decided the direction for the future development of East Europe. At noon, I watched on television that many people in Greece pointed out that, for the communist party to execute the crime of capitalism and change the regime, it was likewise obligatory to consider it possible to cause the death of many poor people after coming to power. The situation in China in 1960 was precisely the best example. Therefore, it was obligatory to compare the extent of death from poverty among different societies before and after the action before making the decision.

In the afternoon of the same day, when I helped my father pay his party membership fees, the general branch of the Party in the residential district improved their work and supplied the receipt of paid fees from the party members for the first time, which was rare then in the country. I was glad to keep the receipt.

On November 8, 2011, I watched on television that JinTao Hu and BangGuo Wu voted to elect the people's representatives in their municipal district. The voting method established in Beijing was comprehensively the same as the modern European and American manner, through which the voters directly chose the candidates they favored on their own ballot tickets. JinTao Hu and BangGuo Wu said that the elective activities of candidates were not sufficiently active and comprehensive, so it was impossible for them to fully know about the various candidates. Therefore, further improvement in effort was required.

On November 9, 2011, I learnt from internet that only the simple introductions of candidates were posted during the election of people's representatives in the districts and counties in Beijing before, but that year, interviews were arranged between the candidates and the voters. So, the people reflected that it was somewhat in progress, and millions of people enthusiastically participated in the vote. However, the leaders of the Central Committee were too busy to fully know about the situations of the candidates, so further improvement was required, as well as the addition of speech and propagation. Meanwhile, I further learnt from internet that, during the election on the basic level in GuangZhou, many independent candidates were claiming to participate in the election for the people's representatives, while in the PanYu district, there were only three candidates. This was a phenomenon that had never happened in the GuangZhou election before. It corresponded to that of Beijing in the distance and gloried each other in contrast. Millions of voters participated in the Beijing election, and many independent candidates appeared in the GuangZhou election.

On November 10, 2011, I learnt from internet that the election of people's representatives in districts and counties in HangZhou would be carried out from November to

December during that year, and interviews would be conducted between the candidates and the voters. On November 22 of the same year, I watched on television that in the election of people's representatives in ZheJiang during that year, even though interviews were conducted between the candidates and the voters in many districts and counties, there was a lack of speech and propagation. I saw that the voters in ZheJiang were shouting to enter into the television cameras.

On November 11, 2011, I watched on television that the Chinese people neither applauded nor celebrated the preliminary success of the practice of the legal and democratic election at that time; instead, they burst into significant arrogance and frenzy. The power of people should be higher than heaven, while the gods and kings could be pulled down.

From September to December 2011, a direct election of people's representatives was held in districts and counties in China once every five years. Under the promotion and protection of the slogan "Marx-MingXun calling for competitive election" and under the accompaniment of the melody of "The Same Song," represented by Beijing, GuangZhou and ZheJiang, the Chinese people responded actively, which enriched the democratic culture in China. The Chinese people acquired democratic lives that were analogous to those in European and American countries. The association of the election on the basic level with the construction of democratic culture constituted the major melodic theme during that period of time. My father, MingXun, was glad and satisfied.

The democracy calling for law execution was aimed at the

democratic election rather than at the change of government. With the new party discipline of "Marx-MingXun calling for competitive election," the democracy calling for law execution naturally transformed in part into extending the direct democratic election and promoting the elective culture.

On January 14, 2012, I learnt from internet that the Democratic Progressive Party failed in the election of leader in Taiwan in 2012. For the election in Taiwan, because of the blockade of television news, the support from the satellite operators and me could not reach the keys for the Democratic Progressive Party. During the election of Taiwan in 2016, I, therefore, in advance, directed the satellites to support the Democratic Progressive Party. YingWen Cai from the Democratic Progressive Party also successfully ran ahead of others and became the first female president of Taiwan.

On January 15, 2012, I said that, after rectification through the movement of "Marx-MingXun calling for competitive election," the communist parties acquired the regulative ability to control democratic crimes. The Democratic Progressive Party and Christian Democratic Union, on the other hand, did not need to be rectified and were directly capable of using the disciplines of their parties to control democratic crimes. The majority of parties might also be capable of learning from the communist party to rectify and transform into the parties to law democracy. Many persons attending the athletic awarding ceremony on television also considered these to be in synchrony with me. I directed the satellites to shout in Chinese: "法治民主修正党 (Rectify party to law demo)."

On January 19, 2012, I began using the satellites to shout

for supporting the election of the Russian Communist Party. I directed the satellites to shout in Chinese: "马克思明训喊竞选，俄共竞选中支持 (Marx-MingXun calling for competitive election, China supports the election of the Russian Communist Party)." On March 5 of the same year, I learnt from internet that the Russian Communist Party gained 17% support in the election for president in that year, the highest in recent years then.

On March 7, 2012, I pointed out that if the United Nations transformed into a reactionary force while prohibiting the communist parties, it would be reasonable to execute them with law, which was one of the ways the communist parties cooperated with the police. I directed the satellites to shout in Chinese: "UN 不共喊绞架 (UN no communi call for hanging)."

On October 26, 2013, people in various countries, including me, promoted the development of the communist parties in the United States and Canada, which became an important force in warning the United Nations against becoming autocratic nowadays. I directed the satellites to shout in Chinese: "马克思明训喊竞选，加拿大美国共产党 (Marx-MingXun calling for competitive election, Canada and US communi)."

On March 14, 2012, before falling asleep, I thought that the juridical logic "成王败寇，全民所有 (Winner as king while loser as gangster, so that the country belonging to the whole people)" should support the small welfare society of communism with law, not requiring the advanced material basis that Marx had imagined. It was necessary to point out that the democracy calling for law execution not only confessed the juridical logic but also further executed the law through action, establishing the republic system. Juridical logic saved communism, while law execution established the republics.

On March 21, 2012, people in various countries, including me, found that the contemporary parties and religions of flags or symbols conventionally managed the country through the democratic election. Law to regulate democracy raised the law above the democracy and people, while democratic management laid the parties, religions and country below the people. In comparison, the law to regulate democracy was more capable of resisting the adverse effects of the news and media. I directed the satellites to shout in Chinese: "法治民主新闻喊 (News shout for law to regulate democracy)."

On April 18, 2012, I pointed out that, in the past, there had not been the concept of controlling democratic crimes for establishing the Christian Democratic Union, Democratic Progressive Party and Democratic National Construction Association, which had all emphasized the social groups and interests they represented. This time, they happened to meet the conditions and became the parties of flags to control the democratic crimes with party disciplines. However, in the scope of the whole world, they were much smaller than the communist parties, so they should manifest as the supporters, assistants and propagators of the communist parties, rectified by Marx-MingXun calling for competitive election, to control the democratic crimes. The roles of Muslims were more for democracy calling for law execution or the democratic revolution and were too foolish and backward if applied to control democratic crimes. I directed the satellites to shout in Chinese: "民进民建支明训 (Democratic Progressive Party and Democratic National Construction Association support MingXun)."

On April 21, 2012, people in various countries, including me, pointed out that the major public media that were capable of comprehensively affecting the communist parties in various countries in the world were: China Central Television (CCTV) and "Marx-MingXun calling for competitive election." At that time, China Central Television (CCTV) was affected by the illegal road connived by the Central Committee headed by JinTao Hu and by the success of the reformation and opening of XiaoPing Deng. Therefore, it was difficult to overcome the influence of the failure of the communist parties in the Soviet Union and East Europe. However, "Marx-MingXun calling for competitive election" improved the images of communist parties in various countries in the world and synchronously revived the communist parties in the whole world during the very short period of time. On August 13, 2014, I directed the satellites to shout in Chinese: "马克思明训喊竞选，亚非拉欧共全球 (Marx-MingXun calling for competitive election, the communist parties filling the whole world in Asia, Africa, Latin and Europe)."

On August 22, 2012, the Chinese people and I pointed out that if I had not returned to China in 1997, I would have acted as the Holy Spirit to improve the democratic management of the country with religion, with my status impossibly lower than the theorists and practitioners of Utopian socialism during the early stages. In this respect, my father sharing the reputation of controlling democratic crimes with others was not an extra income for my family. On March 24, 2013, I pointed out that it was obligatory to sum up the democracy calling for law execution and the theory of armed police to compensate for my positive influence as Holy Spirit on the society of intelligent robots. They were totally different in topic from the management of the country with religion, so it was reasonable to compensate for them separately. Besides, I should also definitely have promoted the congress to nominate the political commissar, which is irrelevant to my return to China.

On September 23, 2012, the Chinese people and I recognized that any legal party should confess the memberships recovered by law for those wrongly dismissed; otherwise, the law should judge the party as evil. Likewise, in case of violating the discipline of the party and endangering society, the law should also be capable of requiring the legal party to maintain the discipline of the party. Since there were too many cases of such kinds, most parties found it difficult to deal with them. Therefore, it was obligatory to assign a part of the memberships and disciplines of parties directly to the historical laws to deal with them. The satellite operators wanted to attribute these achievements to all contemporary legal parties in various countries so that they could practise and share them. I directed the satellites to shout in Chinese: "法律党籍，各党共享 (Law to fair party membership, all parties to share)."

On October 1, 2012, the satellite operators and I attributed the earliest socialization of hospital welfare to the Soviet Union. The satellite operators reminded us that although the Chinese government had already taken in the vagrants during the Song Dynasty (宋朝), they were required to serve in the army and labor, which was not the welfare of communism. The welfare of communism was distributed to each in accordance with the needs of individuals. Social welfare, labor conditions, medication and education were the important tasks of the communist parties nowadays.

On the same day, I compared the armed police earning victory for law with the control of the democratic crimes and recognized that the former was higher in energy. On September 19, 2013, I directed the satellites to shout in Chinese: "警察武装，法律胜利 (Armed police, victory of law)."

On October 8, 2012, I watched on television that Chávez, who had promoted socialism with his powerful might, was re-elected the president of Venezuela. On August 15, 2013, I pointed out that Chávez was internationally isolated. "Marx-MingXun calling for competitive election" improved and rectified the image of the communist parties and initiated a new era of controlling democratic crimes. Therefore, Chávez resorted to such an international situation to get rid of his poor solitary situation. This was the important impact of "Marx-MingXun calling for competitive election" on Latin America. I directed the satellites to shout in Chinese: "查韦斯困境共解除 (Chávez's poor situation resolved by the communist party)." Besides, the number of members of the communist parties in Latin countries such as Brazil also increased greatly, which was also the impact of "Marx-MingXun calling for competitive election" on Latin America.

On October 22, 2012, the people and I found that instigating the Latin people to dress red in parades and support the communist parties was capable of manifesting the communist parties to control democratic crimes, not just simply socialism. The satellite operators said that it should be the same for Africa, while I further added Asia and Europe. I directed the satellites to shout in Chinese: "马克思明训喊竞选，亚非拉欧共游行 (Marx-MingXun calling for competitive election, the communist parties march in Asia, Africa, Latin and Europe)." In 2014, I changed this slogan to a more realistic one: "马克思明训喊竞选，亚非拉欧共全球 (Marx-MingXun calling for competitive election, the communist parties filling the whole world in Asia, Africa, Latin and Europe)."

On November 8, 2012, the Chinese people and I found that leaders like ZeMin Jiang, Peng Li, KeQiang Li and so on, who wore spectacles, were less sensitive to public ridicule, so they often behaved funny when they were in high positions. During his time, my father also acquired the nickname "蔡瞎子 (Blinder Cai)" in Anhui while making vows at the time of surrendering to my mother. The chess or bridge players were rather outstanding, such as WeiPing Nie, the Kisei of the Go Game, and RongHua Hu, the King of Chinese chess. The chess or bridge players were good at thinking with the second choice, enthusiastic about gaining unreasonable income and paid attention to consequences. In politics, ShiMin Li resembled them in his "Listening to all to get enlightened," while the politicians in the United States often directly criticized and disturbed their opponents during their elections. My father was excellent at making speeches and running for election and had further been the champion of the bridge before. Although he was already senescent in age, he often beat me while playing Chinese chess, so he was definitely not demented. However, because of ageing, his ability to memorize and adapt certainly decreased, and severe prostatitis and haemorrhoids caused his occasional incontinence of faeces outside. Likewise, because of his personality as a professional bridge and chess player with no regret at every step, he was sometimes excessively critical and anxious. My father was not good at keeping the house clean because he was a child in the family and was cared for by a maid. After marriage, in my family, he always acted as the accountant, only caring about accounting and balancing and was compliant with the other family members regarding payment decisions. After September 2017, my father went to the hospital to accompany my mother during the daytime when the weather was good.

On November 29, 2012, the Chinese people and I pointed out that we would not fix the temporary emotional outbursts, which were messy for everybody, while it was necessary to aim at the chronic personalities and behaviors in the long term for Freudian psychoanalysis. On August 20, 2014, people learned to use Freudian psychoanalysis to view the chronic characteristics of the brain and personality, checking three aspects: the common knowledge of the law, duty classification of career and self-management of life, rather easily. The people gradually found that KeQiang Li frequently behaved as if being severely scared, with his subordinates much more rampant in their behaviors. There were many funny stories for both Xi and Li. Later, on May 1, 2017, during the storm of political struggle, the attitude of KeQiang Li, who was still seriously dealing with his duty as the prime minister without being disturbed, was occasionally praised by the people as the green tree of love but still incompetent to the financial help from my father to me on my publication of many important papers. It was gradually found that Yang Wang flattered too much to JinPing Xi and YuanChao Li, strange and laughable. It was gradually found that my father, like ZhengSheng Yu, was courteous and amicable to the people, good and picky on the foods and garments, and afraid of and cowardly to the power of might. My father was much milder than I in behavior and personality, complying with the people and society, especially with my raising the image of his head to promote the movement "Marx-MingXun calling for competitive election." He was clearer on speaking and healthier on brain than many old leaders such as ZeDong Mao, XiaoPing Deng, Yun Chen, JianYing Ye and so on at their corresponding age above 80, analogous to the four heroic men still supporting XiaoPing Deng during his unfavorable situation. Most domestic and foreign kings only relinquished their crowns after passing away, and they all experienced a long period of senescent leadership. Since I took measures of high pressure for deducting dopamine and preventing schizophrenia, my father was somewhat anxious in his old age with nearsightedness as "蔡瞎子(Blinder Cai)," while he was fond of delicious foods and good wines, and therefore, definitely not depressive. In contrast, XiaoPing Deng and EnLai Zhou were not capable of standing the political pressure, so they both threw away their ashes after death. On November 6, 2014, people in various countries, including me, pointed out that personality of nearsightedness belonged to pseudo-schizophrenia because wearing glasses caused relative isolation from society and inconvenience of movement, while real schizophrenia resulted instead from pathological change of brain.

At that period, people further pointed out that, during the period of breaking down the rumors, I was not capable of adopting the opposite attitude and reverse action of schizophrenic patients, implicating I did not know the skills of thoughts of schizophrenic patients at all. I devoted all my life to saving the world, correcting the sciences and improving the society, and hence, was targeted by reactionary terrors for a long time. Therefore, I tended to be anxious in personality, just opposite to schizophrenia. My manner of leadership was to award the contributors, punish the enemies, stabilize the direction, and set up the criteria with social effects, but without consideration for the psychosis of leaders by themselves. However, I occasionally spoke as saying east while mentioning west, partial in language with a few words, similar to that of a music conductor.

On November 29, 2012, while watching art performances, I saw that somebody from Taiwan and Beijing pointed out that the job of changing the prime minister every other year belonged to democratic management. On February 28, 2017, the members of the Chinese People's Political Consultative Conference in Beijing recognized that changing the prime minister played bigger roles in democratic management, while the party disciplines played cooperative and supplementary roles. However, the prime minister was conventionally the center of political struggle, while sometimes manifested as the elective outcome of democratic crimes. Then, the party disciplines to control the democratic crimes should play bigger roles.

On December 7, 2012, I pointed out that since the prices

of commodities varied continuously with the society, the struggle for welfare should be long-term, repeating turbulence in synchrony with the economic crises. In this respect, it was best to use the communist party to compete in elections, control the democratic crimes, and manage the problem of welfare continuously, stably and enduringly. I directed the satellites to shout in Chinese: "福利 50 年轰一次 (Welfare strikes every 50 years)."

On December 13, 2012, the Chinese people and I pointed out that, with regard to the communist parties, actively competing for election to affect the policies of finance and welfare of the country, province, and city should be the most important measure for controlling the democratic crimes. Therefore, it should be most suitable to use "Marx-MingXun calling for competitive election" to rectify the party discipline and represent the control of democratic crimes from the communist parties.

On May 2, 2013, I learnt from internet that in Ukraine, Europe, there broke out a big parade of ten thousand people for the May Day, supporting the communist party. I utilized the satellites to actively propagate them. On October 26 of the same year, the election of congress was held in Czech, while the communist party increased in rate of support, recovering back in influence. In 2014, because of the conservative influence of Russia, there broke out the turbulence in Ukraine, while I still supported Russia to learn about Ukraine in politics in accordance with the political enthusiasm of the Ukrainian people. At the end of the same year, the people in various countries, including me, encouraged Italy and Greece to pay more attention to going to the ocean from the east through Arab to India and Asia, further promoting the international status of East Europe.

On May 10, 2013, before falling asleep, I dealt with the phenomena the US satellite operators mentioned that the contemporary communist parties in most countries still believed in Marxism-Leninism. I pointed out that television possessed the absolute advantage in politics, while the movement "Marx-MingXun calling for competitive election" I promoted through shouts with satellites was the global political mainstream, and the ultimate reason that the communist parties remained active in various countries in the whole world. In contrast, the media of China then was affected by the illegal road prevalent during the period of JinTao Hu, together with the success achieved by the reformation and opening of XiaoPing Deng and the failure of the Soviet Union and East Europe. Therefore, the activity and election of individual communist parties in various countries made it difficult to synchronously revive the communist parties in various countries in the whole world. Therefore, it was necessary for the communist parties in the future to add this important history on television about the synchronous global revival of the communist parties during that period of time. I directed the satellites to shout in Chinese: "马克思明训喊竞选，电视明训共产加 (Marx-MingXun calling for competitive election, communists adding MingXun on television)." On August 13, 2014, I directed the satellites to shout in Chinese: "马克思明训喊竞选，亚非拉欧共全球 (Marx-MingXun calling for competitive election, the communist parties filling the whole world in Asia, Africa, Latin and Europe)."

On July 27, 2013, I watched on television that the Asian

country Cambodia, a bigger influence from the communist party, was active in the election, learning the democratic culture of China and the United States. On May 16, 2014, I watched on television that riots broke out against Chinese in the southern area of Vietnam. Several days later, the Chinese people and I supported Vietnamese companies in the area with the influence of the Communist Party of Hanoi, which had more potential prospects.

On March 27, 2014, the people in the United States supported Europe in developing communist and liberal democratic parties and constructing numerous small countries of constitutional monarchy. On August 9 of the same year, I learned from the internet that the Spanish Communist Party and King Carlos had once cooperated in history to accomplish the political democratic reformation of constitutional monarchy. Therefore, I collected it as a model.

On December 3, 2014, I watched on television that the domestic and foreign people supported me in timely declaring that the international communist parties had already recovered and, therefore, were capable of segregating the movement "Marx-MingXun calling for competitive election" into the early period of practice on history that the communist parties in various countries resorted to the party disciplines to control the democratic crimes for the first time, guaranteeing safety. After all, my father was far more friendly to the communist parties than Gorbachev and XiaoPing Deng, so it was certainly also the ardent expectations of most international communist parties. Since there was unfavorable influence from some relatives in Shanghai, and my father sometimes contended dominance with me, and the people in

Beijing shouted that the future democratic general secretary might usurp the achievements of my father on international communist parties, I consented to take this measure for safety. In accordance, the movement "Marx-MingXun calling for competitive election," therefore, ended and became history, while I, in addition, began to promote "Democracy of communists San monitors" and "Competitive election of communists San requires" for the purpose of deducting the influence of autocracy from China Central Television (CCTV) on the international communist parties. I directed the satellites to shout in Chinese: "国际共产已恢复，共产民主圣监督 (International communists have recovered, democracy of communists San monitors)." Promulgated in 2016, the new disciplines of the Communist Party of China prohibited its party members from making speeches and expressing opinions incompatible with the Central Committee, manifesting this safety measure as very appropriate. Because of the same reason, Yang Wang was also subjected to the constraint by the new disciplines of the Communist Party of China.

On February 12, 2015, the Chinese people and I actively promoted the functions and status of the people's congresses on the district level, which were elected directly in cities of China. They were capable of controlling the plan of estates and the attraction of factories in the cities. I directed the satellites to shout in Chinese: "房地产工厂区人大 (Real estate and factory, people’s congresses in district)." On the next day, I watched on television that the people in Beijing and the soldiers of the People’s Liberation Army considered that DaWei Zhang in Anhui had timely subsidized and arranged the householders during the relocation and reconstruction. So, he had already compensated more for the losses of the relocated householders, which was certainly legal and had a useful contribution to the rapid construction of the city in the situation of the public owning the land, manifesting that owning the land by the public was beneficial to the construction of cities.

On February 21, 2015, I pointed out that although the communist parties in democratic countries had practised for hundreds of years in competition for elections, at that time, I created a new concept of law to control democracy for the first time and actively promoted the various parties to practise the control of democratic crimes with party disciplines for the first time. I further rectified the discipline of the communist parties with "Marx-MingXun calling for competitive election." So, for the first time, the communist parties were transformed into political parties with their party discipline to control democratic crimes. The synchronous revival of the communist parties in various countries around the world just manifested the historical effects of "Marx-MingXun calling for competitive election" to rectify the discipline of the party and control democratic crimes through the party discipline.

On April 15, 2015, I watched Italian football players on television say that many social and regional affairs required democratic decisions, so it was impossible for democracy to be totally substituted by the law.

On July 13, 2015, I raised the issue that I wanted to utilize the force of the Christian religion to increase the organizational force of democracy in China. On April 4, 2016, I called for the Demo-League of China and the China Association for Promoting Democracy to unite with the Christian religion to monitor the Military Committee so that the democratic parties and religions could expand greatly in force. I directed the satellites to shout in Chinese: "民盟民进基督教 (Demo-League and Demo-Promoting unite with the Christian religion)."

On September 3, 2015, the people and I recognized that it was not appropriate to argue about two such concepts as the law to regulate democracy and democratic management. Therefore, whichever of these two concepts would become formal depended on their usage in future. I directed the satellites to shout in Chinese: "法治民主，民主治理，以用为准 (Law to regulate democracy or democratic management, whichever utilized is formal)." On June 15, 2016, I pointed out that the law to regulate democracy belonged to the democratic management, and it was further the most outstanding portion of the management, even dealing with the crimes and destructions from the democracy itself. On February 28, 2017, people in various countries recognized that it should be more suitable to use "Democratic crimes, party disciplines to control" to manifest such a concept. I directed the satellites to shout in Chinese: "民主犯罪，党纪治理 (Democratic crimes, party disciplines to control)."

On August 4, 2016, people in various countries, including me, pointed out that the theories of Marxism represented the poor people, emphasizing the consciousness of communism and reprimanding luxurious needs. Therefore, the needs of individuals requiring accommodation by communism should be compatible with social welfare. I directed the satellites to shout in Chinese: “奢侈需求共批判，共产需求是福利 (Communists reprimand the luxury needs, the needs of communism are welfare).”

On January 6, 2017, I pointed out that communism required distribution to meet the needs, and it was certainly obligatory to accommodate the needs of individual persons. So, it contained the characteristics of the marketing economy, while the planned economy might only be the characteristic of some countries of socialism. I directed the satellites to shout in Chinese: “社会主义计划经济，共产主义市场经济 (Socialism planned economy, communism marketing economy).”

On June 4, 2017, I recognized that installing the computer programs to realize the control of democratic crimes would still be incompetent to the method of party disciplines in congress demonstrated in this chapter because whichever computer program it was, it should constrain a lot on the invasion of army and police, and would definitely cause the death of the country.

The movement “Marx-MingXun calling for competitive election” overcame the tendency of contemporary communist parties to despise democracy and emphasize revolution under the direction of Marxism-Leninism, and rectified the flag and discipline of communist parties, which improved the democratic reputation of communist parties in the whole world and resorted to the party discipline to practise the control of democratic crimes in various countries in the world for the first time. Besides, the movement “Marx-MingXun calling for competitive election” concurrently constructed the democratic culture in China and successfully transformed the

Chinese army into a solid democratic skeleton. Social welfare, labor conditions, medication, and education were the important tasks of communist parties that they had been practising for a long time, while the communist parties in democratic countries had also been practising for hundreds of years in the competition for election. Therefore, the global synchronous revival of communist parties in various countries at that time just fully manifested the significant social effects of "Marx-MingXun calling for competitive election" in rectifying the discipline of the party and resorting to the discipline of the party to practise the control of the democratic crimes for the first time, considerable on historical significance.

In all, after I tried to act as the Holy Spirit in the United States and dreamed of improving the democratic management of the country with religious kindness, there were parties with flags and symbols, such as the communist parties in various countries in the world, the Democratic National Construction Association in China, the Christian Democratic Union in Germany, the Democratic Progressive Party in Taiwan and so on, practising to control the democratic crimes with the party disciplines for the first time. Besides, there were further added measures such as rectification of party disciplines, the parliamentary proportional system of representatives, replacement of prime minister and other ministers, and so on, altogether comprising the major methods and forms of contemporary democratic management and control of democratic crimes. In democratic management, changing the prime minister played a huge role, while the party disciplines only played cooperative and supplementary roles. However, in controlling democratic crimes, the party disciplines played a huge role.

End poem of the illustrated chapter:

The communist parties for competitive election Marx-MingXun advocating,
The global revival of communist parties synchronously showing,
The democratic crimes the party disciplines capable of controlling and regulating,
The democratic management of the country both law and discipline capable of assisting.

Chapter | 17

Defects of Administration,

Demonstration to Make Up

Musical Background of Rhythmic Writing: The Same Song

Please read the following text sentence-by-sentence to feel the music background of the rhythmic framework.

On September 16, 2008, I considered the supplement of another half deficient in the contemporary European and American system of democracy and law and extended the application of examination and assessment in the country. Although it was common and regular nowadays that the civil servants and police were admitted through examination, it was not sufficient in its influence on politics and the country. A male Beijing satellite operator pointed out that to make sure that it was not controlled by the parties, it was obligatory to change the proposals from Congress to the whole people. I perceived that there must be too many in quantity if the proposals from the whole people were adopted, so it was reasonable to adopt the method of proposal from the whole people plus the standard examination. I directed the satellites to shout in Chinese: "全民提案加统考 (Proposal from the whole people plus the standard examination)." Many athletes of the Beijing Paralympic Games were likewise discussing this topic, while there was a lack of audience on television with little influence.

On September 17, 2008, I carried out an inspection and evaluation of the democracy and examination. Both the civil servants and police needed to take the examination and accept the low salary. Therefore, it was impossible to hire the most excellent candidates. The raisers of proposals needed to take the examination. However, during the review of the examination, it was more prevalent for the priority of the country and, therefore, favorable neither to the benefits of people nor to the democracy of parties and religions.

On November 9, 2008, I watched on television that the Taiwanese recognized that the substitution of congress election with examination might be equivalent to the governing of the Nationalist Party in Taiwan for a long time, manifesting that the system of examination should be more monotonous and inflexible than that of election. Therefore, the congress should still use the system of election in future. I directed the satellites to shout in Chinese: "考试单调选举优 (Examination monotonous while election advantageous)." On March 7, 2013, I pointed out that the examination only assayed personal ability, while the debate was then capable of considering comprehensively. Therefore, on intelligence, the autocratic examination was incompetent in the democratic debate. I directed the satellites to shout in Chinese: "考试失败辩论喊 (Debate shouts, exam fails)."

On July 10, 2009, I was required to constrain the police on their suppressing the demonstration of people with shots. As per law, the police were only capable of using tear gas and high-pressure water jets to deal with the people; they were not allowed to hurt any person with a shot at ease, and it was their obligatory duty to sacrifice themselves for the public affairs. On February 15, 2010, people in various countries, including me, recognized that the demonstration and occupation of public squares was analogous to the army without food and money. Therefore, so long as the suppression from the army and police was tenacious and persistent, they should be capable of realizing clearance without shots and victims. I directed the satellites to shout in Chinese: "无伤亡清场军警顽强 (The army and police must be tenacious to clear without victims)." On January 4, 2012, I directed the satellites to shout in Chinese: "警察机枪摄像机 (Police machine gun with video camera)."

On August 3, 2009, a US satellite operator said that Congress was the channel of the market for society, so the election should possess more social advantages. I consented and supplemented by saying that if the examination for Congress was adopted, the members of Congress would reversely run for their own benefits and might even start a personal movement beneficial to themselves and harmful to others. Before then, I had also considered that point belonging to the defect of examination, but after that moment, I began promoting this reason up to the major defect of examination. I directed the satellites to shout in Chinese: "私人运动，考试弊端，台星圣喊叫 (Personal movement as a defect of examination, Taiwan, San and satellites shout)."

On May 25, 2010, I became aware that the biggest defect of examination and personal movements was that the examinees flattered for their own benefit, licking the boots of their supervisors and examiners and even plundering the local properties without bothering the fates of people at all. I directed the satellites to shout in Chinese: "私人运动拍马屁 (Personal movement flatters)."

On March 13, 2011, I learnt from internet that, during the era of AnShi Wang of the Song Dynasty, the Chinese were already aware of the defects of examination, which included complying with and flattering the higher officers, avoiding and escaping reality, and calling a deer a horse. On March 14 of the same year, I directed the satellites to shout in Chinese: "考试弊端宋问题 (Exam defects as a problem during Song Dynasty)."

On June 24, 2012, I believed that the communist parties in India and Europe should promote their own influence by demonstrating that they were more advantageous on social feedback than the traditional administrative bureaucrats. On October 22 of the same year, the people and I encouraged the Latin communist parties to go on demonstrating the important role of communist parties in giving feedback with demonstrations. The satellite operators and I further added Asia, Africa and Europe. I directed the satellites to shout in Chinese: "马克思明训喊竞选，亚非拉欧共游行 (Marx-MingXun calling for competitive election, the communist parties march in Asia, Africa, Latin and Europe)."
On August 29, 2012, while watching television, I saw that the Beijing artistic actors said that the audiences might take after me and likewise consciously preserve the political dominance. I believed that the obsequious and flattering actors and audiences would shout more loudly, so it was obligatory to have a leader like me with a clear political purpose to specifically coordinate and maintain.

On September 17, 2012, I found on the internet that, on the 15th and 16th of the same month, the people in SuZhou, GuangZhou, Shanghai, Beijing, ShenZhen, XiAn, ChangSha, NanChang, WuHan and so on spontaneously hurried to go on parade before September 18, protesting the recent invasion from Japan and the United States onto the Chinese DiaoYu Islands. In the evening, while watching television, I saw somebody in Shanghai point out that the domestic parade should be accompanied by a speech.

In the middle of July 2013, an artistic performance was carried out for Confucius in Shandong, eliciting the people and me to make use of the theory of Confucius and Mencius about governing the country with kindheartedness to counter the crimes of bureaucrats then. On July 28 of the same year, the Chinese people analogized the demonstration for the livelihood of international communists to the governmental kindheartedness of Confucius and Mencius, glorifying the Confucian theorem of governing during the feudal era in China. On August 1 of the same year, I directed the satellites to shout in Chinese: "中华游行，孔孟现代 (Demonstration in China, Modern Confucianism and Mencianism)."

On August 10, 2013, while watching television, I saw that the Brazilian people said that in the next presidential election of the big country, they should not vote for those from the factions of demonstration and democrats, while the leaders of the demonstration should be appropriate to be elected as the parliamentarians and vice president. I directed the satellites to shout in Chinese: "游行领导副总统 (Demonstration leader to vice president)."

On September 24, 2013, since the people in the domestic

parade were too small in scale and too few in quantity, I threatened and said that if there were too few people in the parade, the bosses might immigrate out. I directed the satellites to shout in Chinese: "游行太少，老板移民 (Parade too few, the bosses immigrate)."

So far, in this regard, the main forces for the democracy calling for law execution in China during the early stage had been the satellite shouts I directed, the responses of the leaders in Shanghai, the GuangDong people threatening and revenging the retired bureaucrats, and the geographic and religious influences in XinJiang, Tibet, GuangXi and the old liberated area of the New Fourth Army. During the later stage, they transformed into the rectification of the communist parties with "Marx-MingXun calling for competitive election" I directed, and the People's Liberation Army admitting the republics, while on the basis of them, there even synthetically emerged the slogan of high pressure "共和镇央党代会 (Republics down the Central Committee with the Representative Meeting of Party)," directly improving the democratic rights of the republic country. China had never reached the high violence as in the regions of the Middle East, nor was it big in the force of demonstration from the people.

On October 22, 2014, people in various countries in the world, including me, recognized that mayors and government officers of various ranks should learn to make vows to the people, changing their habits like the armored warriors and changing their styles of work. The Beijing people said that the attitude of ZiYang Zhao to the students in demonstration was correct in 1989. Soon, the people and I utilized the famous phrase of ZeDong Mao "Serving for the people" as the behavioral criteria for public servants in China.

On January 23, 2015, people in various countries, including me, found that the examination on internet in the future would be more reliable than the brand of university nowadays, supplying various talents on the basis of qualification and comparable ranks to employers such as the government, enterprises, hospitals and so on. The Chinese people expected to inherit the examination as an excellent culture rather than the political system, which paralleled the assessment of achievements while glorifying each other in contrast.

On April 4, 2017, after waking up early in the morning, I pointed out that the television university should definitely be more successful, while its public examination happened to correspond to the traditional Imperial Examination System in old China, fairer and more open. I directed the satellites to shout in Chinese: "电视大学科举喊 (The Imperial Examination System shouts for the television university)."

End poem of the illustrated chapter:

The flatteries as defect of examination existing,
The social situations and public opinions the democracy undertaking,
The examination choosing talents while it being more comprehensive for debating,
The administration blocking while the demonstration altogether shouting.

Chapter | 18

Provincial and Municipal Legislation, Republics and Armed Police

Musical Background of Rhythmic Writing: Blue Danube Waltz

Please read the following text sentence-by-sentence to feel the music background of the rhythmic framework.

In 2005, I set up a matrimonial agency on my own. I personally experienced how difficult it was to pair a male and a female to marry willingly and live together all lifelong. I also observed that there were a great number of people who were unable to marry and reproduce. Accordingly, it was necessary to encourage the sexual business to become legal and professional to reduce the threshold of reproduction. Merely in this way, it was possible to make most of the people realize reproduction fluently.

In many dance halls in Suzhou, there was a dance service in the dark. It was necessary for a man to pay ¥10RMB to a miss if he asked her to accompany him in a dance in the dark. The man was allowed to fumble on every part of the body of the miss. In this way, many men were able to fumble the miss, whereas the miss was able to have more than ten dances in the dark a day with a considerable monthly income. Since January 2006, I have been frequently going to the dance hall and dancing in the dark.

On December 30 2006, I learned from internet that it was legal for the whorehouses in Australia, the Netherlands, Germany and Nevada in the United States, whereas Great Britain and Italy were trying to make them legal.

On October 29 2007, I was worried that it could increase the burden of people to revenge with the law as I shouted for democracy without a child. I directed the satellites to shout in Chinese: "喊民主强迫生孩子 (Shouting democracy be forced to reproduce)."

Several years ago, in the face of the satellite terrors, I did not adopt the measure of fast marriage and fast reproduction; instead, I adopted the publicly recognized but wrong measure at that time, which was the reproduction of children after arresting the satellite criminals. On November 11 & 12, 2007, I rectified this issue to reasonably reproduce more children as early as possible to reduce the burden on people. Presently, in China, even newly-born children are allowed to become citizens, showing a dark side of the society.

Due to the dual shocks from the entrepreneurial resistance and economic crisis of Europe and the United States, it was very difficult for my company to run the headhunting business. After June 2008, I relied on my father's retirement pension to maintain my daily life, and it took several years for me to translate and email the Chinese and English versions of my two books on armed police and physics colloquia. In 2009, the swing of Obama to the eastern side of the United States made less fortune to my European and US business. Before 2010, I had been living outside of my company for safety purposes. However, after the Spring

Festival in 2010, I was unable to pay the rent. Accordingly, I had to move back home to live with my father and started to cooperate with him in writing the principles and lists of Chinese chess. After 2014, to resist the rumors, I restarted writing many scientific papers, and spent time in writing, translating and dubbing this book of memoirs, with a desire to publish it in early 2018. Unfortunately, the popularization of internet influenced the market of printed literature, and accordingly my economic remuneration from the writings was very little.

On March 23 2009, I equalized the revenge of extinction against East China with that against Beijing in regard to my being unable to marry and reproduce to reduce the burden merely on East China. In 2010, I registered in many marriage agencies in SuZhou and required very low without considering the female appearance. Whereas, I was still unable to get any girlfriend for marriage, which elicited the opposition between me and the people in SuZhou. Actually, many single and divorced persons in the agencies of marriage possessed the psychology of misanthropy, enthusiastic to devastation and extinction. Accordingly, I was forced to turn to the dancers.

On August 14 2009, I discovered that, in the period of national succession in the future, if the southwestern three provinces, namely GuangXi, YunNan and GuiZhou, in China, apprehended the chance to declare independence, they could indeed develop better, as a consequence of natural geography. On October 14, 2010, the Chinese people and I actively promoted the internationalization of GuangXi. In 2011, GuangXi was excellent as the manifestation in the competitive election at the basic level. On February 14 2012, I saw many Chinese say that SiChuan and XinJiang would not be willing to become independent; instead, they would be willing to join and constitute a big country like China. On June 16 of that year, while watching the news on the television, I saw many people in China saying that if China could occupy Myanmar, there would be an additional exit to the sea in the western area, and it would acquire the same geographic advantage as the United States with two sides facing the sea. Accordingly, it was possible to constitute a big country like China. On March 26, 2013, people in various countries, including me, noticed that the regional livelihood in Inner Mongolia wished to follow a big country like China, whereas, in a big northern country in the shape of a long tail with northeastern China and Mongolia, it was relatively difficult in livelihood. Accordingly, it was possible to appear as a small country in northeastern China without anybody being interested in it.

On March 26 2010, the Chinese people thought BangGuo Wu should also be eligible to take over as the general secretary in the next term, competing with JinPing Xi. I directed the satellites to shout in Chinese: "下届总书记吴邦国 (Next general secretary BangGuo Wu)." On April 26 of that year, while watching the news on television, I saw that BangGuo Wu was willing to take over as a major leader of the Central Committee, and accordingly, the whole country was warmly supporting him.

On May 22, 2010, people in various countries, including me, encouraged Asia to colonize California and influence the inland of the United States. On the afternoon of June 18 of the same year, while watching the Football World Cup, I saw the

Mexicans reiterate the friendship I had communicated with them. Mexico became the new market of Asia and India in northern America. The western part of the United States could ally with Mexico to further internationalize. I directed the satellites to shout in Chinese: “加州亚印墨西哥 (California to Asia, India, Mexico).”

On November 21, 2010, I supported the United States to relocate the capital and directed the satellites to shout: “US Denver capital.” On May 8, 2013, a US satellite operator reminded me that the support to relocate the capital would increase the rumours about me in the United States. So, I decided to give up the relocation of capital. I directed the satellites to shout in Chinese: “美国迁都圣放弃 (San gives up the relocation of US capital).”

On the evening of March 27, 2011, since it was necessary to get pregnant for reproduction, I required the Gods in various present religions to bless me with a sexual life to overcome sexual difficulties in the future. I directed the satellites to shout: “Home sex bless.”

On the evening of November 4, 2011, while watching the news on television, I saw the Central Committee rudely depose the democratic governor HuaHua Huang in GuangDong, who was still in his term. The people in GuangDong strongly required the Communist Party to dismiss the party member YongQing Liu, the wife of JinTao Hu, to demonstrate the revenge and punishment. The next day, while watching the news on television, I saw that JinTao Hu confessed that it was he who disposed of HuaHua Huang. On December 31 of that year, I learned from internet that the Standing Committee of the National People’s Congress voted to nominate HuaHua Huang as the vice chairman of Oversea Chinese Affairs Commission in the National People's Congress. Accordingly, I decided to withdraw the revenge on the party member YongQing Liu, the wife of JinTao Hu. I directed the satellites to shout in Chinese: "黄华华人大共永清 (HuaHua Huang to National People's Congress, YongQing to Communist Party)."

On November 29, 2011, before falling asleep, I pointed out that it would be one of the characteristics of Muslims to be glorious in the army and police. XinJiang in China had also contributed much to the movement of democracy calling on law execution I directed in China, standing shoulder to shoulder with GuangDong, GuangXi, and East China. That morning, I directed the satellites to shout in Chinese: "印尼发展警武装 (Indonesia develops armed police)."

On the evening of December 2, 2011, the satellite operators and I realized that to build the armed police, it was unnecessary to wait until the legislation of direct election of municipal congresses. The provincial leaders, as the Members of the Central Committee, would have both the courage and might to operate. In the areas, such as the old liberated regions, GuangDong, Shanghai and so on, all were courageous to arm their own police. I directed the satellites to shout in Chinese: "警察武装老区响 (Armed police sonorous in the old liberated areas)."

On December 3, 2011, the Chinese people and I further realized that the infantry truck of the present army was incompetent to the police car and motorcycle in both maneuver and combat abilities. It was necessary to gradually equip the infantry with police cars and motorcycles and eventually substitute the infantry with police. I directed the satellites to shout in Chinese: "步兵卡车换警车 (Infantry truck changed to police car)," "直升机高炮城市警 (Helicopter and antiaircraft artillery to municipal police)," "沿海市警火箭炮 (Rocket artillery to coastal municipal police)."

On December 7, 2011, while watching the news on television, I saw that WeiFa Liang, a member of the Provincial Standing Committee and director of the Public Security Department in GuangDong, called on the provincial and municipal police in GuangDong to increase the heavy pieces of equipment, such as the helicopters, patrolling boats, antiaircraft artilleries and so on, to contribute a part to the construction of armed police.

On February 28, 2012, while watching the news, I saw many people in China say that it was reasonable to add the United States to the construction of armed police to repay the US satellites for their assistance to me. I agreed with them immediately and directed the satellites to shout in Chinese: "美国军队参加警 (US army joins police)." In July of that year, I learned from internet that the strategic reserve force of the United States was the United States National Guard, supervised by the states, equipped with heavy weapons, and originated from the early militia. On May 8, 2013, I learned from internet that the members of the United States National Guard usually held their own jobs and occasionally took part in the militia, different from the professional armed police. Accordingly, it was necessary for the United States to change its organization and set up armed police. In contrast, the US army had already realized the dual commands from the president and congress, while half of the land army was the United States National Guard supervised by the states, and in addition, there were Christian priests to coach the soldiers. Accordingly, the US army exceeded the Chinese army and became the strongest army in the current democracy.

On May 5, 2012, while watching the news, I saw the domestic and foreign people point out that if JinPing Xi and Beijing murdered me and resulted in my extinction without offspring, Hebei would be the place of his birth to be extinct to compensate for me. On September 14 of that year, I said that it was the natural right protected in law for me to reproduce offspring, and I was not willing to bargain it with any achievements made with satellites. In addition, the Holy Spirit had the right to reproduce offspring, just as Jesus was the son of God. Later, I learned from internet that HongZhi Li, the God of FaLun Gong, reproduced offspring, while XiuQuan Hong, the self-declared brother of Jesus, had also reproduced many offspring. On December 21 of that year, the Beijing people and I developed a method to realize the revenge of subspecies with the party disciplines to reduce the population via birth control in the long term.

On May 14, 2012, I learned from internet that the Provincial Standing Committee of GuangDong headed with Yang Wang changed on succession. ZhiHeng Xiao, WeiFa Liang and GuangNing Zhang, the original members of the Standing Committee, were all excluded, with none reaching the retirement age. They were all the leaders the GuangDong people were fond of. WeiFa Liang had even called for the construction of armed police. The people and I called on revenge. In the evening, while watching the news, I saw that

JinTao Hu denied that he was involved in the change of the Provincial Standing Committee of GuangDong, and I saw that Yang Wang and YuMei Li said that YuanChao Li from the Organization Department of the Central Committee stressed to them the image of leadership of JinTao Hu as general secretary, following which Yang Wang changed them out. I assumed that Yang Wang would be responsible for half liability without protecting the benefits of people in GuangDong, whereas YuanChao Li was responsible for another half liability. Accordingly, the co-operators of democracy calling for law execution in the GuangDong Provincial Party Committee were HuaHua Huang as the principal and Yang Wang as the accessory. On August 16 of that year, I learned from internet that Xiong Lin in GuangDong was degraded from the Minister of Propaganda to the United Front. Yang Wang and the Central Committee punished the GuangDong Satellite Television for ignoring "Marx-MingXun calling for competitive election" and resisting to report the election at the basic level in GuangDong in 2011, which indicated that the mind of Yang Wang on democracy and law had not turned to reactionary. Accordingly, Yang Wang was still accepted as the co-operator of democracy calling for law execution in GuangDong, sharing with HuaHua Huang, whereas necessarily subjected to continual observation.

On November 15, 2012, while watching the news, I saw JinPing Xi use his power to exclude Yang Wang from the new Standing Committee of Political Bureau in the 18th Congress of the Communist Party of China. On the evening of November 16 of that year, while watching the news, I saw somebody in Beijing think in the daytime that Yang Wang could take over as the National President of Supreme Court to ameliorate the embarrassing situation that was created after JinPing Xi excluded Yang Wang from the Standing Committee of Political Bureau. I directed the satellites to shout in Chinese: "法院院长喊汪洋 (Shouting Yang Wang to the President of the Supreme Court)."

In the second half of the year 2012, the people and I started to adopt "Marx-MingXun calling for competitive election" as the new flag and discipline for the communist parties to restrict the National People's Congress, skipping the dangerous general secretary, and placing him on the high pavilion, just as the autocratic president was expelled. On the evening of November 24, I pointed out that the kids and siblings of JinPing Xi had all gone and settled abroad, whereas he held the power of the military in his hand and behaved highly dangerously in the 18th Congress of the Communist Party. Accordingly, the democracy calling for law execution did not aim at him to avoid the disaster. On November 29, 2013, to overcome the infestation and tyranny from the majority of the highest leaders in China at the present time, the Chinese people and I objected to the direct election of the national chairman. We criticized the direct election of the president in the United States, which might result in the difficulty of communist parties in election and politics and designed the Republic country of China to govern on the basis of power division with provinces and cities in the future, temporarily giving up the competitive election of general secretary.

On the evening of December 20, 2012, I saw many Chinese people say that at the foot of the Great Wall, the

Beijing people behaved like gangsters and captives, shouting for bullets and terrifying the family. In this regard, the women there should be compensated for marrying me as San Force, whereas the duty of Eastern China would be less.

On January 15, 2013, before falling asleep, I learned from internet that both China and Russia encouraged North-eastern China to exit to the sea in the east via the Tumen River. Vladivostok was the important economic center of Russia in its Far Eastern Region, whereas other regions of Russia were far away from the Chinese regions of high density in population, difficult to develop. Accordingly, it would be more humane to allocate it to Russia. I directed the satellites to shout in Chinese: "图们江出海中宣传 (China propagates to exit to sea via Tumen River)." On March 1, 2015, on schedule, I assisted in promoting the development of Tumen River and directed the satellites to shout in Chinese: "东北开发图们江 (Northeast develops Tumen River)." On December 16, 2017, I directed the satellites to shout in Chinese: "韩国开发图们江 (South Korea develops Tumen River)."

On February 21, 2013, the Japanese prime minister and I realized that since Asia significantly influenced the western regions of the United States, as soon as Latin America and Mexico influenced the United States from the south, it would be feasible to dominate the majority of the United States. On July 4 of that year, while watching the news, I saw many people in the countries in Southern America actively suppress Washington DC as the capital of the United States. On March 8, 2014, while watching the basketball games in the United States, I saw that the blacks in Texas recovered, rose up, cooperated, and united with California. On October 26, 2015, the American people and I proposed to the United States to relocate Huston as the center of financial investment. I directed the satellites to shout in Chinese: "投资中心休斯顿 (Investment center Huston)."

On March 15, 2013, I learned from internet that the National People's Congress did not elect Yang Wang the President of the Supreme Court, whereas the new National Chairman, JinPing Xi, nonetheless, promoted YuanChao Li, who was not within the Central Standing Committee, as the Vice Chairman, despising the country, violating the nomination of the Second Plenary Session of the 18th Central Committee and the discipline of Party, and accordingly losing his Party membership in the law of history. On the next day, Yang Wang was elected the Vice Prime Minister in charge of trade, tourism and agriculture.

YuanChao Li degraded and extruded WeiFa Liang, calling for the construction of armed police out of the GuangDong Standing Committee in 2012, which should be treated with the historical law, dismissing his Party membership. On February 11, 2015, due to the malicious prohibition of the expression of opinions and views, the people and I appealed to the law in history to dismiss the membership of the Communist Party of LiQun Deng in the time of XiaoPing Deng in a conservative school.

In addition, in the earthquake in SiChuan in 2008, the China Central Television broadcast in a large quantity that the local officers of Party and government were afraid of the threats of Beijing gangsters and yellow perils, whereas not active in disaster relief. The ChengDu Military District reversely shouted ZeDong Mao, resulting in the death of

60000 people in SiChuan that year. Accordingly, it was necessary to inform the historical law later to consider using the discipline of the party to treat ChangChun Li and YunShan Liu as the leaders of Central Propaganda Department. YunShan Liu was elected a member of the Standing Committee of the Political Bureau in the 18th National Congress of the Communist Party of China, and accordingly, could be inspected within the Party and treated in the integration of his total contributions and mistakes. In 2017, he supported YanAn in taking over power and correcting the political attitude. ChangChun Li was better in ethics, whereas unable in management. In contrast, JiaBao Wen and QingLin Jia were strange and odious, numerous in ridiculous and ugly behaviors in the later stages. It was necessary to compare to make treatment with the discipline of Party. JiaBao Wen made a severe mistake by rescuing BeiChuan. Whereas, according to the integrative situations of his duty as Prime Minister for ten years, he could either be treated on probation within the Party or dismissed from the Party, leaving to the historical law to judge. In 2017, when SiChuan turned to the Central Committee, another earthquake occurred there. The Chinese people and I were similarly inactive to rescue them, and were similar to JiaBao Wen as belonging to the natural reduction in rescue of illegal people. QingLin Jia, during the last several years in his position, said on television several times that he would not be willing to keep his membership in the Communist Party, as he was leaving history later to deal with.

On March 30, 2013, I thought that, since Inner Mongolia followed the big country China to reduce the risk of splitting, it was necessary to promote the legislation by provinces and cities, improve the people's livelihood with democracy, and facilitate the construction of republics. I directed the satellites to shout in Chinese: "省市人大，民生立法 (Provincial and municipal congress, Legislation for people's livelihood)." While watching the news, I saw that in the domestic basketball games one day earlier, many people had wished me to start the provincial and municipal legislation movement as early as possible. On December 20, 2016, people in various countries realized that the provincial and municipal legislation in China would help in the development of the sex industry in the future. A European satellite operator said that the country would be more similar to the European Union after the provincial and municipal legislation, certainly better than the National People's Congress in legislation.

On April 11, 2013, the people and I increased the surveillance and prevalence of the People's Congress over the government while gradually decreasing the personal influence of the general secretary and prime minister of the country.

On March 9, 2015, the satellite operators and I similarly increased the monitoring from the People's Congress to the army, which encouraged the two National Conferences being held in sessions: The democratic parties synchronous with the Communist Party, and the democratic might superior overall. After 2016, the people and I further started monitoring from the Christian religion, which the People's Liberation Army dared not deal with crudely.

On July 8, 2013, I discovered that it would be difficult for the congresses of various provinces and cities to actively share the budgets of armed police, as the budgets belonged to the expenditure of national defence, without any reward to the provinces and cities. On September 15 of that year, I learned from internet that the Chinese militia were supervised by the Headquarters of General Staff as well as the various military regions, whereas the armed police were nonetheless compliant to the commands from the Bureaus of Public Security in provinces and cities. Accordingly, it was the key to the construction of armed police in China to transform the militia with poor equipment into the reserves of police. On December 23 of that year, the Chinese soldiers and I discovered that the armed police were better trained in running and fighting than the militia. On May 6, 2014, the Chinese people and I realized that the General Logistics Department could directly issue a notice and ask the provincial and municipal police to store and monitor the weapons of the militia.

On September 4, 2013, while watching the news, I saw the People's Liberation Army say that the naval and air forces were subjected to the protection and surveillance of the armed police in various provinces. The next day, I saw the senators in the United States say that the US Air Force also belonged to the National Guard.

On the evening of January 29, 2014, while watching the news, I saw that JinPing Xi was suffering from twitching while speaking and had a trance appearance. I required the Chinese army to segregate him as early as possible; otherwise, he might manifest more dangerous behaviors. Segregation and fighting were the duties of the army, aiming at the criminal words and deeds of the Chairman of the Military Committee, irrelevant to the democracy calling for law execution. After the second half of the year 2012, I no longer aimed at the general secretary of great danger for the democracy calling for law execution, as the People's Congress was the legislative organization of democratic election. On February 25, 2015, the people and I associated the general secretary as the real secretary of the Communist Party with the segregation of the chairman by the People's Liberation Army. I directed the satellites to shout in Chinese: "总书记秘书党员喊，隔离主席解放军 (The party members shout general secretary to real secretary, the People's Liberation Army segregates chairman)."

On February 19, 2014, people in various countries, including me, noticed that the local provincial and municipal banks were constrained by the people in deposit and withdraw and were accordingly folksier. In contrast, the national banks would foster the authority of the prime minister and government. On March 1 of that year, I adopted the local banks to improve the situation in the United States. I directed the satellites to shout: "US bank state." On October 26, 2015, I encouraged the people in the United States to construct Houston, Texas, as the center of finance and investment.

On May 6, 2014, while watching the news, I saw that people in Africa said that the armed police were strong in their image and could reduce the terrific organizations in Africa. Accordingly, they backed the armed police. In the afternoon, I directed the satellites to shout in Chinese: "中美非洲警武装 (Armed police in China, US and Africa)." Mauritius, a small country in Africa, was also one of the earliest countries to realize the armed police. On August 17, 2017, people in various countries realized that in India and Africa, the soldiers were very active at the basic level, and accordingly, the armed police were more efficient than the second command from the congress to control the army.

In June 2014, Yang Wang reversely flattered to JinPing Xi in public situations, such as meetings, and reversely complained about me as an obstacle on his way to being promoted to the Standing Committee. In the ordinary time, he was slow in reaction and sometimes behaved as an embarrassment, and accordingly, the people and army were all unsatisfied with Yang Wang becoming the important image of the country in the future. In the news, I saw many people in China remind me that Yang Wang had dismissed WeiFa Liang in GuangDong and hindered the construction of armed police there, and called on the army and police to cooperate to suppress his status in the country in the future. On the evening of June 19, 2015, while watching the news, I saw that Yang Wang agreed with the wrong opinion of YuanChao Li in the meeting. After getting the permission to rumor my papers, he vented and revenged for his not being promoted because of me, flattering JinPing Xi in attendance. China was really hard to suffer from the duty of compensation. On April 29, 2016, I proposed that the army would not tolerate any behavior to connive for rumor in light of the award to the military achievements of battle.

On July 5, 2014, while watching the news, I saw that JinPing Xi strangely thought in fantasy to detour the army and resort to the armed police in province to assassinate me. Several days later, he further imitated the German footballers and required ShanXi to assassinate me and die along with me. On September 28, 2015, JinPing Xi even asked Ban Ki-Moon, the General Secretary of the United Nations, to send me to prison as a gift. All of these increased the difficulty of my marriage.

On August 12, 2014, while watching the news, I saw that people in various countries thought that in World War II, the Japanese had surrendered after being hurt by two atomic bombs. It would be more embarrassing this time if JinPing Xi terrified as yellow perils and resulted in my extinction. I, on the other hand, required the parties of law to take revenge and abuse the two cities, namely Beijing and Suzhou, to be extinct for compensation with one district from each of them. Soon, the Chinese people wished to remember the history of XianZhong Zhang in SiChuan as he had slaughtered the people there. On February 8, 2016, I glorified my political achievements, just as the United States dropped the atomic bombs on Japan in World War II to reduce the casualties. I directed the satellites to shout in Chinese: "警杀减杀超 2 区 (Police reduce killing more than killing 2 districts)." On December 18, 2017, the people and I proposed that the required decrease in population in a district in the period of gradual extinction from the reduction of reproduction would greatly exceed the total population in the district due to the inflow from the surrounding areas, whereas the decrease in the density of population in the surrounding areas would make up reproduction, and accordingly the net population of extinction would still be equal to that in one district. In the time of XiaoPing Deng, family planning in China would have reduced the population by hundreds of millions.

On October 23, 2014, the 4th Plenary Session of the 18th Central Committee of the Communist Party of China laid stress on running the country with law, ending the fashion of illegal roads during JinTao Hu.

On October 26, 2014, the Chinese people considered that the national flag and emblem of China indicated the leadership of the Communist Party in the country. To change them, it was necessary to resort to the referendum, and it was uneasy to practise. Accordingly, the republic system, along with the provincial and municipal democratic legislation, was actually the outlet of China. In addition, with the discipline of the Communist Party in welfare, it would be impossible to address the disaster of livelihood in China at a large scale, while it could further propagate the philosophy of Confucianism as kindness to international societies, which is really a good chance to the provincial and municipal democratic legislation. On November 8, 2016, I said that, as one of the contributors to the theory of armed police, I would naturally promote democratic legislation in provinces and cities to glorify the armed police. I did not impose the flag of five stars and certainly did not have the duty to change it. On the evening of January 5, 2017, while watching the news, I saw that the Beijing people considered that the constitutional monarchy was even worse, and accordingly, the provincial and municipal democratic legislation under the leadership of the Communist Party was also respectable, whereas, in Asia, the ideology of ZeDong Mao to put down the empire with violence was also significant in education. On January 7 of that year, the Chinese people considered that to elect the Chairman with the two sessions as the democratic People's

Congress and the elite Political Consultative Conference, it was sufficient to preserve the flag of five stars without any alteration.

On October 28, 2014, people in various countries, including me, anticipated Afghanistan to comply with Pakistan. In the news, I saw that the President of Afghanistan also agreed and propagated this opinion. Several months earlier, I had already adopted Pakistan to substitute Iran to represent Muslims, gradually increasing the progressive forces of Muslims in various countries in the Middle East. On the evening of February 7, 2015, while watching the news, I saw that the domestic people instigated XinJiang to shout big breasts of Iranians. I said that, with the democratic discipline of the Communist Party, the north-western people in China could unite with Pakistan bravely and promote the secularization of dressing in Iran. On the next day, the people and I actively promoted the women in the airline companies, restaurants and hotels in Pakistan to serve with western suits, and adopted business to strongly promote the modernization of dressing of Muslims. There was even no discipline in the Koran yet to force women to wear the veil, whereas it was the believers in Muslims themselves who abused women. I directed the satellites to shout in Chinese: "巴基斯坦宾馆女西装 (Women in Pakistan in western suits in hotels)."

At the end of 2014, people in various countries, including me, encouraged Italy and Greece to pay attention to exit eastward to the sea via the Red Sea in Arab to India and Asia. On the evening of January 12, 2015, while watching the news, I saw that the first female President in Croatia in Eastern Europe promptly promoted the international awareness of the country. In the middle of that year, while publishing my book on the electromagnetic unification of four forces, the German people recovered in confidence. I guided the German people to back the parliamentary politics in time and, along with other countries in Middle and Eastern Europe, glorify the parliamentary system with both the president and prime minister they had established first. On November 28, 2016, as the whites said to hurt Italy, I decided Hungary and Eastern Europe as the new European center of politics. In December 2017, both Hungary and Austria received support from Italy and Russia.

On February 9, 2015, the people and I adopted the incorruptible manner of "Government no to Beijing companies" to block the bad habit of Beijing companies of borrowing from the government to earn. Later, as JinPing Xi sometimes instigated the terrific expressions inopportune to my marriage without considering the embarrassing situation of Beijing necessary to compensate me for the extinction of one district, the people in Beijing gradually supported my leadership, significantly improving the local habits there. On January 19, 2017, the people and I allied with the more democratic People's Congress and Political Consultative Conference of Beijing at the municipal level. On December 25 of that year, the Chinese people encouraged the teachers and students in universities in Beijing to promote the tradition of monitoring the Military Committee and proposed the universities as the ridge correspond to the army as the prop.

On the evening of February 13, 2015, while watching the news, I saw that the Beijing people and the People's Liberation Army proposed that the arrangement of nail owners in relocation and reconstruction by DaWei Zhang in AnHui would already belong to the overcompensation in law, and would certainly be legal. He provided valuable experiences for the rapid construction of a city under the condition of public ownership of land. The next day, before falling asleep, I recalled that Chicago was the top city constructed in the United States because its lands were planned and scheduled by the municipal government. Accordingly, the public ownership of land was beneficial to the construction of the city. On November 30 of that year, I proposed that the new apartments in the state-owned village were not only cheap in price but also good in quality and grand in style. Under the condition of public ownership of land, it would be the new creation and instance of democratic construction of cities for the People's Congress in districts and counties to plan and construct the real estate with democracy, which supported and supplemented the democratic system first demonstrated in Rome and the United States. In regret, the land in the United States was privately owned at the present time, and accordingly, it was required to promote the public ownership of land there in the future. On the evening of August 30, 2016, while watching the news, I saw that the Chinese people said that Fu Du and Jing Cai corresponded to the welfare of real estate in districts and counties.

On the evening of March 3, 2015, while watching the news, I saw that the people in SuZhou proposed that there was no local person in SuZhou to conspire with the Central Committee headed by Hu and Xi. Accordingly, a district with the lowest reproduction of it would be sufficiently big in scale to compensate for my natural extinction, whereas, in addition, as a premise, it was not necessary for the satellites to be criminal any longer to influence my marriage. On July 31 of that year, while watching the evening news, I saw the people in SuZhou say that they would refer to the villages of the minority to compare with my perspective descendants in scale and utmost compensate one district for my extinction. Whereas, all such organizations located in Beijing as the army and police, Party and government, culture and propaganda, and so on under the direct supervision of the Central Committee conspired against me, and accordingly would not be fewer than SuZhou in compensation.

On July 21, 2015, it was my 50th birthday, but I was still single and unmarried. The terrific expressions of JinPing Xi were the main reason. Accordingly, I asked the law in history to sentence that JinPing Xi would divorce in equivalence. It was definitely difficult to keep the membership of the Party of JinPing Xi, as his fraudulent proposal of YuanChao Li out of the Standing Committee to the Vice Chairman depreciated the country and violated the discipline of the Party. DeJiang Zhang had recommended YuanChao Li, which resulted in a terrific atmosphere for several years, and accordingly should also accompany JinPing Xi to divorce.

On September 6, 2015, I led and started the movement to rescue the race and save Beijing against terror. I directed the satellites to shout in Chinese: "北方嫁圣救北京 (Northern areas marry to San to save Beijing)." On September 10 of that year, I proposed the principle of "Social psychosis treated earlier, personal psychosis treated later," and the Beijing people actively cooperated. Nonetheless, on September 4, 2016, JinPing Xi even threatened terror in further to my father MingXun in the G20 summit meeting, whereas my father shouted at the communist parties and me. Fortunately, the chief of general staff, FengHui Fang, was indifferent to terror. On December 28, the Chinese people utilized the manner of framing drugs or even assassinating to threaten the sister of JinPing Xi, who went abroad to counter-attack JinPing Xi for his expressions about terrors.

On September 7, 2015, the Chinese people and I started the movement of "Republics down the Central Committee." The force of democracy became stranger than ever and dominated the whole country. On September 13 of that year, I pointed out that the Central Committee would eventually be substituted by the representative meetings elected via democracy in the future.

Several months after November 2015, I went to the prosperous shopping streets in SuZhou several times, wishing to solicit donations to establish a website for the democratic election, but I did not succeed. The Chinese people were very stingy and unwilling to give even a single yuan toward the construction of democracy and republics of China.

On July 1, 2016, JinPing Xi maliciously appointed Qiang Li from ZheJiang as the top leader of JiangSu province, who relied on struggling against me to get the promotion. ZhiJun Luo, the former secretary of JiangSu Provincial Committee, had assigned TaiFeng Shi from Beijing to SuZhou, severely violating the regulation, whereas he was promoted to Beijing by JinPing Xi. On March 31, 2017, while watching the evening news, I saw Qiang Li, promoted by JinPing Xi, relocate Mayor FuTian Qu away from SuZhou, who was good at science and technology. The people in SuZhou and I required Beijing to explain and compensate.

On September 4, 2016, I nominated the leader LeJi Zhao from YanAn, who respected republics, to become the third candidate of successors of 2022 for the upcoming 19th Congress of Party in 2017, along with ChunHua Hu and ZhengCai Sun. The Chinese people and the soldiers of the People's Liberation Army actively supported this idea. As it opened to India and Europe, along with the old liberated area of YanAn and the glory of Muslims, the north-western part of China rapidly rose up to the rank of leading the whole country. In history, under the leadership of ZeDong Mao, YanAn had been the sacred place to salvage the country and people. On October 7 of that year, the Chinese people shouted on television that they lived happily under ZeDong Mao and it seemed that they were living in Brazil. Since 2016, the communist party has been one of the main accounts of Brazilian people's lives and democracy. The friendship between China and Brazil also gradually improved my relationship with the Catholic religion, whereas Notre Dame was just one subordinate of the Catholic religion, not big in influence.

Several months earlier, in the old liberated area of the New Fourth Army, the municipal bureaucrats of the NanTong government and Party, low in quality, maliciously resisted and put off my proposition to establish the Nantong Institute of Neuropsychology. SuZhou was not the old liberated area, whereas I belonged to the democratic school opposite to the autocracy of the Central Committee. So, even if an institute in SuZhou was set up, it would still be difficult and unfeasible to apply for financial support for scientific research in the later years. Even though the republic of Mao and Cai was established in 2017, it was still in its initial stage. The Open Access Journals Hans in WuHan still rejected my relevant Chinese paper on history in television. In addition, the universities southern to YangZi River were quite conservative, and closed their doors to society, and as a result, the progressives frequently reprimanded them. I was already far away from them, and since I also lacked a PhD degree, I was irrelevant to them. In this regard, the time I spent in scientific research and writing earned me no reimbursement to influence my getting married and having a family in time. I had to consider promoting the establishment of the Nantong Institute after 2018 when Jinping Xi finished his nomination at a high level, and the domestic situation turned more opportune for me.

After October 2016, I turned to the Chinese Academy of Sciences to contend for the reward of the sciences of mine to make it opportune for my marriage and reproduction. The physics turned to Shanghai, and the neuropsychology to Beijing. To those resistors, law appeal was the major measure. Along with my promotion of law to science and technology to take advantage of my own, the people also followed the law and the reactionary conservatives for the construction of the republic country. On June 29, 2017, the people and I discovered that lawing the bureaucrats with the procuratorate in assistance to the court was more efficient than the discipline of the Party.

On October 27, 2016, while watching the news, I saw that the representatives of the 6th Plenary Session of the 18th CPC Central Committee said that Christianity educated the bourgeoisie with kindness and atonement, and accordingly, the Communist Party would naturally encourage them. In regret, the 6th Plenary Session of the 18th CPC Central Committee inappropriately put forward the Central Committee having JinPing Xi in its center, infringing the image of the Communist Party of China. In December 2017, the people and I referred to the United Nations and Muslims to promote the general secretary to be the real secretary. I directed the satellites to shout in Chinese: "总书记秘书联合国 (UN requires the general secretary to be the real secretary)," "总书记秘书安拉喊 (Allah shouts the general secretary to be the real secretary)."

On November 11, 2016, I encouraged YanCheng of the New Fourth Army to ally with TianJin, with both progressing out of the low valley hand in hand. On December 17, 2017, while watching the news, I saw that in YanCheng, China and Korea cooperated to establish the Developing Area. Besides, in the area of New Fourth Army of northern JiangSu, there were, in addition, LianYunGang for the Belt and Road Initiative to exit to sea, as well as NanTong learning ShenZhen, prosperous in the whole area.

On December 3, 2016, while watching the noon news, I saw that the people in Beijing said that Pence's partner, Trump, came from Indiana, where the University of Notre Dame was located, and would take over the role of the vice president and speaker of the congress, which would postpone the United States from supporting my marriage. In this regard, the United States should compensate the county, Goddard, having shouted about breaking the earth. On December 8 of that year, I asked the historical law to sentence

US President Obama to divorce after retiring to severely punish him for not having tried his best in his term to support my marriage before the age of 50 and for giving up several states adjacent to the borderline of Mexico. In China, I had already appealed to the historical law to sentence JinPing Xi to divorce.

On December 8, 2016, due to the demand for public ownership of land in the United States, people in various countries, including me, instigated the blacks to siege and promote. On January 14, 2017, while watching the news, I saw that the American people said that the blacks were free to be better than the whites. Since the liberation of blacks, the conflict of races in the United States had been fierce. The wise leaders, such as Washington and Lincoln, disappeared as whites, and accordingly, the whites in the United States were similar to those in Great Britain and South Africa. The Chinese people said that the United States and Great Britain oppressed the freedom of culture, science, and technology in various countries around the world. On March 25 of that year, while watching television, I saw that the people in various countries encouraged the Spanish in the United States to lead the Democratic Party there, allying with the hospitals and Open Access journals while pushing aside the academic professors.

On December 12, 2016, the people in Beijing said that if those from the north continued to make use of the capital to disturb the whole country, they would pass down to HeBei their two northern districts: MiYun and HuaiRou. Several months later, they changed to construct a defensive area of forest there. On January 19, 2017, the people and I reinforced and allied with the more democratic People's Congress and Political Consultative Conference of Beijing at the municipal level. On April 1 of that year, JinPing Xi held a newly established developing area called XiongAn among Beijing, TianJin and BaoDing to increase the influence of Beijing on mainland China. On July 14 of that year, the people in Beijing realized that the talents in Beijing and TianJin were willing to immigrate to work in ShanDong but not willing to go northward. As a result, Beijing, TianJin and ShanDong were naturally united, belonging to a part of the traditional China, whereas the North-eastern China was relatively far away. After September of that year, the people in TianJin learned to call on Cao Cao. On October 20 of that year, the people in Beijing admired HongZhang Li in the Qing Dynasty and his opening to the world.

On January 22, 2017, I learned from internet that the China Central Television Station (CCTV) was the subordinate of the State Administration of Radio Film and Television, and belonged to the country in characteristic. Accordingly, I immediately required them to eulogize the republic of Mao and Cai, as well as the democracy of the country. But, they did not turn good in time. On that evening, I said that it was well-known that it would be distressing to Mao and Cai if the Nationalist Party in Taiwan reversely reprimanded Liao and Meng for destroying the country. Accordingly, it would reduce the reprimands to Mao and Cai if Taiwan went to independence. On March 20 of that year, while watching television, I saw that the people said that it would have been better for GuoFeng Hua if he had not actively resigned but naturally stepped down after finishing his term. His crash of the illegal Gang of Four belonged to the adoption of similar measures in return for the opposite parties on their own. As I did not belong to any party, the Republic of Mao and Cai improved the status and influence of the democratic parties and religions in China. In contrast, I also wished to consolidate my status in the republic of Mao and Cai from the democratic parties and religions.

China rapidly exceeded the countries in Asia and Middle Europe, having supported the open economy in the time of XiaoPing Deng, while science and technology in China rapidly rose. Accordingly, the international economic relationship of China had also been gradually returning to export addressing Asia, Africa and Latin in the time of ZeDong Mao, and resisting the reactionary faction of the United Kingdom and the United States. As resistance to Chinese democracy, the Singaporean Park located in SuZhou was also defined by me as hostile to the country of Chinese Communists. On September 16, 2017, the people in Beijing shouted that the talents in HaiDian preferred socialism. On November 15 of that year, while watching television, I saw that the people in Thailand admired the construction of cities of socialism in China, as their own cities lagged behind those in China in that field.

On January 29, 2017, aiming at the trend of the new US President Trump to be friendly to kings and, at the same time, extend the armaments, the people in various countries, including me, reiterated the defect of the US army liable to fear death without justice as consisting of multiple races, and propagated the tradition of the white flag of the US army. I directed the satellites to shout in Chinese: "美国军队白旗响 (US army resonant on white flag)."

In the early morning of March 18, 2017, a British satellite operator said that they would argue that most of the international terrors previously were from the satellites of the United States, and accordingly, the compensation of extinction would not count to them. I said, in this regard, that it would not be reasonable to require a woman in SuZhou to marry me as a man with terrors from satellites and substitute the duty of extinction of SuZhou with one county of Goddard as the US center of satellites if I was not able to reproduce any offspring. The compensation of Beijing for the terrors from JinPing Xi remained the same as one district. In this way, it was possible to apprehend the other criminals of satellites, severely punish them, and, accordingly, consider my marriage. I directed the satellites to shout in Chinese: "美国绝种英国咬 (US extinction British biting)." In addition, I spent much time on science, whereas the United States had always been oppressing my academic status, naturally influencing my marriage. On June 7 of that year, I considered that there could also occur an illegal event hurting me or my family in SuZhou in the future, and accordingly, in that situation, it would require one county in SuZhou to extinct and compensate me, even though it was much lower in possibility with regard to that situation. I directed the satellites to shout in Chinese: "苏州美国，绝种一县 (SuZhou US one county to extinct)."

On March 28, 2017, I sent an email to the Shanghai Institute of Applied Physics to further investigate nuclear physics along with them, but I did not get any reply. On May 3 of that year, I had to appeal to the Shanghai Branch of Academy of Sciences of China about their bad attitude, but I did not get any reply either. I planned to contact Beijing to study neuropsychology with them after 2018. On December 27, 2017, people in various countries, including me, severely repressed the domestic scientific and technological talents with the crime of anti-humans, not allowing them to shout against the autocracy of Central Committee, whereas the University of Science and Technology of China (USTC) as the old university I had studied previously was most obvious in this mistake of anti-democracy and anti-humans after 2010. The USTC repressed their LTD opportune to my theory of sleep, promoted their communication with quantum entanglement, resisting the movement as the unification of physics with electromagnetism of mine and the global people, and propagated their linguistic vocal automation cooperative with the Singaporean autocracy. There were also many world champions in the domestic athletes, and most of them were afraid of anti-humans to shout for republics and support me, whereas USTC was less competent to them in agility after achieving ahead of the world in the period of these years. The Chinese people and I considered that the attitude of anti-democracy and anti-humans of USTC was even worse than mine in Chicago not agreeing to commit suicide to save the humans.

On April 7, 2017, US President Trump said that the people in the United States would help the Chinese people inhibit the Northern culture of yellow perils to improve the condition of Beijing and me. The conspicuous behaviors of yellow perils were the assignment of ShanDong to the Northern Military Area under the supervision of Northeast China. The translocation of the center of sciences and technologies of Beijing to the HuaRou District near Inner

Mongolia is inconvenient to applications and communications and the investment of DaQing to Volvo and amicable to the constitutional monarchy, giving up their flags and images on their own.

On April 23, 2017, the Chinese people and I decided that I would actively promote the direct election of municipal congress along with the democratic parties and religions, while the relatives of Mao and Deng, along with the old cadres, would be assigned to promote the dual commands onto the army from the congress, proceeding separately forward. I would utilize the satellites to shout to help both of them.

On the evening of May 16, 2017, I considered that businessmen were good at finance and conservative and accordingly, I shifted to using intellectuals. Several days later, the Chinese people shouted out their intelligence and military talents to serve the republics. They spun the silk like the spring silkworm, bent the back to exhaustion, and recorded the red heart in glorious history. On July 20 of that year, the Chinese people welcomed the Hindu talents to reinforce ShenZhen and Hong Kong.

On June 17, 2017, I received a letter from a Swiss madam, Janine Eberhardt Knappich, doing business in England, saying that she believed in religion and kindness and was internationalized in her habits, willing to donate to me a huge amount of money as much as 15 million British pounds. 40% of it would be donated to orphanages in China, and 60% would be donated to me. Two weeks later, I received recognition from the corresponding company, but it was in freezing status. As another European woman could possibly be required to marry me as a priority, I was worried that the leaders of the Republic of Mao and Cai might be too much westernized, which might influence the feelings of Chinese people to the donor Janine. Accordingly, I, in turn, donated 60% donation to me to set up a foundation for graduate students on reality analysis in social and historical studies, whereas I just got a higher annual salary from the management of the foundations, sufficient to marry the domestic nurses and dancers not afraid of the satellites.

On July 18, 2017, European Consultants Limited, located in England, declined my reasonable requirement to deduct the costs of transferring the donation from the fund via the efforts of several months the company yielded. In contrast, they changed their tactics, exchanged the donation into cash, and sent it to my home via the affiliated Palace Company. As the law in China was violated, I asked to pay post-service and declare to customs afterwards to clear myself. On November 7 of that year, the British part lay that the fund cash was intercepted at the Phuket airport of Thailand and informed me of the name of the relevant customs officer. On the evening of November 14 that year, I went to the Phuket airport. On November 15, after confirming that the interception and the name of the officer of customs were both fake, I reported to the police in Thailand in time. On November 23 of that year, the British part said that the fund was returned to London, but they were not willing to return it to me as it did not arrive to them. Accordingly, I had to consider appealing this company to the police and court in London, where the company was located. As soon as I lost the lawsuit, it might result in a change in Janine's philanthropic will and hurt the benefits of not only me but also the orphans in China and East Europe.

If it was possible to legally transfer this huge amount of money from a British company to me to operate the foundations, with my annual salary from them and my investment of a small proportion of the foundations to my company of artificial intelligence, it would be sufficient to offset the negative influence of the United States to my not getting married for a long time, and the higher requirement of SuZhou people to the economic condition, and accordingly, neither of them would be liable to compensate my extinction from staying unmarried. The mere factor that influenced my marriage was the terrific expressions around Beijing. On June 24 of that year, while watching television, I saw that the army in ShanXi continually shouted terror at me without considering the miserable circumstances that Beijing needed to compensate for my extinction from staying unmarried in one district.

In early September 2017, as the donation from Janine could come to nothing, I turned to accelerate to look for investors in Shanghai and Beijing to invest in a software company for the automation of language processing and translation, taking advantage of my theory on neurolinguistics. Despite the early efforts of half a year, there had not been any progression. This was one of the directions of my growth in the future, along with such directions of my growth as promoting the Chinese Academy of Sciences to study my neuropsychology and physics, continuing to apply for the establishment of the Nantong Institute, and so on, to try to make the progressions gradually one by one and marry and reproduce before reaching 60. As I had very high scientific achievements and status, I was not afraid of getting old.

On October 25, 2017, I learned from internet that, after the end of the 19th CPC National Congress, ChunHua Hu did not appear in the newly elected highest Standing Committee of the Political Bureau, but LeJi Zhao and Yang Wang did. Accordingly, they were relatively older. As Yang Wang entered the Standing Committee of the Political Bureau, it was no longer necessary for JinPing Xi to compensate him for his previous position as Vice Chairman.

Looking retrospectively to the five years after the 18th CPC National Congress, there were many violations and strangeness on nomination and dismissal of cadres, such as ZhiJun Luo, Qin Xu, ZhengLong Wu and so on, whereas the Organization Department of the Central Committee did not correct them. Accordingly, there were many calls requiring historical laws to dismiss the party membership of the several relevant vice ministers, while Minister LeJi Zhao was promoted and appropriate to be subjected to continual observation within the Party. QiShan Wang, the secretary of the Central Committee for Discipline Inspection, was indifferent to all of these. He did not even stop some inappropriate nominations and dismissals at the higher level after the 18th CPC National Congress. Accordingly, there were also many calls requiring historical laws to dismiss his party membership. In the fields of sciences and technologies, there was full of reactionary psychosis and arrogance, but YanDong Liu was not controlling them, which resulted in the consequence of anti-humans from the University of Science and Technology of China. So, it was also reasonable to consider dismissing her party membership. In the Military Committee, Chang Long Fan and Zhong Tian were responsible for the reverse leadership of North-eastern China to ShanDong, while it could also be difficult for the Reform and Establishment Office in the Military Committee to clear themselves. So, it was also necessary to dismiss all their party memberships.

On December 3, 2017, I required the Chinese democratic parties and religions to vigorously strive for the realization of provincial and municipal direct election and legislation to gradually lead the republic country to a healthy road. I directed the satellites to shout in Chinese: "民主党教，奋勇拼搏 (The democratic parties and religions, vigorously strive)." On December 10 of that year, I directed the satellites to shout in Chinese: "共和镇央党代会，民主党教大喊叫 (Republics down the Central Committee with the Representative Meeting of Party, The democratic parties and religions shout vigorously)."

On December 31, 2017, I stopped adding the contents in 2018 and afterwards to this book of memoirs. The victory of Chinese democracy and the current political trends in various countries made it clear that there will not be any big political change in the near future. Therefore, I decided to publish this book of memoirs as early as possible. In addition, the publication of this book of memoirs could reduce my terrors and decrease the evil imagination to kill the leader and mess with history, making it convenient for me to marry and reproduce as early as possible.

End poem of this chapter:

The republics down the Central Committee with the Five Stars to the representatives of parties,
The provincial and municipal legislation with brightness and glories to the army and police,
The democratic parties and religions in the ocean of people fragrant and vigorous,
The anxiety of no offspring from the foggy hazes of terrors.

Epilogue

At last, let us review and chorus "The Same Song."

The flowers once told me how you passed by.
The land knows every corner of your heart.
Your sweet dreams nobody would miss.
After all, here comes the gathering time for today.
Hundreds of rivers and thousands of mountains we have walked across.
Every meeting and smile is engraved to each other.
On happy days of brilliant sunlight,
We, hand in hand, hope to say a lot.
Starlights sprayed all of childhood,
Storms have wound to all corners of the world.
The same feeling gives us the same thirst,
The same happiness gives us the same song.
Sunlight wants to penetrate all language,
Spring spreads the story of friendship.
The same feeling gives us the same thirst,
The same happiness gives us the same song.

References

❖ Books of Zi-Jian Cai:

i. Cai Z-J. (2015). Electromagnetic Unification of Four Forces. Lambert Academic Publishing, Saarbrücken, Germany. ISBN: 978-3-659-76798-2.

ii. Cai Z-J, Cai M-X. (2015). The Natural Principles and Gists with Nuisance on Chinese Chess from Two Cais. Golden Light Academic Publishing, Saarbrücken, Germany. ISBN: 978-3-639-82094-2.

iii. Cai Z-J. (2016). Weapons, Armed Troops and War—The Armed Police Winning over the Army. Lambert Academic Publishing, Saarbrücken, Germany. ISBN: 978-3-659-95272-2.

iv. Cai Z-J, Cai M-X. (2016). Initial Launch of Three Rhythmic Literatures of Music Backgrounds. Lambert Academic Publishing, Saarbrücken, Germany. ISBN: 978-3-659-95614-0.

❖ Published Papers of Zi-Jian Cai:

i. Cai Z-J. (1990). The neural mechanism of declarative memory consolidation and retrieval: a hypothesis. Neuroscience. Biobehavior. Rev. 14(3): 295–304.

ii. Cai Z-J. (1991). The functions of sleep: further analysis. Physiol. Behav. 50(1): 53–60.

iii. Cai Z-J. (1995). An integrative analysis of sleep functions. Behav. Brain Res. 69(1–2): 187–194.

iv. Zu JS, Deng HX, Lo TP, Mitsumoto H, Ahmed MS, Hung WY, Cai Z-J, Tainer JA, Siddique T. (1997) Exon 5 encoded domain is not required for the toxic function of mutant SOD1 but essential for the dismutase activity: identification and characterization of two new SOD1 mutations associated with familial amyotrophic lateral sclerosis. Neurogenetics. 1(1): 65–71.

v. Cai Z-J. (2015). A new function of rapid eye movement sleep: improvement of muscular efficiency. Physiol. Behav. 144: 110–115.

vi. Cai Z-J. (2015). Termination of organogenesis as an intrinsic constraint on animal development and evolution: A theory. OALib. J. 2: e1646.

vii. Cai Z-J. (2015). Semantic memory association, procedural grammar syntax and episodic modality coordination as three interactive neural processes organizing language: A model. OALib. J. 2: e1718.

viii. Cai Z-J. (2015). Extending psychoanalysis with theories on sleep functions. J. Sleep Disorder. Ther. 4(6): 217.

ix. Cai Z-J. (2015). Advocacy for extension of microwave and infrared to detect the brain activities. J. Med. Diagn. Meth. 4(4): 188.

x. Cai Z-J. (2016). Two types of Korsakoff alcoholism in reference to habenula: A new opinion. J. Neurol. Neurosci. 7(Special Issue): 68.

xi. Cai Z-J. (2016). Regulation of both cell state and gene expression with nutrient gradient as conserved mechanism differentiating the cell fates for embryonic gastrulation: A theory. OALib. J. 3: e2348.

xii. Cai Z-J. (2016). The electrophysiological memory function of hippocampus different from O'Keefe and Mosers. J. Neurol. Neurophysiol. 7: 362.

xiii. Cai Z-J. (2016). Review of milestone book: Electromagnetic unification of four forces. Res. Rev. J. Pure Applied Phys. 4(2): 20–27.

xiv. Cai Z-J. (2016). Principles derived from neurolinguistics of brain for design of translation machines. OALib. J. 3: e2704.

xv. Cai Z-J. (2016). The hypothetic post-sensory nociceptive-sympathetic coupling necessary for pain sensation from NBA. J. Neurol. Neurosci. 7(4): 141.

xvi. Cai Z-J. (2016). A hypothetic ageing pathway from the skin to the hypothalamic suprachiasmatic nucleus via slow wave sleep. Sleep Sci. 9(3): 212–215.

xvii. Cai Z-J. (2016). Progressions of sleep, memory and depression applicable to psychoanalysis: A review. Curr. Psychiat. Rev. 12: 240–245.

xviii. Cai Z-J. (2016). Proposal of the electromagnetic structures of the most important particles from decays. Res. Rev. J. Pure Applied Phys. 4(4): 9–19.

xix. Cai Z-J. (2016). Advocacy on the fascinating integrative neuroscience. Res. Rev. Neurosci. 1(1): 15–17.

xx. Cai Z-J. (2016). The advantage of asymmetrical handedness in cooperation with heartbeat: A hypothesis from the Chinese member of satellite group. OALib. J. 3: e3253.

xxi. Cai Z-J. (2017). Two types of REM sleep: The atonic and brain REM sleep. Sleep Hypn. 19(1):1–9.

xxii. Cai Z-J. (2017). The adipose cause of senescence of male hypothalamic preoptic nucleus: A European view. Res. Rev. Neurosci. 1(2): 21–26.

xxiii. Cai Z-J. (2017). Political history necessary to use television. OJPS. 7: 353–367.

xxiv. Cai Z-J. (2017). The cholinergic-regulated thalamocortical imagining as mind differentiated in two phases of sleep: A view from the Guangdong people. OALib. J. 4: e3748.

xxv. Cai Z-J. (2017). The neurobiological models of language: An updated review. Psychol. Neurosci. 10(3): 297–306.

xxvi. Cai Z-J. (2017). Significant contribution of neural regulation to immune recognition of self and else: A hypothesis from the US member of satellite group. Res. Rev. Neurosci. 1(3): 1–2.

xxvii. Cai Z-J. (2017). The impact of television on democratic politics. IJSSHR. 5(4): 740–747.

xxviii. Cai Z-J. (2017). Three types of episodic associations for the semantic/syntactic/episodic model of language prospective in applications to the statistical translation. OALib. J. 4: e3830.